Indigenous Communication

Eno Akpabio

Indigenous Communication

A Global Perspective

Eno Akpabio
University of Namibia
Windhoek, Namibia

ISBN 978-3-031-41765-8   ISBN 978-3-031-41766-5 (eBook)
https://doi.org/10.1007/978-3-031-41766-5

© The Editor(s) (if applicable) and The Author(s), under exclusive licence to Springer Nature Switzerland AG 2024
This work is subject to copyright. All rights are solely and exclusively licensed by the Publisher, whether the whole or part of the material is concerned, specifically the rights of translation, reprinting, reuse of illustrations, recitation, broadcasting, reproduction on microfilms or in any other physical way, and transmission or information storage and retrieval, electronic adaptation, computer software, or by similar or dissimilar methodology now known or hereafter developed.
The use of general descriptive names, registered names, trademarks, service marks, etc. in this publication does not imply, even in the absence of a specific statement, that such names are exempt from the relevant protective laws and regulations and therefore free for general use.
The publisher, the authors, and the editors are safe to assume that the advice and information in this book are believed to be true and accurate at the date of publication. Neither the publisher nor the authors or the editors give a warranty, expressed or implied, with respect to the material contained herein or for any errors or omissions that may have been made. The publisher remains neutral with regard to jurisdictional claims in published maps and institutional affiliations.

This Palgrave Macmillan imprint is published by the registered company Springer Nature Switzerland AG.
The registered company address is: Gewerbestrasse 11, 6330 Cham, Switzerland

Paper in this product is recyclable.

I dedicate this to my wife, Imafon, and our four children: Abasiama, Prisca, Etietop and Stephanie. These are my joy and strength.

Preface

This journey started at the University of Lagos where I was allocated a module – African Communication Systems (ACS) – to teach as well as when I wrote a study pack for the distance students on the same module. This served to galvanize my interest in indigenous communication and I have not looked back since then. That journey has resulted in my making contributions from an African and now a global perspective to scholarship in the area. Importantly, communication must not be left out in the ongoing revival of Indigenous Knowledge Systems (IKS) and this is my humble contribution to the effort.

Windhoek, Namibia

Eno Akpabio

Acknowledgement

In my acknowledgement I must have recourse to my mother tongue – Ibibio – as it would be disingenuous to put together a book on indigenous communication without any reference to an indigenous language.

Me kom Abasi ye Eyen esie ke ukeme se amo eno mien adi wet nwed ami.

Contents

1 Indigenous Communication: Introduction — 1
Introduction — 1
Background — 2
Indigeneity — 6
Indigenous Knowledge — 8
Indigenous Communication — 11
Conclusion — 12

2 Researching and Classifying Indigenous Communication — 17
Introduction — 17
Philosophical Worldview of Indigenous Knowledge — 17
Indigenous Research Methodologies — 19
Models and Classification of Indigenous Communication — 22
Conclusion — 26

3 Instrumental Communication — 31
Introduction — 31
Drums — 32
Chordophones (Lutes, Zithers and Harps) — 35
Aerophones (Whistles, Flutes, Reeds and Pipes) — 38
Bells, Gongs and Cymbals — 42
Trumpets, Clarinet and Animal Horns — 43
Clappers and Rattles — 47
Conclusion — 48

4 Demonstrative Communication — 57
Entertainment — 60
Religious — 62
Dirge — 64
Work Songs — 65
Lullaby — 67
Love Songs — 69
Wars and Conflict — 69
Praise Songs — 70
Travelling Songs — 71
Education — 71
Conclusion — 72

5 Iconographic Communication — 77
Introduction — 77
Types and Uses of Iconographic Communication — 77
Misuse of Indigenous Signs and Symbols — 80
Indigenous Forms of Writing and Communication — 82
Message Sticks — 82
Iconic — 83
Indexical — 84
Numeric — 84
The Khipu System — 85
The Yapana Matrix, Cilka and Maya Scripts — 86
Nsibidi and Mud Cloth of Mali — 88
Conclusion — 89

6 Extra-mundane Communication — 95
Introduction — 95
Global Outlook — 96
Bottom-Up Communication — 102
Top-Down Communication — 104
Conclusion — 108

7 Visual Communication — 115
Clothes — 115
Accessories — 118
Colours — 119
Body Art — 120
Conclusion — 126

8	**Institutional Communication**	133
	Introduction	133
	Marriage	133
	Masquerade	135
	Kinship and Age Grades	138
	Chieftaincy and Leadership	140
	Secret Societies	142
	Conclusion	144
9	**Venue-oriented Communication**	149
	Settlement Patterns	150
	Markets	155
	Conclusion	159
10	**Taxonomic Communication**	165
	Personal Names	166
	Tribal and Ethnic Names	172
	Conclusion	175
11	**Axiomatic Communication**	181
	Introduction	181
	Myths	182
	Legends	186
	Conclusion	190
12	**Conclusion – Indigenous Communication Around the World**	195
	Conclusions and Way Forward	200
Index		205

Abbreviations

ACS   African Communication Systems
IKS   Indigenous Knowledge Systems
STEM Science, Technology, Engineering, and Mathematics

CHAPTER 1

Indigenous Communication: Introduction

INTRODUCTION

Colonised and oppressed peoples are in every continent, nook and cranny of the world we live in. It is estimated that there are 350 million indigenous people in 70 countries worldwide.[1] The oppression they were subjected to was not only intended to break their spirit but to ensure that they discard their tried and tested ways of life for those of the oppressors and colonizers. In many instances, the new way of life has damaged the environment and decimated indigenous peoples and impaired their way of life irretrievably. The ray of hope is that indigenous studies and research are reviving these cultural practices and showing to Western scholars and others that their existence is no threat as the sky is big enough to accommodate all viewpoints. This work is another attempt to decolonize and breathe new life into indigenous knowledge albeit from a communication angle. But justice would not be done if one does not locate the communication perspective in the larger context of indigenous marginalization and the work in progress to revive and restore indigenous knowledge to its pride of place.

Background

A lot of disservice has been done to colonized and subjugated peoples with some of wounds being reopened by actions and inactions of the former overlords hence their continued reverberation as we speak. The comfort women saga between Japan and Korea is a case in point[2] but this example goes to show that this was indeed a global phenomenon that is not restricted to former colonial masters and the colonized peoples. The Australian scenario was not any different. Not only did the newcomers not wipe their feet when they arrived hence bringing diseases that decimated the local population,[3] they behaved in a most uncivilised way by supplanting their hosts and imposing their world view even though they claim to be the civilized and proper people.[4] The Sámi people in the Nordic environment were seen as research subjects and treated as the "other" by Western scholars.[5]

In a similar vein, White South Africa's divide and rule policy in Namibia involved "grand apartheid, with self-governing and eventually independent homelands for the different black ethnic groups. Petty apartheid – segregation on grassroots level…"[6] These and other colonialists perpetrated cultural genocide,[7] dehumanization and physical genocide. For the former the colonial infrastructure tried its utmost best to kill off indigenous cultural knowledge and the oft repeated assertion that because it is primarily oral and "elders are dying" are not a true reflection.[8] Simpson asserts that "elders have always passed into the next realm and IK systems have always been primarily oral, yet they sustained complex social, cultural, spiritual, and political systems long before the arrival of the Europeans."[9]

Genocide and dehumanization took various forms. Indigenous women and girls were placed under domestic service by government policies in Australia and the US.[10] Namibians suffered at the hands of the Portuguese, South Africans and Germans. The Germans[11] for instance waged 'a war of extermination', during which they ruthlessly killed any Namibian they could find, whether soldier or civilian. When the war ended, the population in parts of" … [the] country was reduced by two-thirds." Men and women were whipped on their buttocks in public after they had been forced to undress with a six-foot long palm tree cane.[12] Forceful removal of the original owners and placing them in **Katutura** as in the case of Namibia[13] seem to be a global phenomenon.

The Wounaan people of Columbia, for instance, survived the Spanish colonial overlords, Marxist guerillas and nationalists armies perched on stilted huts above the river banks but not warring factions of coca growers, gold miners, paramilitaries, guerillas, and government troops that sent them packing out of their ancestral land to El Cristal Sports Arena in Buenaventura, Colombia for twelve months.[14] The difference is that in the case of Namibia it was only after the Apartheid era that Blacks could venture into formerly White-only residential areas. Thankfully, this took a much shorter period but the damage remained nonetheless as the Wounaan's "cultural survival signals a critical humanitarian and environmental emergency in which Indigenous people living sustainable lives have been caught in a resource war for coca cultivation, gold mining, and control of key river tributaries."[15]

The Australian Aborigines suffered a worst fate than the Wounaan. The cattle industry and the entire European economy caused them untold hardship from uprooting them from their traditional communities to making them rudderless as the colonialists upset their "psychic balance" so much so that life was no longer worth living more so perpetuating their lineage as summed up by a member of the group:

> why should we have children? They are a drag on our scanty rations, they evade their responsibilities when grown (sometimes not through their own fault as they were transferred from their home camp, or absent for long periods); and why should we breed more natives for the **whites** (emphasis added) to work and treat in the same way as they do us?[16]

The inhuman and degrading treatment of Indigenous Australians was rationalized by placing them "close to the developed nonhuman animal world and at the bottom of the hierarchy within the human species."[17] European incursion into Canada ensured an end to the indigenous governance and governance practices overtly and covertly hence the existing atmosphere of mistrust.[18] In the US, the continuing and relentless strategy is the eugenic idea to make the first people less native with less claim to the dispossessed land so that settlers can assume ownership.[19]

Sacred sites did not evade the reach of the new entrants. Mount Graham in Arizona where the Western Apache (Nneé) people collect materials for their religious ceremonies was taken over by a consortia of international research institutions led by the University of Arizona.[20] They wanted the sacred site to build astrophysical observation stations whose location had doubtful value yet they pressed on thus recording a number of firsts in infamy: It's observatory is the only one protected by police attack dogs; it was the first "to fight in court against an endangered animal species; to litigate against traditional American Indian religious practice rights; to require 'prayer permits' and then arrest for trespass an American Indian accessing his ancestral sacred ground."[21] This is in spite of the UN's position that "at the core of indigenous peoples' struggles are their rights to lands, territories and resources. Ancestral lands are the source of indigenous peoples' cultural, spiritual, social and political identity and the foundation of traditional knowledge systems."[22]

There have been attempts to romanticize the evil perpetrated against indigenous people through frames such as paternalistic behaviour,[23] civilizing the natives that was dominant among colonialists[24] that involves applying salve to their conscience and other narratives. Even some scholars are of the view that too much focus on "warfare, disease, loss of land, culture and language"[25] obviates the resistance and victories achieved in some instances by indigenous people. But this itself proves the point in spite of the fact that these scholars' reasoning that "concentrating on such themes has too often depicted Indigenous groups from Australia, New Zealand, and the United States as powerless, as victims of history with little ability to chart their own futures."[26] But such sophistry flies in the face of the reality of the situation. In fact, Wilson refers to such persons and scholars as "parroting" their European colonizers.[27]

The Sámi's people way of life, language and culture was severely impacted by European colonialism in the Nordic countries.[28] The Viliui Sakha's way of life in Siberia was disrupted by Russian military outpost and colonization in the mid 1600s.[29] They were forced to pay fur tribute and the colonialists would seize their land, gold fur and salt as well as enroll them in the collectivization process. The 1991 breakup of the Soviet Union and the dissolution of the Elgeeii centralized farm system resulted in food shortages with the saving grace being their tried and tested "cows-and-kin" smallholder food production system that involves "accessing elder knowledge about cow care, land use and production technologies."[30] Which meant that if they had let this indigenous knowledge go, by following the typology of the "noble savage"[31] they would have suffered the fate of other indigenous groups that the colonialists' way of life had decimated.

It was clearly a survival of the fittest situation as colonialists ran riot and it was only when they realized that their extermination attempts were irreversible, or they met with violent or ideological resistance that they stopped to rethink their strategies. Hence the difference in the way indigenous peoples is treated can be the distinction between life and death. A case in point is Indigenous groups within the Ecuadorian Amazon. They are allowed to apply for land tenure thus precluding division among households and private land sales hence the Kichwa, for instance, have done a good job managing their own affairs.[32] The Māori signed the Treaty of Waitangi guaranteeing them sovereignty over their land, but this did not stop the European settlers from stealing large swathe of territory.[33]

But even rival indigenous and settler groups can also negative impact on the group at the receiving end. Hence the official Chinese view that indigenous rights are only applicable to "countries where European colonization had marginalized indigenous peoples" does not hold water.[34] The Moros, for instance which has been agitating for an Islamic state within The Philippines, has had the upper hand over and above the Teduray and the Lambangian tribes and this has forced them to move from the ancestral domain into the mountainous hinterland thus altering their established ways of life with deleterious effect.[35] The Hoklo or native Taiwanese are known for destroying indigenous communities like European colonialists hence the pejorative referents such as "bailang" and "Mugan".[36]

But we agree with the Chinese position as regards policies that were that were put in place even though we place a caveat that the behaviour was not peculiar to Europeans alone. The end result of such policies being that: "many indigenous peoples were dispossessed of their ancestral homes and lands, brutally oppressed, exploited and murdered, and in some cases even deliberately exterminated. To this day, many indigenous peoples still suffer from discrimination and diminished status."[37] An instance is the Green Revolution policy that privileged modern agriculture and pushed small scale farmer and indigenous landowners out of their holdings to the point of extinction and decimated their sovereign knowledge.[38]

The case of the Irish is ambiguous but still a sad reminder of the evils perpetrated by settlers so much so that it becomes a vicious cycle:

> Irish people sometimes quite actively participated in these settler colonial formations, in such ways as fighting in the Indian wars, settling on Indian land, or encouraging American expansion. But even descriptions of how the Irish flourish in America naturalize these formations because they work to claim the land. As one correspondent to the Nation phrases it, "In every state in the American union – in every town, city, hamlet through these states, you will meet the honest, industrious Irish peasant a new and an altered man." The Irish peasant became "a new and an altered man" by

actively accepting, inhabiting, and extending the structures of settler colonialism in America.[39]

Yet the Irish want to identify with their precolonial past and proud culture and question the assumptions behind British inaccurate discourse painting them as savages and lacking in history.[40]

INDIGENEITY

The conception of indigeneity is complex and shifting but the connection to land seems to be a recurring decimal. Johnson captures this fluidity when he argues that it is imagined

> (1) as practiced by a discrete, bounded social group that clearly marks insiders from outsiders by genealogical descent; (2) as practiced on a discrete, bounded land site since beyond the Western historical record; and (3) to consist of traditional beliefs and practices, uniquely that group's, which are not invented, borrowed, or syncretic. This ideal-typical indigenous community fuses, in a pure, logical sense, a people, a place, and a set of beliefs and practices within clear limits. **But let me repeat: There is no such purity in the world, nor has there ever been** (emphasis added). In history, there is always mixing, always migration, always exchange; the question is only one of degree.[41]

According to Tallbear, it is not only connected to biology and settlement patterns, but it is also encompasses political self-determination and mutual networking to ensure their survival in the global scheme of things hence the increase in the number that self-identify as indigenous.[42] Others see it as embracing "indigenous societies' practices, languages, histories, landscapes, and ways of living."[43] The UN recognizes that indigenous peoples "relationship to their lands, territories and resources is at the heart of their identity, well-being and culture"[44] as well as the need giving them the right to determine "what and who is indigenous."[45]

But a note of warning has also be sounded on the indigenous and non-indigenous divide based on the premise of purity.[46] Virtanen, Olsen, and Keskitalo (2021) argue that talking of indigenous as local and global raises the question of whether someone from one indigenous group can be an "insider" in the understanding of another indigenous group from another part of the world.[47] It also embraces items and persons from a fixed

location in relation to other contenders hence we can talk of local, native, original vis a vis migrant, alien and settler.[48]
According to the UN[49]

> Indigenous communities, peoples and nations are those which, having a historical continuity with pre-invasion and pre-colonial societies that developed on their territories, consider themselves distinct from other sectors of the societies now prevailing on those territories, or parts of them. They form at present non-dominant sectors of society and are determined to preserve, develop and transmit to future generations their ancestral territories, and their ethnic identity, as the basis of their continued existence as peoples, in accordance with their own cultural patterns, social institutions and legal system.

Other factors it identifies as a qualification are:

(a) Occupation of ancestral lands, or at least of part of them;
(b) Common ancestry with the original occupants of these lands;
(c) Culture in general, or in specific manifestations (such as religion, living under a tribal system, membership of an indigenous community, dress, means of livelihood, lifestyle, etc.);
(d) Language (whether used as the only language, as mother-tongue, as the habitual means of communication at home or in the family, or as the main, preferred, habitual, general or normal language);
(e) Residence on certain parts of the country, or in certain regions of the world;
(f) Other relevant factors.

The occupation of ancestral lands and domination by settlers or other groups as well as spiritual connection with the earth also features in definitions of indigeneity or indigenous.[50] Clearly, in postcolonial nations indigenous people possess what has been referred to as *undeniable national category membership*[51] (emphasis author). Their claim to their land is firm and uncontestable, period.

But the buffeting by the powers that be continues to this day. Constructs such as aboriginals, ethnic groups, natives (example Native American) are still intended to make indigenous communities identify with the "political-legal relationship to the state rather than any cultural or social ties" to their communities of origin.[52] This is precisely why long discarded identities are staging a comeback. It is no longer the label Aboriginals but Yolngu or Wurundjeri, Kanaka Maoli, Ngempa, Budjidi, Wangkamara etc.[53] The bag of tricks of colonialists and their successors include the tried and tested divide and rule. Other tactics are "creating a bogus 'we are you' agenda, calling for a vote to legitimize their occupation, referring to state camps as 'economic development' and 'new communities', and offering amnesty to resistant military leaders and their forces in order to co-opt their movement."[54] An example from Bangladesh is instructive:

> ... government of Bangladesh's official position [is] that all of their state inhabitants are "Indigenous" and "Bengalee" despite the existence of 16 different Indigenous communities (collectively referred to as Jumma) in the area of the country known as Chittagong Hill Tracts (CHT) alone. In order to implement this "we are you" mythology, Bangladesh, with the assistance of international agencies, has engaged in a tactic of "swamping" by initiating a massive ethnic Bengalee settlement of the CHT region since 1971 consequently, the area has been purposefully overloaded with over 400,000 Bengali Settlers who have dislocated the much smaller Jumma population (approximately 50,000) from their homeland. From comprising just three per cent of the population of the CHT in 1947. Bengalee Settlers now constitute roughly half the total population of the area.

In Nicaragua, the hypocrisy and ambivalent relationship is clear as daylight: indigenous groups are looked down upon as "Indians" possessing indigenous "things" yet they are seen as reflecting the soul of the country with their patrimony considered as reflective of national culture.[55] In the same vein the Japanese Empire classified the Ainu and Taiwan Aborigenes as *dojin* (savages) and deployed "dispossession and legal control with assimilationist education and social welfare."[56] Consequently, "Ainu policy then became a model for policies imposed on Taiwan and Korea, as when the colonial government looked to the way Hokkaido and Karafuto had Japanized Ainu names, for a similar task in Korea."[57]

Indigenous Knowledge

According to Masolo, the growth of the indigenous was given impetus by the criticism of scientific realism and the fact that there are many ways of knowing without privileging one way above the others.[58] Its recovery is driven by the "loss of what was and ... hope for what will be."[59] Māori scholar, Smith's (1999/2012) seminal work *Decolonizing Methodologies*, assisted a great deal by pointing to the social and political contexts undergirding research which meant that it needed to be taken with a pinch of salt.[60] The United Nations Declaration on the Rights of Indigenous Peoples adopted in 2007 added political pressure for its inclusion in academic and scientific discourses.[61] The postpositivist approach has toned down its assumptions and acknowledges that "knowledge is conjectural…absolute truth can never be found."[62] This new dispensation has made IKS come into its own and take its pride of place along with other knowledges which is as it should be. More so now that is widely recognized that the knowledge possessed by inhabitants of a place offers lessons that humanity generally can benefit from.[63]

Indigenous knowledge is tried and tested and has served creditably for millennia before the buffeting it has add to endure and the resulting genocidal effect it has had on indigenous peoples and their livelihoods. Underlining its importance, Christie refers to Indigenous knowledges as what makes possible the "routine practices of everyday life", and which possess the following characteristics:

> performative, something you do rather than have; context specific, differing from place to place; owned, protected and accountable as it is governed by laws; collective; responsive; active and constantly renewed and reconfigured. Language is also integral to these practices and gives meaning to all things.[64]

These practices are so much part of who people are that putting them in silos is unimaginable. An instance is the marriage culture in most parts of sub-Saharan Africa where it is family rather individual-oriented. That is why an uncle for instance can say "convey greetings to my wife" even though it is to the husband of the woman that he is directing his speech to. So in that context she has married into a family and is now "our wife." But these things are not monolithic as you have Tanzania culture where an elderly woman can marry a younger lady but this does not fit the Western definition of same-sex marriage as the objectives are worlds apart.

Mawere defines indigenous knowledge "ideas, beliefs, and practices (some of which have indigenous religious underpinnings) of a specific locale that has been used by its people to interact with their environment and other people over a long period of time."[65] It also includes knowledge of plants and animals and means of propagation as well as expressions of sacred values, beliefs, rituals and community laws and knowledge regarding land and ecosystem management that are kept secret.[66]

This is precisely why Barnhardt and Kawagley call for a change of mindset: from the disdain of Western literature and scholars to indigenous knowledge. This disdain manifested in the wholesale attempt to frame indigenous knowledge and way of life as unscientific, ungodly, anti-progress and development[67] as a precursor to throwing it out because of its "primitive, barbarous and unholy" nature.[68] It was regarded as insignificant, a methodological folkloric, anecdotal and lacking scientific rigour and objectivity.[69] In addition to being savage, superstitious and primitive.[70] African indigenous knowledge was pejoratively referred to as "unscientific", "delusory" and "no more than a bunch of magical beliefs."[71] The same sentiment was used to label indigenous people generally; they were regarded as barriers to scientific, economic and social progress.[72] Anthropological studies were driven by the need to show how different indigenous ways of life were from the better and preferred Western model, thought and philosophy.[73]

Scholars have attempted to address this cultural marginalization to restore the indigenous back to its pride of place in the scheme of things "where it will have greater political and cultural values over what is foreign or imported."[74] Western scholars have been urged to acknowledge along with non-native people "Native worldviews and ways of knowing as constituting knowledge systems in their own right" as well as "recognize the coexistence of multiple worldviews and knowledge systems and find ways to understand and relate to the world in its multiple dimensions and varied perspectives."[75]

The African way of knowing takes a holistic perspective and involves weaving nature, culture and society together.[76] Interestingly this is not something peculiar to Africa. The Sámi of Finland share an affinity as

> relations are based on a detailed knowledge of kinship and peoples' connection to the land. One can distinguish between *gaskavuohta*, which is close to the notion of "relationship" in English, and *oktavuohta*, which is close to the concept of "relations"... This interrelation is cyclic, reciprocal and holistic ...[77]

Other descriptors of indigenous knowledge are inclusive, animate, and pragmatic through the agency of oral transmission that

> allows knowledge to be passed to individuals at the appropriate time in their life journey to safeguard against the offering of noncontextualized teachings.

Personal knowledge is true for the individual but is not necessarily generalizable to the whole community, nor is it expected to be so. Experiential knowledge is that which nourishes the relationship between inner, subjective understandings and the empirical world. Holism is openness to all of the knowledges that our senses offer.[78]

So indigenous culture and way of life may be scattered geographically but they do have a lot in common apart from the attempts at marginalizing and erasing these ways of life.

Indigenous Communication

Since communication involves the sharing of cultural experiences,[79] it stands to reason that a lot of the practices in indigenous peoples' way of life and outlook would feature forms of communication. This is because communication is integral to every aspect of our lives.[80] And this worth studying and featuring because like every aspect of indigenous peoples' experiences, this would also resonate with them thus ensuring its effectiveness is properly leveraged.

So dress, relationship with the land, relations within the community, marriage, family, music, carvings, poetry, signs and symbols, rituals and spirituality etc. of indigenous peoples will be expressed through communication. These communication practices and the ways they have reinvented themselves to cope with changes will constitute the focus of the remaining chapters. These forms of communication have exhibited resilience despite the buffeting they have undergone at the hands of colonialists and others that have tried to paint anything indigenous in bad light.[81]

The African warmth, the holistic nature of indigenous culture in which everything is connected to each other, the various coping mechanisms and practices that have enabled these people live in peace and harmony with their environment will feature prominently in these discussions. Some of these are being revisited because of the disastrous consequences that have attended Western capitalist ventures that have not paid the requisite attention to the balance of forces in the environment. Overfishing, overgrazing, decimation of the land, pollution of rivers and streams were alien to this way of life and the sustainability movement has a lot to learn from indigenous people and the way they learnt for millennia to live in harmony with nature. According to Wilson, "it is about regaining the ways of being that allowed our peoples to live a spiritually balanced, able existence within our ancient homelands."[82]

This is because indigenous communication has a communal origin and it utilizes symbolisms from the community thus readily connects with the people; it is part and parcel of the way of life of a people – in other words, it utilizes what is familiar and conventional; values of the community and age-old institutions come into play in the communication process; and what is communicated is informative, entertaining, educative and integrative.[83]

That is precisely why indigenous forms of communication are important in that they speak directly to the indigenous spirit and way of life and when factored into communication processes ensures relevance, interactivity, engagement and results.

Conclusion

The chapter starts off by addressing the global attempts made to subjugate anything indigenous globally. Addressing this involves going back into the past to show the glorious exploits of indigenous knowledge as a way of inspiring pride among indigenous peoples. The chapter also contrasts the failures encountered when these forms are ignored. It sets the tone for the rest of the discussion which is intended to conceptually clarify and showcase these indigenous forms in their various manifestations as well as their connection to communication through which they are expressed.

Notes

1. Alfred, T., & Corntassel, J. (2005). Politics of identity – IX: Being indigenous: Resurgences against contemporary colonialism. *Government and Opposition, 40*(4), 597–614.
2. Hosaka, Y. (2015, November 18). "Why did the 2015 Japan-Korea 'Comfort Women' agreement fall apart" The Diplomat. Retrieved from…
3. Chalmers, J. (2013). Indigenous as 'not-indigenous' as 'us'?: A dissident insider's views on pushing the bounds for what constitutes 'our mob.' *Australian Indigenous Law Review, 17*(2), 47–55. p. 47.
4. Chalmers. (2013).
5. Virtanen, P. K., Olsen, T., & Keskitalo, P. (2021). Contemporary Indigenous Research within Sámi and Global Indigenous Studies Contexts. In P. K. Virtanen, T. Olsen, & P. Keskitalo (Eds.), *Indigenous Research Methodologies in Sámi and Global Contexts* (pp. 7–32). Brill, p. 9.

6. Scholtz. L. (2006). The Namibian border war: An appraisal of the South African strategy. *Scientia Militaria: South African Journal of Military Studies*, 34(1), 19–48. Scholtz. L. (2006), p. 32.
7. Simpson, L.R. (2004). Anticolonial strategies for the recovery and maintenance of indigenous knowledge. *American Indian Quarterly*, 28(3/4), 373–384
8. Simpson, L.R. (2004), p. 374.
9. Simpson, L.R. (2004), p. 375.
10. Antonellos, S., & Rantall, J. (2017). Indigenous history: A conversation. *Australasian Journal of American Studies*, 36(2), 115–128, p. 115.
11. Melber, H. Namibia's Past in the Present: Colonial Genocide and Liberation Struggle in Commemorative Narratives. *South African Historical Journal*, 54 (2005), 91–111, p. 96.
12. Scholtz. L. (2006).
13. Scholtz. L. (2006).
14. Cappelli, M. (2017). Innovative strategies of indigenous resistance among the Wounaan People of Colombia. *Native American and Indigenous Studies*, 4(1), 89–95. https://doi.org/10.5749/natiindistudj.4.1.0089
15. Cappelli, M. (2017), p. 89.
16. Geoffrey Gray. (2014). 'We know the Aborigines are dying out': Aboriginal people and the quest to ensure their survival, Wave Hill Station, 1944. *Health and History*, 16(1), 1–24. https://doi.org/10.5401/healthhist.16.1.0001, p. 9.
17. Rigney, L.-I. (1999). Internationalization of an indigenous anticolonial cultural critique of research methodologies: A guide to indigenist research methodology and its principles. *Wicazo Sa Review*, 14(2), 109–121. https://doi.org/10.2307/1409555, p. 112.
18. Hanrahan, M. (2016). Making Indigenous Culture the foundation of indigenous governance today: The Mi'kmaq rights initiative of Nova Scotia, Canada. *Native American and Indigenous Studies*, 3(1), 75–95.
19. Arvin, M., Tuck, E., & Morrill, A. (2013). Decolonizing feminism: Challenging connections between settler colonialism and heteropatriarchy. *Feminist Formations*, 25(1), 8–34.
20. Helfrich, J.T. (2014). Cultural survival in action: Ola Cassadore Davis and the struggle for dził nchaa si'an (Mount Graham). *Native American and Indigenous Studies*, 1(2), 151–175. https://doi.org/10.5749/natiindistudj.1.2.0151
21. Helfrich, J.T. (2014), p. 152.
22. Nuorgam, A. (2021). Foreword. *5th Volume State of the world's indigenous peoples: Rights to Lands, Territories and Resources*. New York, NY: United Nations, p. vii
23. Chalmers. (2013).

24. Geoffrey Gray. (2014).
25. Antonellos, S., & Rantall, J. (2017).
26. Antonellos, S., & Rantall, J. (2017).
27. Wilson, W.A. (2004), p. 361.
28. Virtanen, P. K., Olsen, T., & Keskitalo, P. (2021).
29. Crate, S. A. (2008). "Eating hay": The ecology, economy and culture of Viliui Sakha smallholders of Northeastern Siberia. *Human Ecology, 36*(2), 161–174.
30. Crate, S. A. (2008), p. 167.
31. Ellington, L. (2019). Towards a recognition of the plurality of knowledge in social work: The Indigenous Research Paradigm. *Canadian Social Work Review/Revue Canadienne de Service Social, 36*(2), 29–48.
32. Cummins, I., Pinedo-Vasquez, M., Barnard, A., & Nasi, R. (2015). The Napo province: Site description. In *Agouti on the wedding menu: Bushmeat harvest, consumption and trade in a post-frontier region of the Ecuadorian Amazon* (pp. 9–13). Center for International Forestry Research.
33. Carruthers, D. V. (2001). The politics and ecology of indigenous folk art in Mexico. *Human Organization, 60*(4), 356–366.
34. Sturgeon, J. (2007). Pathways of "Indigenous Knowledge" in Yunnan, China. *Alternatives: Global, Local, Political, 32*(1), 129–153. https://doi.org/10.2307/40645205, p. 130.
35. Fischer, M., & Bacani, A. B. (2013). Fighting for land and identity: The perpetual struggle of the indigenous peoples in southwest Mindanao. In G. Wahlers (Ed.), *Minorities – social position and political representation* (pp. 43–67). Konrad Adenauer Stiftung.
36. Simon, S. (2010). Negotiating power: Elections and the constitution of indigenous Taiwan. *American Ethnologist, 37*(4), 726–740, p. 727.
37. Sturgeon, J. (2007), p. 134.
38. Fre, Z. (2018). The case for indigenous knowledge systems and knowledge sovereignty. In Knowledge Sovereignty Among African Cattle Herders (pp. 12–32). London: UCL Press.
39. Mullen, M. L. (2016). How the Irish Became Settlers: Metaphors of Indigeneity and the Erasure of Indigenous Peoples. New Hibernia Review/Iris Éireannach Nua, 20(3), 81–96
40. Mullen, M. L. (2016).
41. Johnson, P. C. (2002). Migrating Bodies, Circulating Signs: Brazilian Candomblé, the Garifuna of the Caribbean, and the Category of Indigenous Religions. History of Religions, 41(4), 301–327. http://www.jstor.org/stable/3176451
42. TallBear, K. (2013). Genomic articulations of indigeneity. *Social Studies of Science, 43*(4), 509–533.
43. Virtanen, P. K., Olsen, T., & Keskitalo, P. (2021), p. 8.

44. United Nations. (2021). Overview. *5th Volume State of the world's indigenous peoples: Rights to Lands, Territories and Resources*. New York, NY: Author, p. x.
45. United Nations. (2004). *The concept of indigenous peoples*. New York, NY: Author, p. 2.
46. Virtanen, P. K., Olsen, T., & Keskitalo, P. (2021).
47. Virtanen, P. K., Olsen, T., & Keskitalo, P. (2021), p. 20.
48. Masolo, D. (2003). Philosophy and indigenous knowledge: An African perspective. *Africa Today, 50*(2), 21–38.
49. United Nations. (2004), p. 2.
50. Sturgeon, J. (2007).
51. Carruthers, D. V. (2001), p. 22.
52. Alfred, T., & Corntassel, J. (2005), p. 599.
53. Phipps, P. (2010). Performances of power: Indigenous cultural festivals as globally engaged cultural strategy. *Alternatives: Global, Local, Political, 35*(3), 217–240.
54. Alfred, T., & Corntassel, J. (2005), p. 602.
55. De Burgos, H. (2014). Contemporary Transformations of Indigenous Medicine and Ethnic Identity. *Anthropologica, 56*(2), 399–413, p. 402.
56. Poyer, L. (2022). "Martial myths" and native realities. In *War at the Margins: Indigenous Experiences in World War II* (pp. 90–100). University of Hawai'i Press. https://doi.org/10.2307/j.ctv2ngx5f5.10, p. 94.
57. Poyer, L. (2022). "Martial myths" and native realities. In *War at the Margins: Indigenous Experiences in World War II* (pp. 90–100). University of Hawai'i Press. https://doi.org/10.2307/j.ctv2ngx5f5.10, p. 94.
58. Masolo, D. (2003).
59. Wilson, W.A. (2004). Introduction: *Indigenous knowledge recovery is indigenous empowerment*. American Indian Quarterly, 28(3/4), 359–372, p. 359.
60. Virtanen, P. K., Olsen, T., & Keskitalo, P. (2021).
61. Knopf, K. (2015). The turn toward the indigenous: Knowledge systems and practices in the academy. *Amerikastudien/American Studies, 60*(2/3), 179–200.
62. Cresswell, J.W. & Creswell, J.D. (2020). *Research design: Qualitative, quantitative and mixed methods approaches*. Los Angeles, CA: Sage, p. 26.
63. Barnhardt, R., & Kawagley, A. (2005). Indigenous Knowledge Systems and Alaska Native Ways of Knowing. *Anthropology & Education Quarterly, 36*(1), 8–23.
64. Muller, S. (2012). 'Two ways': Bringing indigenous and non-indigenous knowledges together. In J. K. Weir (Ed.), *Country, native title and ecology* (Vol. 24, pp. 59–80). ANU Press.

65. Mawere, M. (2015). Indigenous knowledge and public education in Sub-Saharan Africa. *Africa Spectrum, 50*(2), 57–71, p. 59.
66. Dodson, M., & Barr, O. (2007). Breaking the deadlock: Developing an indigenous response to protecting indigenous traditional knowledge. *Australian Indigenous Law Review, 11*(2), 19–32.
67. Mawere, M. (2015).
68. Chinweizu, Jemie, O., & Madubuike, I. (1980). *Towards the decolonization of African literature: African fiction and poetry and their critics* (vol. 1). Enugu, Nigeria: Fourth Dimension Publishers, p. 42.
69. Knopf, K. (2015).
70. Akena, F. (2012). Critical analysis of the production of Western knowledge and its implications for indigenous knowledge and decolonization. *Journal of Black Studies, 43*(6), 599–619.
71. Luyaluka, K. (2016). An Essay on Naturalized Epistemology of African Indigenous Knowledge. Journal of Black Studies, 47(6), 497–523, p. 498.
72. Ellington, L. (2019). Towards a recognition of the plurality of knowledge in social work: The Indigenous Research Paradigm. *Canadian Social Work Review/Revue Canadienne de Service Social, 36*(2), 29–48.
73. Okafor, V.O. (1991). Diop and the African origin of civilization: An Afrocentric analysis. *Journal of Black Studies, 22*(2), 252–268, p. 254.
74. Masolo, D. (2003). Philosophy and indigenous knowledge: An African perspective. *Africa Today, 50*(2), 21–38.
75. Barnhardt, R., & Kawagley, A. (2005), p. 9.
76. Wane, N. (2005). African indigenous knowledge: Claiming, writing, storing, and sharing the discourse. *Journal of Thought, 40*(2), 27–46.
77. Porsanger, J., Seurujärvi-Kari, I., & Nystad, R. L. (2021). 'Shared remembering' as a relational indigenous method in conceptualization of Sámi Women's Leadership. In P. K. Virtanen, P. Keskitalo, & T. Olsen (Eds.), *Indigenous Research Methodologies in Sámi and Global Contexts* (pp. 144–174). Brill.
78. Kovach, M., Carriere, J., Barrett, M. J., Montgomery, H., & Gillies, C. (2013). Stories of diverse identity locations in indigenous research. *International Review of Qualitative Research, 6*(4), 487–509. https://doi.org/10.1525/irqr.2013.6.4.487, p. 490.
79. Ugboajah, F. (1998). *Mass communication culture and society in West Africa*. Munchen, Germany: Hans Zell Publishers.
80. Turner, L.H., & West, R. (2019). *An Introduction to communication*. Cambridge, United Kingdom: Cambridge University Press.
81. Akpabio, E. (2021). *African communication systems and the digital age*. London England: Routledge.
82. Wilson, W.A. (2004).
83. Akpabio, E. (2021).

CHAPTER 2

Researching and Classifying Indigenous Communication

Introduction

Based on the marginalization that anything indigenous has been subjected to, this chapter goes to great lengths to show that indigenous scholarship is at par with that of their western counterparts given the effort put in by indigenous scholars to make it come into its own. These efforts revolve around surfacing indigenous philosophical worldview, research methodologies and designs. This would assist scholars interested in doing research in indigenous communities. We then proceed to discuss models and classification of communication and show their intersection with indigenous communication. The classification of communication drawing from indigenous research and scholarship sets the tone for the rest of the book.

Philosophical Worldview of Indigenous Knowledge

Worldviews are beliefs that guide action, and they are also referred to as paradigms, epistemologies, and ontologies as well as research methodologies.[1] Since indigenous knowledge is just coming in from the cold that Western researchers and scholars had consigned it, one must go to great lengths to show its epistemological basis so that it can take its pride of place in the pantheon of knowledge. There exists the contention that to have been able to administer huge, centralized states in precolonial Africa

© The Author(s), under exclusive license to Springer Nature Switzerland AG 2024
E. Akpabio, *Indigenous Communication*,
https://doi.org/10.1007/978-3-031-41766-5_2

presupposes the presence of scientific knowledge.[2] To support this argument, the looted bronze, iron and other artwork and artefacts from Africa sufficiently impressed the Belgian, English and French colonialists that pilfering them to display in their museums since their societies did not possess such knowledge is another clear pointer to ancient technology. In fact, indigenous knowledge has been appropriated for commercial purposes in artwork, music medicine etc. without consent.[3] It has been pointed out that "many elements of *modern* science (modern medicine, agriculture, mathematics, etc.) are partly rooted in indigenous knowledge principles, a historical truism which is often neglected…"[4]

The manner Western scholars engage with indigenous knowledge when they see it as worthy of study has been called into question. The British in their research of the First Nation Peoples was intended to prove that Australia was terra nullius to justify their occupation and plunder.[5] The dehumanization of indigenous people was also perpetrated through research. These included "measuring" their intelligence, forcing them to eat rotten food or contract diseases so that consequences of these could be studied.[6] This study and "quantification of Indigenous-specific physical and intellectual characteristics was also intended to shape science as an activity aimed at generalization and universality."[7] Research involving the Sámi people in Finnish, Norwegian, Swedish, German, Italian, and French, among other languages were racist and stereotypical.[8] And this was to be expected as outsiders were the experts on Sámi and other indigenous people who were the most studied demographic from the 1940s to the 1990s.[9] Western research emphasis on positivist, materialistic, reductionist and objectivist approaches that involve compartmentalizing knowledge was seen as strange from an Indian perspective in the indices of the understanding of humans and their place in society.[10]

Research on First Nation Peoples in Canada was not any different hence the researchers are referred to by aboriginal researchers as "poachers".[11] This is because they collect cultural gems from the community for their own financial and professional gain, do not impart research benefits to the community and publish their findings in a language inappropriate to the worldview of the natives.[12] This is not all. They also "often miss essential truths as they view indigenous people through the lens of their own culture. Often they cannot discern that indigenous knowledge stands on its own and does not require constant comparison(s) to other ways to be understood or validated."[13] Hence research, to indigenous people, conjures images of imperialism, power and colonialization.[14]

Scholars have called into question how fit for purpose some of the traditional methodologies are for studying indigenous issues because they "constrain descriptions and obscure the hybrid and heterogeneous nature of indigenous or local knowledge and modes of understanding."[15] They dismiss anything that does not fit into pre-existing categories as well as different paradigms.[16] The indigenous people that were at the receiving end of such research have nothing good to say about their experiences. The adjectives they have deployed in describing it includes theft of emotion and spirit; anger and negativity; exploitation and intrusion and; forcing the findings into preexisting categories designed by researchers hence no tangible outcomes for the indigenous people.[17] In Blair's words they were being researched to death.[18]

The constructivist and transformative worldviews that accommodates varied and multiple meanings for the former and the emphasis on inquiry that addresses social oppression and inequities for the latter[19] are quite useful in the context of indigenous knowledge. According to Mertens and Cram, the paradigm "has space within it for many worlds and tolerance of the complexity of subjectivities and identities of inhabitants."[20] But it also a matter of urgency to redress the academy's complicity in racial and colonial genocide[21] as the foregoing aptly demonstrates. Bearing in mind also that these findings also informed government policies and posture towards indigenous peoples.[22]

INDIGENOUS RESEARCH METHODOLOGIES

The racist undertones that informed research of and on indigenous peoples primed the drive towards emancipatory methodologies.[23] Unlike Western research, the epistemology of indigenous knowledge sees a connected whole. It is "constructed through understanding connections of species to each other, to people, ancestors, stories, dances, art, science, politics, economics, power, society and the cosmos."[24] Knowledge in most indigenous contexts is relational and inclusive of land and "other-than humans."[25] It involves going beyond Western modes. This would involve the indigenous people doing the research about themselves based on their knowledge and language as opposed to being studied by outsiders.[26] It should reflect indigenous values and practices such as using the wisdom of elders and serving the community's interests.[27]

In practical terms, this would involve

a method of *muittašit ovttas* 'shared remembering' for collecting of information, and a '*solju*' both as a method and analytical tool, structuring and presenting in an interconnected way the experiences and strategic choices.... These methods are consistent with Sámi orality, value systems and epistemologies, and are grounded in experiences, memories, relationality and spirituality, allowing the establishment of logical connections between actions and values in a way that is peculiar to Sámi ways of thinking.[28]

The authors note that the use of these methods involved the indigenous language. This idea of "talking circles"[29] has parallels in story telling as a research method in another context. This is because the use of the local language and the sharing of experiences is validating, empowering and assists in the epistemological process.[30]

Yarning is also another methodology that is closely related to these. Yarning involves connectedness and relatedness as well as centres the voices and lived experiences of indigenous peoples hence makes for deeper dialogue and learning.[31] Blair outlines it contours:

Yarning has no beginning and no end and is not a process in search of a right answer. It is a process engaging deep listening with thematic ideas engaging and prompting the yarn where necessary. Yarning and reflection were employed as the research process. It centres their experiences and reflections presenting these views verbatim so as not to lose the richness of expression and meaning. I will not analyse the words, classify them nor reorganise them. It is time that researchers *listened* (emphasis author) to the voices of the researched.[32]

Indigenous methodologies involve participatory action research and empowerment evaluation.[33] In the context of the Lakota people, this is

grounded in the ideas of *wopasi* ("inquiry") and *tokata wasagle tunpi* ("something you set up to go to in the future"), which views research and evaluation as the process of creating knowledge in order to accomplish an end that is desired by the people.

This is also in line with Community-Based Participatory Research (CBPR) that are regarded as more culturally responsive in that these methodologies feature equitable involvement of community members and results in changes for the better.[34] It requires long-term commitment to respectful relationship and commitment of resources for capacity building.[35] Thompson, Miller, and Cameron cite the example of Photovoice which assists in advancing the goals of CBPR in that:

> First, participants select what to photograph. They tell their stories to one another but with facilitation by researchers, and they select their own photos for exhibition. Second, participants reflect on larger social issues impacting their lives and identify actions to take both individually and collectively, again facilitated by researchers. Finally, they develop participatory skills within a collective group of other participant researchers.[36]

A number of scholars have encouraged collaboration between indigenous and non-indigenous researchers, but the challenge is that giving the bad blood from the recent past they would speak above each other's head.[37] Weber-PillWax cites a common response by non-indigenous scholars to their indigenous counterparts as "the inarticulate ramblings of schizophrenia," and/or "the whines of dissatisfied and ungrateful children."

Critical Indigenous Research Methodologies (CIRM) is time consuming as researchers coming from outside of the community must build relationships and establish trust; honor respect; engage reciprocity; enact responsibility and; remain accountable with and to Indigenous community members.[38] The focus of CIRM is sovereignty and self-determination.[39] These have some parallels with Tribal participatory research (TPR) involvement of community members through tribal oversight, facilitation and training of research staff as well as use of culturally appropriate procedures.[40]

Principles flowing an Indian worldview such as all living things must be respected and seen as interrelated; there should be benefits to the community being studied; the research must revolve around lived indigenous experiences; theories developed must be grounded in indigenous epistemologies; transformation is expected of all research participants; it should not undermine the integrity of any indigenous people of community; and the language and culture of indigenous peoples are living and breathing organisms.

Similarly, Indigenist Research Methodology is grounded on the following: Resistance, political integrity and privileging of indigenous voices.[41] According to Rigney,[42] it is research undertaken by indigenous Australians to free themselves from the stranglehold they have been subjected to by the British settlers, ventilate their resilience in the face of the oppression they have been subjected to and give voice to their culture and way of life since they are best placed to do this themselves than outsiders. It must have self-locating information that serves two functions

> Firstly, it offers a relational placing, introductory function. For many Indigenous peoples, it is an intuitive act that precedes a formal address, and with our introductions there is often an acknowledgement of place, elders, friends. In oral addresses, this is an opportunity to show respect for place and allows for community to locate us. Within research this introductory function is significant because it gives an initial indication of the researcher's relationship to Indigenous knowledge systems. This provides the first indication of how the research may proceed and the perspective that will be employed. Secondly, self-locating in Indigenous research gives opportunity to explore the influences in our own life, and through the protocol of introduction we immediately bring the researcher self into our research. Introducing and locating oneself are an integral part of Indigenous methodologies and they ask that we as researchers put ourselves out there.[43]

Clearly, there are disparate voices even though there are areas of commonalities in how to proceed in terms of research on indigenous peoples. This is because indigenous people are not a monolithic lot. Hence Weber-Pillwax rubbishes assumptions of standardization of indigenous research methodologies for standardization and comparative purposes as well as that it would enable a more scholarly critique but does concede that that should be a raison détre for such a methodology so that a modicum of sanity prevails.[44]

Models and Classification of Indigenous Communication

By models is meant "a structure of symbols and operating rules which is supposed to match a set of relevant points in an existing structure or process." The concept has been used to capture everything "from physical and fictional objects through set-theoretic structures to mathematical equations, as well as combinations of some or all of these" including mathematical formalism, visual diagrams, as well as theoretical ideas, policy views, and metaphors.[45] They are useful simply because we cannot physically grasp what they stand for.[46] For instance we "use maps or anatomical atlases precisely because we cannot carry complete countries or complete human bodies in our heads."[47]

Modelling involves making judgments so much so that what is captured is what is regarded as salient and important from the purview of the author.[48] The same posture plays out in communication modelling with the background of authors playing a role in terms of how they model the process. For instance, Shannon's, who has an engineering background, model revolves around an information source, a message, transmitter, signal, noise, received signal, receiver, received message, and destination, naturally.[49] Weaver was of the view that this engineering conception of communication could also apply to humanities.[50] But Harrah notes that a translator and semanticist adds "expansion-into-ordinary-idiom to the usual decoding"[51] thus buttressing the point about how background impacts one's conception of the communication process.

The limitation of models is also something to be borne in mind given the narrow lens from which the process is approached. However, the different conceptions and limitations do not detract from the usefulness of models in terms of throwing light on any matter that they cater to. For instance, Laswell's model – who say what to whom with what effect – requires where, when, and in what social situation?[52] In addition, the information processing nature of earlier conceptions of communication are regarded as simplistic as they did not consider the "interactive structure of discourse processes"[53] more so in human communication as illustrated below

> A mother and a son and a daughter, sitting around a table, talking. The mother says she is going to the mountains for the next week. The children will stay at home with father. In this situation, there is not one message. There are at least three. 1) The message the mother means to send. 2) The message received and reconstructed by the daughter. 3) The message received and reconstructed by the son.[54]

The mother may be signaling her independence, while her daughter gets the message that she is not wanted and the son perceives that he will have more time to himself.[55] But even the thought of going to the mountains may not entirely be hers. If it came from "the unconscious" does it qualify as hers thus calling into question whether she indeed qualifies to be designated as the source?[56] This mystery of the unconscious is really at the heart of indigenous communication which Western thought and philosophy have failed to explain.[57]

The discussion so far capture the linear, interactional, transactional and holistic models of communication.[58] The Source, Message Channel, Receiver (SMCR) model that did not have a feedback component is a hallmark of the linear model while models with feedback component that completes the communication loop fall in the second category. How to conceive of the transactional model is to imagine jugglers throwing balls to one another simultaneously as it is marked by mutual giving and receiving of messages.[59] Turner and West's holistic model builds on the transactional model by adding five components: The first three – cultural, historical and situational contexts – references the fact that all communication is made possible by traditions and norms, history and even the situation one finds themselves. While the fourth – field of experience – references the commonalities that make exchange of messages possible and thus produces the fifth component – effect. For example in the context of indigenous communication, if you do not speak an indigenous language, there are two different fields of experience that may not allow for a smooth exchange of messages. But even that language has a context which can be historical, situational and cultural. So, when an Ibibio in South-south Nigeria person says "akpotiki" (meaning Portuguese),[60] it conveys historical contact and the other emotions based on how the new entrants engaged with the indigenous communities.

The models and classification of indigenous communication also reflect these conceptions. Doob's (1961) model is cyclical and consist of twelve variables: The communicator, goal, basic media, extending media, site, restrictions, communication, mood, perception, reactions, changes and ends with feedback.[61] Ugboajah's traditional-urban model aims to exploit indigenous communication and legacy media to their fullest potential by combining the formal urban sector with the informal rural as well as formal/informal nature of the slums for effective communication as well as to achieve the goals of development.[62] Communication resources are combined to produce a news equilibrium that caters for the various sectors.[63] This shares similarities with the trado-modern concept that looks more at effectiveness of message delivery in the sense that the combination of indigenous communication and the traditional mass media would be more effective since the weaknesses of each is made up for by the advantages they each bring to the message dissemination table.[64]

Ansu-Kyeremeh's intra-village communication embraces venue-oriented communication, events as communication modes, games as communication and performance – oriented communication.[65] Similarly,

Wilson's classification of African traditional communication is based on the forms of communication he observes the rural areas of two Nigerian states – Cross River and Akwa Ibom: Instrumental, demonstrative, iconographic, extra-mundane, visual and institutional.[66] However, his classifications have a lot in common with categories of nonverbal communication: Vocal nonverbal sounds such as laughing, yawning etc.; non-vocal nonverbal sounds such shooting arrows or making music amongst others; silence; free gestures such as facial expression etc.; bound or self-adapting gestures such as grooming, jewelry etc.; body-adapting movements such as clothes, headgear etc.; posture such as prostrate, bow etc.; gait such as manner of walking; responses to the autonomic nervous system such as blush, weep etc.; proxemics such as distances between people and orientation etc.; alter-adapting movement such as stroke, kiss etc. and; metaphor.[67]

Other ways in which messages can be transmitted are

1. Gesture: gestures may be numerous or few, expansive or inhibited, free or stereotyped, jerky or smooth. 2. Posture: not just the altitude (lying, sitting, kneeling, standing) and attitude (or angle) of the position, but whether the person is relaxed or tense, steady or unsteady. 3. Facial expression: scowl, smile, nature of gaze. 4. Bodily adornment : clothing, cosmetics, hair or beard style, jewellery, insignia, tattoo. 5. Gait: manner and pace of locomotion. 6. Autonomic nervous system responses which reveal emotional states : blush, pale, horripilate, sweat, tremble, weep. 7. Silence. 8. Eye contact or avoidance: an important source of signals about fear and security, dominance and submission. 9. Spatial arrangements : arrangements of furniture or distance between bodies. 10. Odours. 11. Pictures : painting, sculpture, mosaic, engraving, diagrams. 12. Dance, mime. 13. Architecture. 14. Music. 15. Handwriting (graphology).16. Tone, volume, timbre, pitch, speed of utterance. 17. Nonverbal human sounds: wail, snore, groan, whistle, etc. 18. Touch – self or others: kiss, embrace, stroke, hit, fidget, scratch. 19. Inanimate signalling devices: spears, arrows, stones, flags, mirrors, smoke.[68]

Akpabio has synthesized the indigenous communication in the African setting into instrumental, demonstrative, iconographic, extra-mundane, visual, institutional, venue-oriented, mythological, taxonomic and axiomatic communication.[69] However, to do justice to global indigenous communication which have a number of similarities, but which is by no means monolithic, proxemics which seem to be absent from the categorization will also feature in our discussion going forward.

Based on Akpabio's[70] categorization, the instrumental communication component will feature devices that accompany music, song and dance and that also have ritual and religious uses. Demonstrative communication is about music that has both social and cultural properties. Iconographic communication is all about signs and symbols as well as the messages they communicate. Extra-mundane communication will embrace the supernatural component with is a pervasive element in the indigenous worldview. Visual communication will feature cues supplied by appearance, hairdo, tribal marks, tattoos etc. Institutional communication will report on chieftaincy, secret societies and other structures in indigenous communities that ensures smooth running and harmonious relationships. Venue-oriented communication will play up the role of habitation patterns and markets. Myths and legends and the massages they convey will feature in mythological communication while taxonomic communication will feature significance of personal and place names. Folktales and proverbs will be the highlight of axiomatic communication. To be added to the classification is proxemics which is about distances between persons and orientation.

Conclusion

The chapter calls into question Western philosophical assumptions, methodologies and designs that have been evil wind in the context of indigenous research and scholarship. The saving grace being the constructivist and transformative worldviews which rightly offers redress. It then locates and properly situates indigenous paradigms, methodologies and designs in any investigation into indigenous communities. The chapter also features categorization of communication by indigenous researchers – instrumental, demonstrative, iconographic, extra-mundane, visual, institutional, venue-oriented, mythological, taxonomic, axiomatic communication and proxemics for a fuller treatment in the book going forward.

Notes

1. Cresswell, J.W. & Creswell, J.D. (2020). *Research design: Qualitative, quantitative and mixed methods approaches.* Los Angeles, CA: Sage.
2. Luyaluka, K. (2016). An essay on naturalized epistemology of African Indigenous Knowledge. *Journal of Black Studies,* 47(6), 497–523, p. 498.

3. Dodson, M., & Barr, O. (2007). Breaking the deadlock: Developing an indigenous response to protecting indigenous traditional knowledge. *Australian Indigenous Law Review, 11*(2), 19–32.
4. Fre, Z. (2018). The case for indigenous knowledge systems and knowledge sovereignty. In Knowledge Sovereignty Among African Cattle Herders (pp. 12–32). London: UCL Press.
5. Rigney, L.-I. (1999). Internationalization of an indigenous anticolonial cultural critique of research methodologies: A guide to indigenist research methodology and its principles. *Wicazo Sa Review, 14*(2), 109–121. https://doi.org/10.2307/1409555
6. Ellington, L. (2019). Towards a recognition of the plurality of knowledge in social work: The Indigenous Research Paradigm. *Canadian Social Work Review/Revue Canadienne de Service Social, 36*(2), 29–48.
7. Ellington, L. (2019), p. 32.
8. Virtanen, P. K., Olsen, T., & Keskitalo, P. (2021). Contemporary Indigenous Research within Sámi and Global Indigenous Studies Contexts. In P. K. Virtanen, T. Olsen, & P. Keskitalo (Eds.), *Indigenous Research Methodologies in Sámi and Global Contexts* (pp. 7–32). Brill.
9. Ellington, L. (2019).
10. Duane Champagne. (2015). Centering indigenous nations within indigenous methodologies. *Wicazo Sa Review, 30*(1), 57–81. https://doi.org/10.5749/wicazosareview.30.1.0057
11. Struthers, R. (2001). Conducting sacred research: An indigenous experience. *Wicazo Sa Review, 16*(1), 125–133, p. 127.
12. Struthers, R. (2001).
13. Struthers, R. (2001), p. 127.
14. Lemley, C. K., & Teller, J. H. (2014). Reports from the field: "Eneq's Ke:s – Kake:ketikuaq Omae:qnomene:wak" ("The Menominee have spoken"): Mentorship and collaboration in an indigenous community. *Journal of American Indian Education, 53*(1), 42–53.
15. Carothers, C., Moritz, M., & Zarger, R. (2014). Introduction: conceptual, methodological, practical, and ethical challenges in studying and applying indigenous knowledge. *Ecology and Society, 19*(4), p. 43.
16. Muller, S. (2012). 'Two ways': Bringing indigenous and non-indigenous knowledges together. In J. K. Weir (Ed.), *Country, native title and ecology* (Vol. 24, pp. 59–80). ANU Press.
17. Blair, N. (2015). Researched to death: Indigenous peoples talkin' up our experiences of research. *International Review of Qualitative Research, 8*(4), 463–478.
18. Blair, N. (2015), p. 463.
19. Cresswell, J.W. & Creswell, J.D. (2020).

20. Mertens, D. M., & Cram, F. (2016). Integration tensions and possibilities: Indigenous research and social transformation. *International Review of Qualitative Research*, 9(2), 185–191, p. 185.
21. Morgensen, S. L. (2012). Destabilizing the settler academy: The decolonial effects of indigenous methodologies. *American Quarterly*, 64(4), 805–808.
22. Riley, L. (2021). Community-led research through an Aboriginal lens. In L. Riley, V. Rawlings, & J. L. Flexner (Eds.), *Community-led research: Walking new pathways together* (pp. 9–38).
23. Rigney, L.-I. (1999). Internationalization of an Indigenous Anticolonial Cultural Critique of Research Methodologies: A guide to Indigenist Research Methodology and its principles. *Wicazo Sa Review*, 14(2), 109–121. https://doi.org/10.2307/1409555
24. Muller, S. (2012), p. 60.
25. Virtanen, P. K., Olsen, T., & Keskitalo, P. (2021). Contemporary Indigenous Research within Sámi and Global Indigenous Studies Contexts. In P. K. Virtanen, T. Olsen, & P. Keskitalo (Eds.), *Indigenous Research Methodologies in Sámi and Global Contexts* (pp. 7–32). Brill, p. 12.
26. Porsanger, J., & Seurujärvi-Kari, I. (2021). Sámi dutkama máttut: The Forerunners of Sámi Methodological Thinking. In P. K. Virtanen, P. Keskitalo, & T. Olsen (Eds.), *Indigenous research methodologies in sámi and global contexts* (pp. 33–64). Brill.
27. Dana-sacco, G. (2010). The indigenous researcher as individual and collective: Building a research practice ethic within the context of indigenous languages. *American Indian Quarterly*, 34(1), 61–82. https://doi.org/10.5250/amerindiquar.34.1.61
28. Porsanger, J., Seurujärvi-Kari, I., & Nystad, R. L. (2021). 'Shared remembering' as a relational indigenous method in conceptualization of Sámi Women's Leadership. In P. K. Virtanen, P. Keskitalo, & T. Olsen (Eds.), *Indigenous Research Methodologies in Sámi and Global Contexts* (pp. 144–174). Brill, pp. 145–146.
29. Keskitalo, P., Rasmussen, T., Rahko-Ravantti, R., & Äärelä-Vihriälä, R. (2021). Gáfestallan Talks of the Indigenous Research Paradigm in Sámi Research. In P. Keskitalo, P. K. Virtanen, & T. Olsen (Eds.), *Indigenous Research Methodologies in Sámi and Global Contexts* (pp. 65–83). Brill, p. 67.
30. Iseke, J. (2013). Indigenous Storytelling as Research. *International Review of Qualitative Research*, 6(4), 559–577. https://doi.org/10.1525/irqr.2013.6.4.559
31. Blair, N. (2015).
32. Blair, N. (2015), p. 464.
33. Robertson, P., Miriam Jorgensen, & Carrie Garrow. (2004). Indigenizing evaluation research: How Lakota methodologies are helping "raise the

tipi" in the Oglala Sioux Nation. *American Indian Quarterly*, 28(3/4), 499–526.
34. Thompson, N. L., Miller, N. C., & Cameron, A. F. (2016). The indigenization of photovoice methodology: Visioning indigenous head start in Michigan. *International Review of Qualitative Research*, 9(3), 296–322.
35. Dana-sacco, G. (2010).
36. Thompson, N. L., Miller, N. C., & Cameron, A. F. (2016), p. 298.
37. Weber-Pillwax, C. (1999). Indigenous research methodology: Exploratory discussion of an elusive subject. *The Journal of Educational Thought (JET) / Revue de La Pensée Éducative*, 33(1), 31–45.
38. Lemley, C. K., & Teller, J. H. (2014). Reports from the field: "Eneq's Ke:s – Kake:ketikuaq Omae:qnomene:wak" ("The Menominee have spoken"): Mentorship and collaboration in an indigenous community. *Journal of American Indian Education*, 53(1), 42–53.
39. Lemley, C. K., & Teller, J. H. (2014).
40. Dana-sacco, G. (2010).
41. Rigney, L.-I. (1999).
42. Rigney, L.-I. (1999).
43. Kovach, M., Carriere, J., Barrett, M. J., Montgomery, H., & Gillies, C. (2013). Stories of diverse identity locations in indigenous research. *International Review of Qualitative Research*, 6(4), 487–509. https://doi.org/10.1525/irqr.2013.6.4.487, p. 497.
44. Weber-Pillwax, C. (1999).
45. Ciula, A., Eide, Ø., Marras, C., & Sahle, P. (2018). Modelling: Thinking in practice. An introduction. *Historical Social Research/Historische Sozialforschung. Supplement*, 31, 7–29, p. 8.
46. Deutsch, K. W. (1952). On Communication Models in the Social Sciences. *The Public Opinion Quarterly*, 16(3), 356–380.
47. Deutsch, K. W. (1952), p. 358.
48. Deutsch, K. W. (1952).
49. Harrah, D. (1956). A Model of Communication. *Philosophy of Science*, 23(4), 333–342.
50. The Communication Process: Conceptual Models for Research and Teaching. (1956). *College Composition and Communication*, 7(3), 165–166.
51. Harrah, D. (1956), p. 337.
52. The Communication Process: Conceptual Models for Research and Teaching. (1956). *College Composition and Communication*, 7(3), 165–166, p. 166.
53. McHoul, A. W. (1983). Announcing: A Contribution to the Critique of Information Systems Models of Human Communication. *Human Studies*, 6(3), 279–294, p. 279.

54. Gozzi, R. (2004). Where is the "message" in communication models? *Etc: A Review of General Semantics, 61*(1), 145–146, p. 145.
55. Gozzi, R. (2004).
56. Gozzi, R. (2004).
57. Gozzi, R. (2004).
58. Turner, L.H., & West, R. (2019). *An Introduction to communication.* Cambridge, United Kingdom: Cambridge University Press.
59. Turner, L.H., & West, R. (2019).
60. Urua, E., Ekpenyong, M., Gibbon, D. (2004). Uyo Ibibio dictionary. Uyo, Nigeria: ABUILD Language Documentation Curriculum Project.
61. Doob, L (1966). *Communication in Africa: A search for boundaries.* New Haven, Connecticut, CT: Yale University Press.
62. Ugboajah, F.O. (1972). Traditional-urban media model: Stocktaking for African development. *International Communication Gazette, 18,* 76–95.
63. Ugboajah, F.O. (1972).
64. Akpabio, E. (2021). *African communication systems and the digital age.* London England: Routledge.
65. Ansu-Kyeremeh, K. (2005) Indigenous communication systems. A conceptual framework. In K. Ansu-Kyeremeh (Ed.). *Indigenous communication in Africa: Concept, application and prospects* (pp. 39–61). Accra: Ghana Universities Press.
66. Wilson, D. (2005). A taxonomy of traditional media in Africa. In K. Ansu-Kyeremeh (Ed.). *Indigenous communication in Africa: Concept, application and prospects* (pp. 39–61). Accra: Ghana Universities Press.
67. Newbold, R.F. (1990). Nonverbal communication in Tacitus and Ammianus. *Ancient Society, 21,* 189–199.
68. Newbold, R.F. (1990). Nonverbal communication and parataxis in late antiquity. *L'Antiquité Classique, 55* (223–244), p. 225.
69. Akpabio, E. (2021).
70. Akpabio, E. (2021).

CHAPTER 3

Instrumental Communication

INTRODUCTION

The category embraces devices which serve as "accompaniment in music, song and dance as well as dissemination of messages."[1] They say a lot about society in which they found in that they have symbolic roles and meanings as well as play significant roles in ritual, music and dance.[2] Musical instruments have a critical role to play in cultural research in addition to communicating about the mental and spiritual life of a people through their secular and ritual deployments.[3] They speak to the musical achievement of a people as well as the cultural importance of their music.[4] They are also very dynamic in that they "interact dialectically with surrounding physical and cultural realities, and as such, they perpetually negotiate or renegotiate their roles, physical structures, performance modes, sound ideals, and symbolic meanings."[5] Instruments can be reflective of society and its belief system.

In the African setting these instruments serve a variety of purposes. Wachsmann acknowledges that there are many uses, but he focuses on three: Social function, belief and physiological factors.[6] The social function has to do with ensuring order in society and this orderly nature of society reciprocates with the continued use of the instrument. Examples are the Nnam who use the skin drum and gong for law enforcement as well as the horn or bell man who was a palace messenger among the

© The Author(s), under exclusive license to Springer Nature Switzerland AG 2024
E. Akpabio, *Indigenous Communication*,
https://doi.org/10.1007/978-3-031-41766-5_3

Yorubas, both of Nigeria.[7] The belief component involves the sacred nature of the instrument which is not seen as just any musical instrument:

> Their powers may relate to healing, physical strength, farming and hunting, safeguarding villages, or help with family problems, and musical instruments may facilitate spirit possession and exorcism, or serve as vehicles for communication between the worlds of the seen and the unseen.[8]

The physiological component speaks to a strong bond between instrument and musical form and this bond complements the "cultural system."[9] Let us take a closer look at the instruments and the meanings they communicate.

Drums

The Afghan circular frame drum has rings of bells on the inside and is regarded as being the only one for females and is used for singing, dancing and ritual with different rhythms based on the event such as weddings and processions.[10] The rhythm is achieved by "striking the centre or the edge of the drum, by 'walking' the fingers across the membrane, and by snapping the little finger of the hand that supports the drum, sharply against the rim."[11] Gender exclusivity and empowerment at work, clearly. This frame drum which goes by various names across the middle East has been described as the "regions most characteristically feminine instrument" and is associated with women's dance tradition across the region.[12]

Music performance in some Punic (consisting of western Mediterranean – mainly Ibiza, South Iberia, North Africa, Sicily and Sardinia – Phoenician inhabitants of Carthage's colonies and Carthaginians themselves) rituals depended upon female expertise.[13] More so as there exists a relationship between women and music not just in terms of musical performance but also to the never ending cycle of managing birth, care and death.[14] This is corroborated by figurines unearthed from the Eastern Mediterranean (Greece, Samos and Boeotia), the Sicilian and Greek South Italian as well as Punics from Ibiza that show females playing drums.[15] It has been posited that the figurines playing hand drums represented the Punic goddess Asarte who played drums to ward off evil spirits as well as to purify the environment.[16]

Ancient Chinese drums were employed for entertainment along with other ancient musical instruments.[17] In Malawi, names of drum communicate "rhythm and timbre rather than… pitch; a few have connotations of a characteristic, most commonly steadiness or firmness, regarded approvingly in the instrument or its performance." Drums in the Baltic region were beaten during wars and with glee if victory was achieved.[18]

Bombitos or little drums are used in Cauzúlor festival that marks the release of water into the communal irrigation canal in the Atacameñas localities in Chile.[19] The Kultrùn is a drum made of a single skin of which a symbolic figure with four parts is painted with its body made from a hollowed-out piece of wood that contains small rounded pebbles.[20] The figure communicates the supernatural world as well as terrestrial reality.[21] Afro Cuban drummers are said to leave out "certain rhythmic patterns that communicate with the orichas" in public performances as they are not allowed to perform these "secrets parts" outside of a ritual and religious setting.[22] In Vodou ceremonies in Haiti, worshippers call on Outo the god of drumming who is also the guardian of the sacred ceremonial drums.[23]

The Stone drum or Keho in Easter island Chile is an interesting variations from the traditional skin or wooden hollowed-out drums as it involved digging a hole "about a meter in depth and a meter in diameter, at the bottom of which a large open gourd was placed, supported by some sand; one covered it by a flat stone on which a single person danced."[24] The drums of the Mohica of Peru also had some unique features. Apart from the large drums, there were those with no rims or binding that makes it possible to tighten the drum rather "the skins are attached directly on the body of the instrument and are stretched by means of a thin leather strap which links them together."[25] The Pohnpei of Micronesia's drum has an hourglass shape and is made from hollowed-out wood and covered in sharkskin.[26] It was beaten during difficult terms, to proclaim victory in war and installation of chiefs.[27]

The Marquesan drum was a very elaborate one with extra-mundane properties. They were made from a single piece of wood and those used in temple grounds could measure up to eight feet in height and 19 inch in diameter.[28] There were also a variety of sizes, but they also had carvings of religious figures (Tiki), sennit lashings as well as human hair and bone.[29] These have some similarities with the Li of China. They have the Nangnong which is a barrel-shaped, double-headed skin drum.[30] The drum is made from a log of wood which is carved into a barrel shape and the skin is that of cattle or yellow water-deer and decorated with paintings of pre-historic animals, birds, fishes and human beings.[31]

Ghana also has a variety of drums. In the Ga community hourglass and closed cylindrical drums as well as heavy drum (Obonu) and talking drum (Atumpan) are used in music associated with chiefs while small and medium-sized drums are using in cult and traditional engagements.[32] The drums are used to herald the approach of a chief in a procession, imitate speech ala talking drum and for dancing.[33] The Jembe (Djembe, Jembe), a goblet-shaped drum is popular in West Africa and is used for communal and family celebrations.[34] In Malaysia the major shapes of drum are tube, kettle and frame and they are mostly deployed in traditional music performances.[35]

The Li's people Nangnong communicated status as "it was usually hung by the door of the village head's house to symbolise its keeper's social status as the authority of the community."[36] It also had other uses with different signals used to communicate an attack on the community, call community meetings, call home cattle herders, add to the celebratory atmosphere during the new year celebrations, funerals etc. in the Hainan island of China[37] The slit drum among the Igbos of Nigeria had similar uses: To spread information, for ceremonial uses as well as sacrificial festivals.[38] The Marquesans single and double-headed membrane drum are also used for communication and could echo their "tone-words."[39] The Alak of Laos used their drums for processions as well as "group movements in rituals."[40]

Kettle drums were in wide use in fifteenth century Europe and were deployed as "signal instrument in church towers" thus the term "leather bells."[41] Drums made of a single shark skin was also used as signals among the Marquesans.[42] The other uses were for war, to sound an alarm, religious rituals such as human sacrifice, feasts, funerals and songs.[43] The religious and veneration attached to drums is also seen in India. The Mrdangam is said to the father of India instrument and the capture of a drum meant the defeat of the enemy.[44] This barrel drum was restricted only to boys.[45] Similarly, among the Ankole kingdom in Uganda was Bagyendanwa, a conical kettle drum, that was highly revered so much so that it had "its own household with its own servants, herds of cattle, musical instruments (!), and musicians. The drum's wealth was used to help those who turned to it for support."[46]

The master drummers of the Akan of Ghana are able to exercise musical authority as they direct proceedings in musical performances including sanctioning dancers who exceed the bounds of good taste: "the drums stop playing in the middle of a phrase and thus expose the offender to public ridicule."[47] Drums of various sizes among the Kavangos of Namibia are used to accompany singing.[48] Only men and boys are allowed to play the drums[49] unlike the situation in the middle east. The two-headed cylindrical drum of the Nawals of Guatemala called K'jom is regarded as a female instrument and represents the earth. Among the Malay, the slit drum is a part and parcel of traditional music performances.[50] Drums can also represent family. Among the Yorubas of Nigeria Bata drums you have "the biggest ... Iya Ilu 'mother'; next comes omele, 'the child that follows'; and the smallest is kudi, 'little one'."[51] A range of drums from the smallest to the gigantic war drums are lined up and played by the Machinga of Malawi during the Malambe festival in honour of the dead.[52]

The slit drum called Mondo or Mbudikidi in Congo is "made from a small log, with a short, narrow slit in the middle and a wider, rectangular opening at either end of the slit."[53] The drum is played with two sticks whose ends are wound with rubber thus giving the instrument a distinctive sound and it is used in judicial hearing in Eastern Congo.[54] The long standing drum called Ndembo was used in execution and was played all night on the eve of such an event.[55] The long drum Ndungu or Nlambula communicates arrival in the market of a person who elects to be a slave to the chief, poison ordeals, judicial hearings as well as summons the community to war.[56] An initiate into the Lemba cult group receives an Nkonzi drum as a sign of their new status which they hang on the door of their house as a sign of prestige and beauty.[57] Miniature drums are packed with medicines and worn as amulets.[58]

Chordophones (Lutes, Zithers and Harps)

Chordophones in Malay music consists of lutes, zithers, and harps. The most important bowed lute is the Rehab tiga tali that is used in storytelling.[59] Zithers consist of stick, ground and tube.[60] The first consists of a string attached to an arched stick with a resonator; the second called "batak (or gendand keba tak) which consists of one rattan string stretched between two pegs that are inserted on either side of a pit dug in the ground" and covered by a stretched layer of bark which then serves as a resonator; while the third is made of bamboo and takes the shape of a tube with strings that "are cut from the surface of the bamboo tube and are made taut by bridges that are placed under the string."[61]

Zither, which in Botswana is known as Segaba, is made up of a rod of barked wood, which is fitted with a string wire and resonator and ranges in length from 90 to 110 cm and with a width of 5–7 cm.[62] Phuthego does acknowledge that there are variations of the instrument across the continent such as Setinkane which the author describes as a truck ideophone or lamellaphone also known as Mbira in Zimbabwe and Sansa in other parts of Africa.[63] Other local names for the same instrument other than Setinkane are Sekanguru among the Tswana of southern Africa, Dinudi, Siwumba, Sebinjolo as well as do n!a o (Zu/wasi of Namibia), Isigankuri (Mpondo), Isicelekeshe (Zulu), Gorita (Damara) and ikatari (Xhosa).[64] In the Botswana context, the instrument is mainly used for relaxation and to pass time hence it is put out of sight when there is mourning or bereavement. In terms of communication, herders play it while herding cattle as the grazing cattle stay within earshot of the sound and are not likely to wander away.[65] So no need to chase after cattle when you can herd them with music from the Segaba.

The Chinese version (sê) consists of twenty-five strings of varying thickness and movable bridges and it was played resting on the body or on the floor.[66] The Han sê was used to produce religious music but when played along with another zither – Ch'in – it served a romantic purpose by promoting harmonious relationship among couples as well as being features in folk music, dancing and acrobatic orchestra as well as feasts.[67] In the Baltic region, string instruments from Riga was called Cythara Rigensium which was regarded as perhaps "a metaphor for the townsfolk's sorrow."

The zither is described as the most significant instrument in Baltic traditional music and produces music that is contemplative hence it is played in the evening.[68] The Koto which is the Japanese zither is also well regarded. It is described as the "most important national and traditional instruments."[69] Among the Cewa of Mali you have Bangwe and Pangwe which refer to zithers with tendons stretched across a board.[70] Among the Kavangos of Namibia the trough zither called Shivumba and thumb pianos, Sitandi limodumo and Sitandi ndingo, serve entertainment functions.[71] The Indian Zither – Vina – represent Sarasvati, the goddess of learning "with its curved neck, two gourds or breasts, and frets or bracelets."[72]

The thumb piano called Deza among the Lemba has various communication functions. It is a seen as a model of their community and it differentiates between different classes of people, their dwellings, the "python that encircles their village" as well as interpersonal relationships.[73] The keys of the piano communicate about people – "high notes are men, low notes are women. The sound is the crying of a newborn; child-that is, creation itself."[74] The raft-zither, among the Marogoli women of Kenya, is played as accompaniment to their harvest songs.[75] The thumb piano serves as companions to lonely travelers and is also said to keep evil spirits at bay.[76]

The Jew's Harp is found all over the world and they take the form of wood, metal or bamboo.[77] The bamboo version is common in southeast Asia, and it is possible that the harp itself originated here before spreading all over the world.[78] In Malay music the harp takes the form of wood and bamboo. The Jew's harp

> is made of a narrow strip of wood or bamboo with a "tongue" cut in the center but attached to the main piece of wood or bamboo at one end ... The player's Jaws hold the instrument and the "tongue" is plucked with the finger white the player changes the size of the mouth cavity to produce different pitches or timbres.[79]

Lithuania is another location where one can find the harp.[80] The instrument was popular in Estonia and Latvia but was said to have irregular use. Excavations have placed them mostly at the vicinity of medieval castles "which might explain some aspects of early history and provenance in the region."[81] The Bamboo Jew Harp among the Marquesans was used for simple past time, courting, private communication and dance performance.[82] An instance is when the Pakoko, the Hakahi'ki chief was arrested by the French, his wife would come and sit outside the prison and play the harp and the message among others was that the prisoners should "seize the first occasion to escape and to fear no obstacle."[83] The Jew Harp among the Li of China called Zhai is made of metal or bamboo.[84] The Kavango of Namibia's Jew Harp called Ruwenge is made from a section of a single stalk of sorghum stalk "cut to form a tongue, plucked by the player, and with a hole through the body of the ruwenge through which the player can blow and amplify the sound."[85]

Kalirangwe among the Cewa of Malawi refers to a single string plucked instrument played with the finger of still blade of grass. Pango in the same environment references an instrument that has only "one string, stretched along a stick to one end of which a gourd is attached; it is played by plucking with a piece of wood."[86] The Zeze harp is found among the Tumbuka as well as in Tanzania.[87] P'i p'a is a Chinese lute played by ballad-singing troubadours.[88]

Ginguru, the harp-lute of the Dogon of Mali is rich in communication. The trough-shaped wooden resonator is the image of the world,

> the concave floor of the resonator is the vault of the sky, with its acoustic equivalent being the high tones. The flat resonator table (a tight skin across the mouth of the trough) is the earth, with its acoustic equivalent the low tones. The inside of the trough is the atmosphere or ether. The four strings, spread out by a bridge (of a kind unknown in Western instruments), are the four cardinal points.[89]

The same instrument also communicates a weaver's loom as well as human anatomy.[90] Harps accompany lonely travelers and also keeps evil spirits away.[91]

The vina lute is associated with Saraswati, the Hindu goddess of wisdom, learning and the arts.[92] As a consequence, it has gender connotations and girls and women have adopted the instrument as theirs more so as "the vinas long neck represents her slender figure, its two gourd resonators imitate her breasts, and the metal frets resemble her bracelets."[93] The three string plucked lute in Tunisia is deployed in Stambeli possession ceremonies because of its ability to transcend the human and spirit world.[94]

Aerophones (Whistles, Flutes, Reeds and Pipes)

Pipes and flutes are also widespread and have various uses. In the Baltic region (comprising Latvia, Lithuania and Estonia), unearthed clay tablet depicts a piper with a conical pipe having four fingerholes.[95] Unearthed Punic figurines in addition to playing drums also were depicted playing double pipes or flutes which were "made of wood, reed, bone or even metal and played with a reed, probably a double reed."[96] In ancient China, the reed mouth organ is classified as belonging to the "gourd" category and is associated with funerals.[97] But this along with drums and zithers also served entertainment purposes.[98] Reeds, pipes and whistles were used as tools for amusement during herding in the Baltic region.[99] The mouth organ in Malaysia consist of a number of bamboo tubes that are sealed into a gourd and are used for music, dancing and chanting.[100]

Whistles in the Baltic region were made from different physical as well as spiritual materials

Single-pitched whistles (pajupill EE, svilpe, svelpïte, düda LV, švilpukas LT) are made of a willow or osier branch; they have a wooden block (or fibbie) at one end, while the other is stopped. A "piston- type" whistle with sliding stopper is also known. In making the whistle, a kind of **"symbolic" or "magic" technology is applied** (emphasis added): a spell is chanted during the loosening of bark from the branch. Vessel-shaped whistles without fingerholes or with one to six fingerholes (savipiilu, pardipill EE, svilpaunieks, pïlïte LV, molinukas LT) are made of clay in the form of a bird, horse or devil.[101]

In terms of their use, they are deployed for imitating birdsongs as well as playing variations of simple motifs. Wooden flutes were made from different types of wood preferably ash, apple, maple or lime trees. Clay flutes were made in eastern Latvia and Lithuania but bone flutes dating from the tenth to seventeenth century are of Baltic-wide origin.

The nose flute in Micronesia which goes by the name Aangún was made from mangrove or bamboo root prior to the mid-twentieth century.[102] The name which translates to "soft sounder" communicates its "delicate tone" as well as its "quiet place" in the history of the people.[103] One such history tells of the story of war directed at the village and someone who became privy to the plan sounded an alarm using the instrument but because villagers could not decode the meaning the instrument having been discarded it resulted in deaths.[104] The reason for its abandonment was because Catholic missionaries felt it did not have a good reputation and was an instrument of "licentiousness."[105] This is because when it played quietly in front of a woman's house by an admirer, if she fancies him, "she tiptoes out of the house and disappears with the man into the palm forest in the mountains."[106] The way she recognises who it is, is based on each islander playing and having his own unique sound so that it can be picked out even in the dead of the night by the woman of his dreams.[107]

There are several flutes made from bamboo among the Li of Hainan Island in China. These include Tsoh, an end blown duct flute; Vai, a double reed end blown pipe; Lilieh, a single reed end blown pipe and Bi which is another single-reed end blown pipe which when bound together forms the Bida that varies the sound.[108] Like the Marquesans, young Li men play these flutes outside the hut of their love interests who is able to pick out their distinctive sound and then invite them in or they stroll out playing the instruments in turn to express their love and affection.[109]

The Lilieh is also used to communicate with spirits in charge of agriculture. "According to Li traditional belief, when the paddy rice bears grain, the lilieh should be played. Li elders say that beautiful melodies played on the lilieh please the spirits, thus ensuring favourable weather and a good harvest."[110] The instrument also features at weddings, festivals and harvest celebrations while simultaneously serving to please the ancestors and drive out evil spirits.[111]

Among the Li people of Hainan Island, China the nose flutes called Tunkah "has a very soft sound which is virtually impossible to keep at a steady volume throughout an entire performance. This variable volume confers a unique gentleness and charm on the music of the instrument."[112] Tuned bamboo flutes are used in Malay traditional music.[113] The nose flute in this environment is associated with magic and the supernatural as

> the use of "nose breath" attaches special magical significance to the instruments. The turall, for example, is used to play music for the Pesta Menual (celebration to honor the spirit of the rice plant) and for other traditional ceremonies in Sabah.[114]

In the western Caroline Island there is a bamboo flute called On Yap and Ngael.[115] The Yapese Ngael had four finger holes and was played using an external duct.[116] Its soft sensual sound made it an ideal communication medium for lovers.[117] The mouth flutes among the Marquesans was used more for spontaneous and intimate occasions.[118] The same group used the single reed aerophone and whistle for dance accompaniment, private communication, courting and simple pastimes.[119] Among the Acholi of Sudan, flutes are used to relay one's personal motif which can range from "slogans in praise of his clan's distinction or of his personal strength and bravery."[120]

Flutes were relegated to the lower caste in India but not the Murali which was played by Krishna.[121] A special type of flute is dispatched to in-laws the morning after a wedding to communicate that the woman was not found to be a virgin.[122] Flutes among the Bunyoro was used to awaken the king in the morning and were also played last at night as they were regarded as life-giving.[123] In Malaysia, the Kata batang is a flute made of bamboo that is used in rites such as circumcision, sunset and funerals.[124] Reed instruments in Malaysia were made from rice stalk and were deployed in music performances.[125] The cane flute among the Nawals of Guatemala called Xul is a male instrument that symbolises "the axis of the world."[126]

Khweru is a dog whistle in Malawi made from reed and the horn of a kudu and is used to summon persons to a meeting.[127] Quena which is found among the Andean Indo-South American territory – Ecuador to Chile – is a reed-wind instrument suited for melodic music.[128] The people of Easter Island Chile also have a reed flute called Hio. The Chinese mouth organ from Laos in the second or third century is characterized as "the ancestor of all free-reed instruments, including the modern American organ."[129] Odu-achala among the Igbos of Nigeria is a bamboo reed instrument that is adorned with spider eggs hence it gives a supernatural sound to masquerades who represent ancestors.[130]

Pipes, on the other hand were made from bark or wood in late spring or early summer. In north-eastern Lithuania, there are homogenous single-tone pipes made from tubular plants of trees – ash, lime, willow bark etc. – so that when played, it results in "an endless musical cloth … with major seconds or tone clusters as the dominant harmony."[131] They are used in celebration as well as for relaxation while work is going on.[132] Oja among the Igbos of Nigeria is made of wood or bamboo and are used for masquerade music (Oja-mmwomwu), ceremonies marking attainment of manhood (Oja-okolobia) and for women dances (Oja-ukwe).[133]

The bagpipe is regarded as the "most beloved instruments of Latvians and Estonians." Its use at a wedding is shown in "Adamus Olearius's Vermehrte newe Beschreibung der Muscowitischen und Persischen Reyse" of 1647. The bagpipes are made from the skins of animals such as sheep, goat, lynx, dog, cat, or the stomach of a cow or sheep.[134] But Latvian and Estonian seaside villages use the stomach of the grey seal to make the bagpipe. The bagpipe was used for entertainment (weddings, processions etc.) as well as religious purposes – "ritual singing, is described in Latvian weddings of the 1780s."[135] In Denmark, the bagpipe was associated with beggars.[136] India is said to be the home of the bagpipe that "appears either as a primitive oboe or with both a chanter and a drone."[137] Expert Oboists were well regarded and were paid handsomely.[138]

The Panpipe is also associated with Lithuania[139] as well as the Andes comprising Ecuador, Peru and Bolivia.[140] The mouth bow, Mkangala, is found mostly in areas of large Ngoni population and is played by women only.[141] The musical bow among the Zulu is used by females to propose to men and so when a woman is married she is expected to cease playing the instrument as this "would send out a message that a woman was interested in men other than her husband."[142] The pan flute whose generic names are halumeaux or pusas or lacas among the indigenous peoples of Chile is played to accompany the dance huaino.

BELLS, GONGS AND CYMBALS

Bells in the Baltic region are of two types: Wooden and metal.[143] The former is made from a single piece of hardwood and possess one to five wooden clappers while the latter were fashioned from bronze or metal plates with a hanging metal clapper inside it.[144] Church bells in the Baltic region served a variety of purposes. They are called Campanas or war bells and they were used to warn of an enemy attack in addition to being considered good "war trophy."[145] A big bell, Gōzen Glocken, was used to mobilise soldiers.[146] The bells wrung doing war time in Europe were called "the bells of horror."[147] They had very interesting uses in animal husbandry. The bells were tied to the necks of cattle so that through the jingling sound they could easily be located in forested areas as well as used to ward of wolves and evil spirits.[148]

Mngwili in Malawi refers to small metal bells tied to a dancer's ankle.[149] Small metal bells are also deployed in Talátur which involves agrarian petitions as well as prayers for prosperity and general wellbeing in Chile.[150] Small bells were attached to the belt of warriors and were worn around the ankles and clothing of musicians in battles and dances among the Mohica of Peru.[151] Pellet bells made of copper or brass are tied to the wrist of children suffering from nightmares.[152] The same bells are tied to the ankles of children to encourage them to take their first steps and socialize them into dancing as they come to associate the leg movement with sound.[153] Keel or Kerincing, are cymbals made of metals that are deployed in Malay traditional music.[154]

In the Ga community in Ghana, gongs are time keepers and accompanying instruments.[155] This is done in these ways:

> One or two gongs may be used, each one playing a different rhythm pattern. These rhythms are treated in two ways. In the first case each gong plays an *unchanging* (emphasis author) rhythm pattern, maintaining a steady tempo throughout the entire performance. The beginning of such a rhythm pattern recurs at regular intervals and the inter-relations of constituents of the pattern are maintained throughout… It is thus easy for a singer or a drummer to find his 'bearing' by listening to the beats of the gong. The rhythm pattern is therefore a guiding principle and it is in this sense that the gong

may be referred to as a 'time keeper'. If the gong player falters, he throws everybody. The second method of using gongs emphasises their function as accompanying instruments... One or both of the gongs may play a number of rhythm patterns in much the same way as drums may be used, while maintaining a steady tempo.[156]

Similarly, gongs are also deployed in Malay traditional musical performances.[157]

The Li of China's gong – Lo and Vo – communicated status hence the more a family had, the greater respect they commanded.[158] The latter was more prized that the former as it had better craftsmanship as well as the inscription of a frog on it as this was one of the totems of the Li people.[159] Bells in India are as old as Hinduism and had both religious and professional significance. The hand bell – Ghanta – is embellished with figures and symbols of gods while the ankle bell – Gunguru – symbolize commitment to professional dancing hence the dancer ties on the bell in a solemn ceremony hence the proverb "the dancer who has tied on the bells."[160]

For the Alak of Laos, bells and gongs are of utmost importance hence they are communally owned and can only be used with permission of the village council.[161] When a village wants to move to a new location, a shield fitted with small bells is used for this purpose.[162] The gong is also central in spiritual communication. It is similar to the talking drum in that it requires special skills to ensure "pitch changes" and "non-repetitive patterns" which enables communication with the spirits who, in turn, provide guidance.[163] Similarly, the bronze gong is regarded as the most important instrument in southeast Asia and it is used for a variety of purposes.[164] In Malaysia, it plays a role in singing, dancing, rituals and message transmission from one village to another and even to the spirit world.[165]

The double bell (Ngongi) "the bell of kings" was used to salute the chief in Congo.[166] It was also deployed in making official announcement, in judicial hearings, when the chief travels and for tax collection purposes.[167] Another double bell, Kunda, mediates between the world of the living and the dead.[168]

TRUMPETS, CLARINET AND ANIMAL HORNS

In the Baltic region, Trumpets (karjapasun, tōri, tōru EE, taure, strumpe, trūba LV, trimitas, triūba LT) were made either of bark or wood with two different technologies:

In the first, a band of alder or birch bark is rolled up to make a conical tube about 60–70 cm long. A wooden needle is pierced through the broad end to hold the roll tight, while the narrow end is cut even, or a wooden mouthpiece is inserted into it. It is usual to supply the bark trumpet (lepatoru EE, ganutaure LV, zevês triūba LT) with a single heteroglot reed, in which case the instrument is side-blown and is characterized by a loud and far-reaching tone. To make a wooden trumpet, a slender trunk is sawn longitudinally and each half is hollowed out. Both halves are then put back together and fastened with bast (or other natural fibers) or with birch bark, which is tightly rolled around the two halves. The length of wooden trumpets may vary considerably, from 45 cm to almost 2 m.[169]

The military trumpet Herhorn made of animal horn was used to announce the beginning of a military expedition in addition to other signaling purposes.[170] In India, the Brahmans assign to the trumpet a sacred position in their rituals.[171] A conch-shell trumpet called Sankha is to be blown by Siva on the day of judgment. One of the trumpets – Nyastaranga is "held next to the throat so that the vibrations of the larynx set into action a tough spiderweb hidden in the mouthpiece. In this manner the timbre of the human voice is altered and takes on an oboe-like tone."[172]

The goat horn features in Lithuanian music. Animal horns production involve cutting off the narrow end of the goat, cow, ox and other animals' horn to produce a mouth hole then, then three to four fingerholes are inserted so that the sound covers great distances when played with intense lip pressure.[173] Its modulation is very interesting from a communication standpoint:

> The goat horn is used to play definite tunes that serve as a message concerning, for instance, a lost cow. Also, the shepherd who is the first to drive the herd out into the pasture informs others by playing a tune, and an antiphonal response may follow from the other shepherds. The instrument is played to keep wild animals away from the herd, as well as for herding. Its harsh tone is supposed to have some magical power, and it may be used to protect the herd from beasts and evil spirits. In addition, goat horns have been documented as accompaniment to the scattering of manure onto the fields: a slow-tempo, eight-bar period is played by all while driving their fully loaded carts onto the field, and a fast response is played by those who have finished their unloading first.[174]

Clearly, to the uninitiated it may all the same sound or tune, but to the people in the Baltic region there is richness in the range of messages it communicates.

The goat horn is played in the Baltic region during matchmaking ceremonies and signals the initiation of sexual relations. While in Chile a cattle horn is part of the musical instruments played at the opening of the communal irrigation canal.[175] In Peru after they had "used natural elements like the shell-fish shells to form the marine conchs, the Mochica undertook the fabrication of horns in baked clay." They also have the Quena, a vertical flute with cylindrical tube made of bone and clay.[176] These were used in combats and for sending messages.[177] The Marquesans sounded their shell trumpet as a call to arm against the Spanish invaders' canon fire as well as any other war efforts.[178] The shells were of various colours and were decorated with human hair.[179] In addition to war, the trumpets were also deployed in mourning along drums, shouting, waving, chanting and clapping.[180] Its other uses were to announce arrival in a bay or a feast as well as to sound an alarm.[181]

The Ivory horn among the Igbos of Nigeria is a status symbol and only titled men could own one.[182] They used it to announce their presence as well as to communicate among themselves in meetings of elders known as Ndi-nze. The antelope horn known as Odu-okike has a more mundane purpose as it is used and blown by hunters.[183] Horns of animals such as deer or cow is called Opi and apart from its musical function it was also used to give signals during wars.[184] Metal horns were used to announce arrival of caravans that had crossed the Sahara. In Congo, whistles made from wood or horns of small antelopes are used to hunt down witches.[185] Ntoyo, a whistle carved in the posture of a grieving woman was used to foretell death and whistles were also used to summon the dead.[186]

Horns, wooden trumpets and birchbark were used for amusement during herding by "senior" shepherds.[187] Straw, reed, wooden branch or bird's feather are used to make simple clarinets (roopill EE, birbïne, niedru stabule, düde, spendele LV, birbynè, düdelé, plunksna, siaudelis LT) in the Baltic region.[188] The hornpipe, on the other hand is "a wooden clarinet with a heteroglot reed on one end, a cow-horn on the other, and with three to six fingerholes (sarvepill EE, ganurags, birbïne LV, birbynè trüba su parputu, klernetas LT)."[189] The simple clarinet was used by young shepherds for amusement while the more senior shepherd's preferred amusement tool was the hornpipe which he would also deploy to collect the herd of animals, direct to pasture as well as communicate with other shepherds.[190] Hornpipes' entertainment function embrace "birdsong imitations, song tunes or free improvisations."[191]

The wooden trumpet was also used by the senior shepherd for similar purposes as the hornpipe:

> It is played early in the morning to collect the herd, but especially in the afternoon, when driving the herd home. The trumpet sound signals the location of the herd and the shepherd, and it is believed that wolves keep away from the herd as long as they hear the trumpet.[192]

In north-eastern Lithuania there are five sets of homogenous trumpets made "in such a way that that the second and third harmonics can be easily played, and each player uses two tones, making the interval of a fifth."[193] They are used for celebration with specific uses also embracing "when returning from the night watch of horses, during haymaking, rye harvesting and during entertainment for young people."[194]

Lipenga is a trumpet among the Cewa of Malawi whose name seems to have some association with blowing the nose (penga). The Mpititira is said to be more "authentically local" than Lipenga and "consists of a hollow reed leading into a gourd cup." Among the Yendi of northeastern Ghana, the trumpeter stands behind the Sultan's throne "and blows trumpet phrases from time to time, praising the sultan, radiating a Life Force either audibly or silently, and communicating with the spirits rather than with humans."[195]

In Chile the bugle "a traversal trumpet of reed, with or without reduced bell made of cowhide, decorated with multicolored strands of lama wool" is used in Cauzúlor which is undertaken at the completion of the communal irrigation canal when water is released into it and which also has religious undertones involving prayers for peace and prosperity as well as the worship of Pachamama, the earth mother of the Inca region.

In the eastern Mediterranean, the double reed pipe, Mijwiz, is associated with goat herding in rural areas and features in entertainment.[196] Trumpets are deployed in dances during harvest time among the Aluur of northwestern Uganda.[197] Similarly, the Dogon employ trumpets to belt out virile music which accelerates at the end to indicate growth of crops.[198] The wooden trumpet among Marquesans does speak but it has since taken on more of an entertainment role.[199]

The shell trumpet of the Pohnpei of Micronesia were linked with the chieftaincy institution and were given proper names.[200] The bullroarer and paired flutes of Papua New Guinea were exclusive to the secret cult of manhood and were said to protect these men "from the power and danger of women's bodies and menstrual blood."[201]

CLAPPERS AND RATTLES

Clappers in the Baltic region "are made as a rectangular birch, ash-tree or maple plaque with a handle fastened to the middle of one surface and one to three freely swinging wooden hammers on the other."[202] Their uses include herding and hunting due to their peculiar construction and properties because when they are held by "handle and shaken, the hammers move to and fro, striking the tablet and producing a loud clatter."[203] They are used by shepherds as security in that they scare away wolves so much so that they feel comfortable if they have it with them.[204] So it can be worn on the neck and beaten with two clapper sticks.[205] Another clapper hung on a cross beam and fastened to two poles has very interesting communication functions: "it calls workers from the field for lunch or dinner and announces the beginning or end of communal work in the fields, as well as weddings."[206] They are also deployed as distress signals.[207]

The Langgong among the Li people of China "consists or four, large horizontal wooden bars which are struck with a pair of wooden sticks."[208] Xylophones made of wood and bronze are used in Malay music and there are many types: Jambang, jatung, utang and genggong.[209]

There are a group of stick rattles that is the exclusive preserve of women in western Latvia. These include

> trideksnis, an iron stick with hanging bells and jingles and with a short wooden handle, the eglīte, a fir-tree top decorated with colored feathers and with hanging bells and jingles, and the puškaitis, a wooden stick, 20 to 40 cm long, heavily decorated with colored feathers, strips of cloth, and with bells.[210]

and are mostly used at weddings. But the materials used in making them also have spiritual significance. They are made from fir trees that are evergreen thus communicating life and fertility as well as cock feathers which signify time-cycles, sexual prowess, and fertility.[211]

Their male counterpart play the hammer rattle (iron hammer with jingles) at weddings. These also have spiritual significance. The instrument is struck on the surface of a table while ritual singing is going on and it is also deployed in drawing of the cross sign on doors.[212] The stick rattle in western and central Lithuania is 120–140 cm in length and is made from the Rowan tree which is "believed to be good for countermagic."[213] In addition, it is used in weddings to greet and announce the arrival of guests.[214]

Among the Mapuche and Huilliche of Chile Wada, a gourd rattle and Kaskawilla, which is a rattle of small bells is played by the female Shaman along with other instruments.[215] Among the San of southern Africa you have ankle rattles employed in dances and made from "butterfly cocoons collected on a long cord of plaited fiber. Bits of ostrich shells placed inside create a soft, rattling sound."[216]

The percussion stick called Koufau, Pahu Koufau and Papaki 'akau by the Marquesans had formal and informal uses such singing, planned public occasions as well as specific genre of chants – Uta, Komumu etc.[217] The shaking of rattles can also bring about cures.[218] Among the Malay, Kecerek are a pair of bamboo sticks IS struck together in traditional music performances.[219]

Conclusion

This excursion into musical instruments has featured aerophones, wooden and skin drums; rattles and clappers; trumpets, clarinet and animal horns as well as Bells, gongs and cymbals from various parts of the world. The instruments from the foregoing are deployed in musical performances but that is not the full story. They also serve various communication purposes; some spiritual and mundane. For the former, they are using for various rituals, to curry favour of gods for good harvest, healing etc., to wooing, directing dancers and singers in a musical ensemble, victory parades and so on for the latter.

Notes

1. Akpabio, E. (2021). *African communication systems and the digital age.* London England: Routledge, p. 27.
2. Oliver, P. (1988). Musico-ethnological approaches to musical instruments. *Popular Music,* 7(2), 216–218.
3. Boulton, L. (1974). The Laura Boulton Collection of world music and musical instruments. *College Music Symposium, 14,* 127–130.
4. Boulton, L. (1974).

5. Racy, A. J. (1994). A Dialectical perspective on musical instruments: The East-Mediterranean Mijwiz. *Ethnomusicology, 38*(1), 37–57, p. 38.
6. Wachsmann, K. P., & Kay, R. (1971). The interrelations of musical instruments, musical forms, and cultural systems in Africa. *Technology and Culture, 12*(3), 399–413. https://doi.org/10.2307/3102996
7. Tamuno, T. (1983). Traditional police in Nigeria. In E.A. Ade Adegbola (Ed). *Traditional Religion in West Africa* (pp. 177–183). Ibadan, Nigeria: Sefer.
8. Doubleday, V. (1999). The frame drum in the Middle East: Women, musical instruments and power. *Ethnomusicology, 43*(1), 101–134. https://doi.org/10.2307/852696, p. 102.
9. Wachsmann, K. P., & Kay, R. (1971), p. 399.
10. Oliver, P. (1988).
11. Oliver, P. (1988), p. 218.
12. Doubleday, V. (1999), p. 102.
13. López-Bertran, M., & Garcia-Ventura, A. (2012). Music, gender and rituals in the Ancient Mediterranean: revisiting the Punic evidence. *World Archaeology, 44*(3), 393–408.
14. López-Bertran, M., & Garcia-Ventura, A. (2012).
15. López-Bertran, M., & Garcia-Ventura, A. (2012).
16. López-Bertran, M., & Garcia-Ventura, A. (2012).
17. Mok, R. T. (1978). Ancient musical instruments unearthed in 1972 from the number one han tomb at Ma Wang Tui, Changsha: Translation and Commentary of Chinese Reports. *Asian Music, 10*(1), 39–88. https://doi.org/10.2307/834124
18. Muktupāvels, V. (2002). Musical Instruments in the Baltic Region: Historiography and traditions. *The World of Music, 44*(3), 21–54.
19. Dannemann, R. M. (1977). The musical traditions of the indigenous peoples of Chile. *The World of Music, 19*(3/4), 104–113.
20. Dannemann, R. M. (1977).
21. Dannemann, R. M. (1977).
22. Rios, F. (2012). The Andean "Conjunto", Bolivian "Sikureada" and the folkloric musical representation continuum. *Ethnomusicology Forum, 21*(1), 5–29, p. 8.
23. Doubleday, V. (2008).
24. Dannemann, R. M. (1977), p. 113.
25. Bellenger, X. (1982). An introduction to the history of musical instruments in the Andean Countries: Ecuador, Peru and Bolivia. *The World of Music, 24*(2), 38–52, p. 41.
26. Diettrich, B. (2011). "Keeper-of-the-Drum": Silent objects and musical pasts of Pohnpei, Micronesia. *The Galpin Society Journal, 64*, 219–197.
27. Diettrich, B. (2011).

28. Moulin, J. F. (2002).
29. Moulin, J. F. (2002).
30. Mu, Y. (1997). On musical instruments of the Li People of Hainan (China). *The World of Music, 39*(3), 91–112.
31. Mu, Y. (1997).
32. Nketia, J. H. (1958). Traditional music of the Ga people. *African Music, 2*(1), 21–27.
33. Nketia, J. H. (1958).
34. Polak, R. (2010). A musical instrument travels around the world: Jenbe playing in Bamako, West Africa, and beyond. *The World of Music, 52*(1/3), 134–170.
35. Matusky, P. (1985).
36. Mu, Y. (1997), p. 104.
37. Mu, Y. (1997).
38. Lo-Bamijoko, J. N. (1987). Classification of Igbo Musical instruments, Nigeria. *African Music, 6*(4), 19–41.
39. Moulin, J. F. (2002), p. 149.
40. Jähnichen, G. (2013). Field Note: Musical instruments used in rituals of the Alak in Laos. *Asian Ethnology, 72*(1), 119–142, p. 131.
41. Muktupāvels, V. (2002), p. 24.
42. Moulin, J. F. (2002). Kaputuhe: Exploring word-based performance on Marquesan musical instruments. *The Galpin Society Journal, 55*, 130–160. https://doi.org/10.2307/4149040
43. Moulin, J. F. (2002).
44. Weissmann, A. (1955).
45. Doubleday, V. (2008).
46. Wachsmann, K. P., & Kay, R. (1971), p. 408.
47. Wachsmann, K. P., & Kay, R. (1971), p. 409.
48. Dargie, D. (2013). Kavango music. *African Music, 9*(3), 122–150.
49. Dargie, D. (2013).
50. O'Brien, L. L. (1976). Music in a Maya cosmos. *The World of Music, 18*(3), 35–42.
51. Doubleday, V. (2008), p. 13.
52. Linden, I. (1974). Mponda mission diary, 1889–1891. Part III: A Portuguese mission in British Central Africa. *The International Journal of African Historical Studies, 7*(4), 688–728. https://doi.org/10.2307/216602
53. MacGaffey, W. (2002). Ethnographic notes on Kongo musical instruments. *African Arts, 35*(2), 12–90, p. 12.
54. MacGaffey, W. (2002).
55. MacGaffey, W. (2002).
56. MacGaffey, W. (2002).

57. MacGaffey, W. (2002).
58. MacGaffey, W. (2002).
59. Matusky, P. (1985).
60. Matusky, P. (1985).
61. Matusky, P. (1985), p. 150.
62. Phuthego, M. (1999). "Segaba", an African zither and its potential for music education. *Botswana Notes and Records, 31*, 119–128.
63. Phuthego, M. (1999).
64. Phuthego, M. (1999).
65. Phuthego, M. (1999).
66. Mok, R. T. (1978).
67. Mok, R. T. (1978).
68. Muktupāvels, V. (2002).
69. Johnson, H. M. (1996). A "Koto" by any other name: Exploring Japanese systems of musical instrument classification. *Asian Music, 28*(1), 43–59. https://doi.org/10.2307/834505, p. 43.
70. Nurse, G. T. (1972). Musical instrumentation among the San (Bushmen) of the Central Kalahari. *African Music, 5*(2), 23–27.
71. Dargie, D. (2013).
72. Weissmann, A. (1955). Hindu musical instruments. *The Metropolitan Museum of Art Bulletin, 14*(3), 68–75. https://doi.org/10.2307/3257652
73. Wachsmann, K. P., & Kay, R. (1971), p. 403.
74. Wachsmann, K. P., & Kay, R. (1971), p. 403.
75. Wachsmann, K. P., & Kay, R. (1971).
76. Wachsmann, K. P., & Kay, R. (1971).
77. Matusky, P. (1985).
78. Matusky, P. (1985).
79. Matusky, P. (1985), p. 133.
80. Muktupāvels, V. (2002), p. 26.
81. Muktupāvels, V. (2002), p. 45.
82. Moulin, J. F. (2002).
83. Moulin, J. F. (2002), p. 142.
84. Mu, Y. (1997).
85. Dargie, D. (2013), p. 128.
86. Nurse, G. T. (1972) p. 32.
87. Nurse, G. T. (1972).
88. Boulton, L. (1974).
89. Wachsmann, K. P., & Kay, R. (1971). The interrelations of musical instruments, musical forms, and cultural systems in Africa. Technology and Culture, 12(3), 399–413. https://doi.org/10.2307/3102996, p. 402.
90. Wachsmann, K. P., & Kay, R. (1971).

91. Wachsmann, K. P., & Kay, R. (1971).
92. Doubleday, V. (2008).
93. Doubleday, V. (2008), p. 7.
94. Doubleday, V. (2008).
95. Muktupāvels, V. (2002).
96. López-Bertran, M., & Garcia-Ventura, A. (2012), p. 395.
97. Mok, R. T. (1978).
98. Mok, R. T. (1978).
99. Muktupāvels, V. (2002).
100. Matusky, P. (1985).
101. Muktupāvels, V. (2002), pp. 35–36.
102. Diettrich, B. (2011). "Keeper-of-the-Drum": Silent objects and musical pasts of Pohnpei, Micronesia. *The Galpin Society Journal, 64,* 219–197.
103. Diettrich, B. (2011), p. 283.
104. Diettrich, B. (2011).
105. Diettrich, B. (2011), p. 294.
106. Diettrich, B. (2011), p. 294.
107. Diettrich, B. (2011).
108. Mu, Y. (1997).
109. Mu, Y. (1997).
110. Mu, Y. (1997), p. 103.
111. Mu, Y. (1997).
112. Mu, Y. (1997), p. 98.
113. Matusky, P. (1985).
114. Matusky, P. (1985), p. 144.
115. Diettrich, B. (2011).
116. Diettrich, B. (2011).
117. Diettrich, B. (2011).
118. Moulin, J. F. (2002).
119. Moulin, J. F. (2002).
120. Wachsmann, K. P., & Kay, R. (1971), p. 404.
121. Weissmann, A. (1955).
122. Wachsmann, K. P., & Kay, R. (1971).
123. Wachsmann, K. P., & Kay, R. (1971).
124. Matusky, P. (1985).
125. Matusky, P. (1985).
126. O'Brien, L. L. (1976), p. 41.
127. Nurse, G. T. (1972).
128. Dannemann, R. M. (1977).
129. Boulton, L. (1974), p. 128.
130. Lo-Bamijoko, J. N. (1987).
131. Muktupāvels, V. (2002), p. 38.

132. Muktupāvels, V. (2002).
133. Lo-Bamijoko, J. N. (1987).
134. Muktupāvels, V. (2002).
135. Muktupāvels, V. (2002), p. 44.
136. Koudal, J. H., & Talbot, M. (2010).
137. Weissmann, A. (1955), p. 74.
138. Weissmann, A. (1955).
139. Muktupāvels, V. (2002).
140. Bellenger, X. (1982).
141. Nurse, G. T. (1972).
142. Doubleday, V. (2008), p. 23.
143. Muktupāvels, V. (2002).
144. Muktupāvels, V. (2002).
145. Muktupāvels, V. (2002), p. 23.
146. Muktupāvels, V. (2002).
147. Muktupāvels, V. (2002), p. 24.
148. Muktupāvels, V. (2002).
149. Nurse, G. T. (1972).
150. Dannemann, R. M. (1977).
151. Bellenger, X. (1982).
152. Wachsmann, K. P., & Kay, R. (1971).
153. Wachsmann, K. P., & Kay, R. (1971).
154. Matusky, P. (1985).
155. Nketia, J. H. (1958).
156. Nketia, J. H. (1958), p. 21.
157. Matusky, P. (1985).
158. Mu, Y. (1997).
159. Mu, Y. (1997).
160. Weissmann, A. (1955), p. 75.
161. Jähnichen, G. (2013).
162. Jähnichen, G. (2013).
163. Jähnichen, G. (2013), p. 133.
164. Matusky, P. (1985). An introduction to the major instruments and forms of traditional Malay music. *Asian Music, 16*(2), 121–182. https://doi.org/10.2307/833774
165. Matusky, P. (1985).
166. MacGaffey, W. (2002), p. 13.
167. MacGaffey, W. (2002).
168. MacGaffey, W. (2002).
169. Muktupāvels, V. (2002), p. 36.
170. Muktupāvels, V. (2002).
171. Weissmann, A. (1955).

172. Weissmann, A. (1955), p. 74.
173. Muktupāvels, V. (2002).
174. Muktupāvels, V. (2002), p. 37.
175. Dannemann, R. M. (1977).
176. Bellenger, X. (1982).
177. Bellenger, X. (1982).
178. Moulin, J. F. (2002). Kaputuhe: Exploring word-based performance on Marquesan musical instruments. *The Galpin Society Journal*, 55, 130–160. https://doi.org/10.2307/4149040
179. Moulin, J. F. (2002).
180. Moulin, J. F. (2002).
181. Moulin, J. F. (2002).
182. Lo-Bamijoko, J. N. (1987).
183. Lo-Bamijoko, J. N. (1987).
184. Lo-Bamijoko, J. N. (1987).
185. MacGaffey, W. (2002).
186. MacGaffey, W. (2002).
187. Muktupāvels, V. (2002), p. 35.
188. Muktupāvels, V. (2002).
189. Muktupāvels, V. (2002), p. 36.
190. Muktupāvels, V. (2002).
191. Muktupāvels, V. (2002), p. 36.
192. Muktupāvels, V. (2002), p. 36–37.
193. Muktupāvels, V. (2002), p. 38.
194. Muktupāvels, V. (2002).
195. Wachsmann, K. P., & Kay, R. (1971), p. 407.
196. Racy, A. J. (1994).
197. Wachsmann, K. P., & Kay, R. (1971).
198. Wachsmann, K. P., & Kay, R. (1971).
199. Moulin, J. F. (2002). Kaputuhe: Exploring word-based performance on Marquesan musical instruments. *The Galpin Society Journal*, 55, 130–160. https://doi.org/10.2307/4149040
200. Diettrich, B. (2011).
201. Doubleday, V. (2008). Sounds of power: An overview of musical instruments and gender. *Ethnomusicology Forum*, 17(1), 3–39, p. 5.
202. Muktupāvels, V. (2002), p. 37.
203. Muktupāvels, V. (2002), p. 37.
204. Muktupāvels, V. (2002).
205. Muktupāvels, V. (2002).
206. Muktupāvels, V. (2002), p. 37.
207. Muktupāvels, V. (2002).
208. Mu, Y. (1997), p. 99.

209. Matusky, P. (1985).
210. Muktupāvels, V. (2002), p. 40.
211. Muktupāvels, V. (2002).
212. Muktupāvels, V. (2002).
213. Muktupāvels, V. (2002), p. 40.
214. Muktupāvels, V. (2002).
215. Dannemann, R. M. (1977).
216. Boulton, L. (1974), p. 128.
217. Moulin, J. F. (2002).
218. Wachsmann, K. P., & Kay, R. (1971).
219. Matusky, P. (1985).

CHAPTER 4

Demonstrative Communication

To the ethnomusicologist, music is a vital and significant part of society.[1] Music is bound up with significant parts of the life cycle, serves as a point of reference for members of a society and is also a bond that holds them together.[2] The communal nature of music is seen among the Alak of Laos who have a game involving musicians

> creating a regular rhythmic pattern with pleasing variations while they circle around a fire, a lamp or a jar of rice wine. As the musicians beat the gongs, all with short wooden mallets, someone – usually a woman – serves each one a drink as she sings good wishes. The three musicians have to continue playing without interruption as they imbibe their drinks.... If one of them gets out of rhythm, he has to be replaced by another man.[3]

Music is ubiquitous[4] and its accompanying behaviours are universal but also diverse in terms of roles, structures and cultural interpretations.[5] Music is bound up in every aspect of life such as work, worship as well as play.[6] To the Marquesans, it was bound up with war, human sacrifice, indigenous worship, memorial service, tattooing and feasting.[7]

Botswana traditional music, for instance, can be categorized into vocal and instrumental.[8] Lithuania has village, local original and migrated musical instruments. The village component comprises long trumpets, pipes, clay pipes, kankles (zither) and violins; migrated feature violin, clarinet,

© The Author(s), under exclusive license to Springer Nature Switzerland AG 2024
E. Akpabio, *Indigenous Communication*,
https://doi.org/10.1007/978-3-031-41766-5_4

flute, gensle, bandura etc. while the local original are made up of pipe, primitive clarinet, whistle, dzindzinis, clay pipe, bagpipe, long trumpet.[9]

The Baltic region music can be categorized into: (1) instruments and music accompanying economic activities, social events, religious practices as well as dance.[10] Gwegwe classifies all musical instruments in Malawi into four categories: Those that have skins, those with strings, those that give out air and those that are scratched, tapped or rattled.[11] Among the people of Easter island in Chile the classification of songs embraces spiritual, emotions, mixed genres called Riu, funeral, game and entertainment, satirical, and controversies.[12]

In ancient Egypt, musicians held religious titles and music was used to curry favour and placate gods.[13] In the Chinese context, the use of music for strictly ritualistic purpose and for ordering society marked its decline while those that were not so deployed were able to "absorb and assimilate the musics [sic] of other ethnic groups and other cultures and blossom into many musical forms."[14]

In ancient Egypt, society women including female members of the royal family played music in palaces and temples while tombs of musicians both male and female were close to those of the Pharaohs.[15] Carthaginian women like their Egyptian counterparts also received musical education and a tomb containing two cymbals was identified as that of a priestess.[16] Women from high status families received musical education in ancient Greece but the same also goes for the *hetairai* (women paid for sexual favours).[17] There was no gender discrimination as boys and girls in Mesopotamia received multi-instrument musical education.[18] Musicians from the near East performed on a variety of instruments and their professional names ranged from professional mourners, solo/group singers to lamentation singers etc.[19]

Music was also deployed in the war effort. A remarkable example comes from the Baltic region: "During the Estonian siege of Beverin Castle, a Latvian priest is described as praying to God to the accompaniment of a musical instrument, whose harsh tone in conjunction with prayer surprised the Estonia."[20] In addition, swords were beaten against drums and other musical instruments to keep soldiers awake during an attack.[21]

But music also had more mundane uses. Sensuality and sexuality were also quite common. For instance

> In Tharros (Sardinia), ... a memorial stone has been found in one of the cemeteries that may be dated to between the fifth and fourth centuries BC)

and that shows a scene of four dancing individuals. The three appear to be naked, while the one man is wearing a skirt and a bull's mask. All of them are dancing around a phallus-like pillar stone.[22]

For instance, Sansa, a thumb piano of the Nsenga "it is the motion pattern of the thumbs as they move 'idly over the noisy keys' which provides the primary satisfaction; the sound produced by the keys plays only a secondary role." Processions also involved music, walking and dancing.[23] Latvian folk songs involving hand clapping, feet stomping and dancing represent an unmarried girl's freedom while instrumental music represents married women so much so that "instrumental playing unambiguously connotes the wedding."[24] Women, in addition to musical performances at funerals in Sardinia, also played the role of supplying food for the occasion as well as purifying the dead with perfumes and spices.[25]

The indigenous people of Chile consisting of the Andean, Atacaménian, Mapuche, HuMiche and Alacalufe and the people of Easter Island combine elements of their traditional religion with Catholicism. Hence "in spite of the European Christian motivation which unites and animates them, they are stimulated by the collective euphoria and the considerable consumption of alcoholic drinks and plunge themselves into the hidden leftovers of their earlier world."[26] We see this mixture also in the Baltic region. The Fuegino of Chile folk songs are about wolves and ducks which are wildfire present in their environment.[27]

Music can be an accompaniment to other activities, as a stand-alone one or terminating activity and it encompasses work, cradle, recreational, healing, religious and incidental.[28] African music in particular may be deployed in

> generating social action and for expressing social relationships within the context of performance. Music may be used as a vehicle for expressing or recording a people's history -their dynasties, migrations, hardships and sufferings, defeats and victories. It may be performed as a tribute to a ruler, to an individual who is the focus of a social ceremony, or to a deceased person; it may be performed as an offering or service to a divinity. Above all it is used as a vehicle for making statements likely to provoke action – for registering protests or for criticizing people. Music may even be institutionalized as a means of criticizing people.[29]

Music, among the Yupik Eskimos of Southwest Alaska, is categorized into adult (first six categories) and children spanning seven categories:

1. dance songs
2. shamans' songs
3. hunting songs
4. teasing songs
5. travelling songs
6. berry-picking songs
7. story songs
8. juggling game songs
9. jump-rope game songs
10. ghost game songs
11. bird identification songs
12. fish identification songs
13. inqum 'cooing' songs[30]

Clearly, categorizations of music is complicated by the various ways societies see it and its role as the foregoing discussion clearly indicates. Nevertheless, some level of categorization is still required to be able to do justice to demonstrative communication hence the following:

ENTERTAINMENT

Even though there are various categorizations of Lithuanian musical instrument, whistles, pipes, kokles, bladder fiddle and bagpipes are deployed in dancing.[31] Music used for entertainment can be to honour a visiting dignitary. An example from Lithuania involved "a unique and extraordinary ensemble from the small Suiti district ... that contained seven bagpipers and eight players of goat horns. This ensemble made music on the occasion of the visit of the Russian crown prince to Liepāja."[32] Musical instruments for dancing include bagpipe, goat horn, kanklés, violin.

The Yupik Eskimos employ a drum in group mimetic dance

> The drums are employed in sets of four to eight, the drummers seated in line upon the ground. They beat vigorously in unison as they chant the song words. During breaks between dances, the drum heads must be watered and rubbed to prevent cracking and splitting and a small plastic squirt bottle being kept nearby for this purpose.[33]

The dances have a gender dimension to them as that of males mimic "sledding, hauling, harpooning, scanning the horizon" and is usually aggressive.[34] The females, on the other hand is characterized by graceful movement depicting carcass-cutting, skin-sewing and plucking of feathers.[35]

Emphasis in Yupik dance song is placed on comedy and humour as a copyng mechanism in their harsh winter environment. One of their favourite song is as under:

> I would like to sing but I have no drum
> I would like to sing but I'm not too bright
> Poor me I don't take leisurely steam bath
> Please notice that I don't stand idly around
> I'm going out to dance up there
> In the middle of the hall
> Oh me I have no drum.

Game songs called Kai-kai among the people of Easter Island in Chile are "rhythmic narrations accompanied by a game of forming geometric figures made by stretching a string between fingers and teeth...."[36] Asonogun, Afan, Ivbiagogo among the Edos of Nigeria are social recreation dance.[37] Across the African continent children also have recreational songs.[38] There are even songs for keeping the audience attentive during story telling sessions.[39]

Among the Alak, games involving music is not completely divorced from spirituality as there is need for "continuous flow of sound" to "keep the friendly spirits transcendent" or else audiences "might see the spirits in various shapes."[40] This spiritual component is also present in the Yupik story telling songs as the song "serves a magical overcoming function."[41] The format it takes is that there if there is a scarcity of anything in the community, the hero then embarks on a journey to solve the problem and deploys the song to overcome obstacles before returning home to the proverbial hero's welcome.[42]

The juggling game song that is sung along to juggling pebbles on one hand cuts across the Polar region stretching from Greenland through Canada, Alaska to Siberia.[43] A version of a cat cradle song among the Yupic Eskimos involves the use of a long string loop [that] goes from the hands to the forehead or to the feet (either direction works). During one stanza of the song, twists are wound in the loop in time with the rhythm and the song syllables. During the second stanza, a finger is inserted in the loop in order to preserve the twists already produced, and a second set of twists is put in the loop, only in the opposite direction. With a loud whoop the singer withdraws the finger and proclaims "Where have all the twists gone?."[44]

It is said that apart from its entertainment function, the songs make for hand-eye coordination, balance, manipulation as well as spatial/directional skills.[45]

The jump rope song involves a question such as "Mother will you always love me every day?" with answers ranging from yes/no to yesterday/tomorrow hence the participant ensures that they do not fail at the undesirable answer.[46] This as well as the ghost game song in the same environment makes for good physical conditioning. In the latter game, a question is asked and a series of humorous answers must be provided and the loser becomes the ghost that chases after the other children.[47] The same rigorous routine is found among African Americans in the plantation era. The dance songs which came after a hard day's work also involved hand clapping, chanting and feet tapping.[48]

Religious

A picture of music making in Livonia dating back to 1547 depicts "devils and witches dancing and three musicians – a lutist, a bagpipe and a hurdy-gurdy player- accompanying them."[49] Music that had ritual purposes in Lithuania were made with pipes, horns, violin, drums and trumpet.[50] In the same vein, clapping, stomping and the use of clappers and rattles are associated with the magical aspect of Lithuanian music.[51] Music was deployed in the sacred Umbanda rituals of Port Alegre and there is Afro-Brazilian sacred music in Olinda both in Brazil.[52]

The indigenous people of Chile have the Huaino dance which pays homage to the Queen of Carmen as well as Chacharpaya which "illustrate the ritual farewells of the participants in the Hispano-Chilean religious celebration."[53] Among the people of Easter Island Chile is a dance ritual "celebrating the discovery of the first egg of the bird called Manutara and associated with the nourishment which these eggs of sea-birds represent for the people."[54]

In Ur during the neo-Sumerian period dating from 2150 to 1850 BCE, drums were a feature of ritual sacrifices and parades.[55] In fact, the goddess Inana bestows drums to her Uruk people and the

> drum was used in the sacred marriage drama (hieros gamos) of Inanna and Ishtar's cult; widely attested in poetic and priestly accounts, this was performed continuously for at least two thousand years to assure prosperity and fertility to the land and its people.[56]

Religious music in India can be categorized into liturgical (Upasanasangit), mystical (Gudhatama) and devotional (Bhakti-sangit).[57] Liturgical music's features are "collectivity, ritualism and simplicity of musical structure"; mystical music is characterized by "esoteric cult practices as a part of Mantra culture" and; the devotional category's "compositions ... carry the name of the composer ... names of the güru(s) as well as the worshipped deity."[58]

Among the Alak of Laos, Vietnam, music "keeps the spirits transcendent and transformable."[59] This is done through the use of gongs and bells

> During singing time in the evenings, the leading storyteller, who can be a woman or a man, swings a bell forward and backward to indicate the steady flow of rhythms to which other community members respond. Without the bell, the story cannot be properly told.[60]

Similarly, among the Achumawi and Atsugewi tribes of northeastern California, the shaman starts off the song and it is repeated in unison by a group and this continues until the shaman indicates that he has being possessed by the spirit by clapping his hands to end the singing.[61] It is only then that he speaks in the spirit and performs magical feats.[62] The example below indicates the range of spiritual experiences.

> I the she wolf am rolling against a tree
> From under the ground I the weasel am singing
> On the mountain top I am peeping out; of the grizzly bear I am the child
> Ripples in the water sheet I the mink am spreading far and wide
> The smallpox brought by me the otter is upon you
> I the young wood pecker have brought on sickness
> With shortened steps I the skunk am dancing
> I am the song of evil
> Bones only I rattle[63]

Among the Kavango of Namibia there are dances that have religious undertones: Nyambi relates to the deity Nyambi, Nzongo is also known as the sorcerer's dance, Kakuruka for puberty ritual, Hathimo and Mendengure used for driving away evil spirits and Lipera for healing.[64] Children perform music associated with certain rites of passage in Africa.[65] Women group across the continent also engage in songs that have religious undertones.[66]

The shaman song among the Yupik Eskimos was about the moon and how the shaman would travel in the spirit to the moon to intercede with hunting spirits to allow for success during hunts.[67] The same posture is observable among native Americans and horses: "Horses were honoured in songs and dances. On ceremonial occasions the horse spirit was asked to provide healing powers, blessings and assistance. Equine spirits would appear to certain persons to teach medicine, songs, dances, and ceremonies."[68]

Dirge

Funerary processions were a more serious and sacred affair so much so that the walk and the accompanying music moves the participants into a "non-material world" with crying making an addition to the "ritual soundscape."[69] The role of women in mourning has been pointed out in that

> the specialisation of women as mourners is rooted in their association with activities related to the maintenance, creation and reproduction of life ... Seeing death as the last stage of life, and bearing in mind that it is women who give birth and who exclusively take care of children in many societies, it is likely that they were responsible for the public ritual of lamenting the dead...[70]

And this activity was left to matured women for a variety of reasons: They are experienced caregivers; their fertility cannot be interfered with by the deceased since they would have already had children and; they are best placed to boldly express themselves in an empowering ritual that points to issues of social importance.[71] The caregiving function is still a feature in most societies even though we now have males taking paternity leave to care for children as well as stay at home husbands. But that ancient society gives some pride of place to women to express themselves says a lot about their egalitarian credentials.

But the communication function of the mourning ritual is also worth noting:

> When mourning, women create a pattern of sounds that can be considered music or at least as having some degree of **musicality** (emphasis added). In addition to proper laments, there are also **stylized** (emphasis added) sobbing and breathing, breathlessness and syllabic prolongation as emotional intensifiers. In all cases, mourning materialises pain not only through the **acoustics** (emphasis added) of screaming but also through bodily gestures. In many cases, women embody their pain with tears or by pulling at their hair or through other actions.[72]

This is music to the ears if not for the solemn occasion that is being described here. But also worth noting is that among the people of Easter island in Chile their funeral songs are described as the "most beautiful" among the mixed genre of songs based on how it is performed: "In using one of the voices as a pedal point, they seem like a sort of litany."[73] Drums, in Ur during the neo-Sumerian period, were played in lamentations to the dead.[74]

Among the Li of China, the instrument Seh and dance Tyun-seh were features of ancestor worship during funerals which are "happy events with laughter, song and dance, not in the sense of applauding death but as signs of comforting, pleasing, and showing respect for the spirits of the deceased and the ancestors."[75] These and more emotions are captured in the Kotas of India's mourning songs. The songs are performed by older women, and they communicate memory and evoke feelings of loss while at the same time channeling "the grief of the community in order that the deceased reaches the other world safely."[76]

Work Songs

These are usually done to breathe some excitement into especially repetitive tasks as the action of singing lessens the onerousness of the work at hand and can actually serve as a booster shot to getting the job done on time. Gospel and soul are examples of music genre emanating from a work environment.[77] The exertions and effort required in executing tasks is reflected in Zulu work songs.[78] In practical terms Txalaparta, in the Basque country (Spain), "is a percussion instrument whose origins are linked to the crushing of apples, a long and tedious stage in the cider-making process."[79] The making of barkcloth in Africa involving pounding the bark of a tree with mallet has given rise to barkcloth songs and dances.[80]

The Sicura is of Inca origin and involves twelve men who are lama or sheep shepherds dancing in a continuous circular motion while blowing on flutes and playing small drums.[81] The Cauzúlor performance takes place after the communal cleaning of irrigation canals

> It is divided into two phases: the first is performed in a rural area by a group of men, usually mature or old men, and consists only of a slow chant sung while the officiating priests, kneeling on the ground, release the water into a recently-cleaned canal with great fervour and they throw in corn and wine so that the current will carry these offerings to the Pachamama. In the second phase, which is performed in the village, the slow and rapid parts of the Cauzulo, with song and dance, are executed, in which most of the inhabitants participate.[82]

In India, folk music is deployed in harvesting, pounding of corn and other household and community chores.[83] The Santhal have a song of invocation while sowing.

> Our obeisance to you, Mother Jaher Era
> On the occasion of Erok festival we offer you
> young fowls, and freshly husked rice Accept it in pleasure.
> We pray to you
> For every seed let there be twelve and let not disease attack them.
> If they attack, please subdue them
> Do not allow weeds and grass to grow among our crops
> Bring us the rain-bearing clouds in plenty Bring them in time.
> Let the earth be green with our crops
> Let there be no hindrance to our movements
> Let there prevail among us the spirit of love and goodwill.[84]

And after the harvest is in, this is chanted:

> I reaped and gathered the crop
> I gathered the crop, a bagful of crop
> I brought the crop carrying on my head I put the crop on the daubed ground
> I shall offer you that crop
> O wealth-fetching bullock
> I shall also give it to the milch [y] cow.

Among the Pohnpei of Micronesia, the pounding of Saka is a natural part of the soundscape as men use small rocks to pound roots on basalt slabs. As a consequence

> The metallic-like tones of the basalt slabs are enhanced by raising the stones off the ground slightly using pieces of coconut husks or other ad-hoc materials underneath. After the roots are mashed, the juice is rung from the pulp and mixed with water, then drunk, generally producing a mild narcotic effect.[85]

Each stage of the work is communicated via rhythmic patterns including when it is ready for consumption and cessation of the task.[86] This is like African American corn-songs that set the rhythm for the work to be carried out and aided plantation discipline.[87]

The Yupic Eskimos also have similar songs fitted to the peculiarities of their environment. They were sung while paddling, snow shoeing or sledding and it also assisted in making sure that trapped and wounded animals were bagged by the hunter.[88] In berry picking season among the Yupik Eskimo, women and children sing berry-picking songs whose range "is narrow, making them suitable for young voices."[89]

After a hard day's work involving rounding up cattle, cowboys in the Texas range in 1887 regaled themselves with ribald songs until someone starts their favourite wail "…oh bury me not on the lone prairie, where the coyotes howl and the winds blow free."[90] Music was also used to calm the cattle and avoid a stampede. Example

> Oh, go slow, dogies, quit rovin' around, /You have wandered and trampled all over the ground, /Oh, graze along, dogies, and feed kind-a slow, /And don't for ever be on the go … I've circle-herded and night-herded too, / … But if you get away, I'm sure to get fired. /Botch up, little dogies, botch up….[91]

Lullaby

Among the Mapuches and Huilliches of Chile, lullabies involve a musical instrument – Trutruca – which is a wind instrument

> 2.50 to 3 meters in length and about 3.50 centimeters in diameter, on the average; it is made of a stalk of quila – a native plant of Chile – previously slit lengthwise to extract the heart and thereafter the two halves are reunited by

tying them with a band of horse-gut; a cow's horn is fixed at the lower extremity while an oblique incision is made at the top as a mouthpiece for the musician.

The Yupic Eskimo cooing songs fits roughly in this category. It is directed by parents to their children by mentioning personality or special features of the child such as "little fingernails, little fingernails", the child's nickname, noteworthy events as well as family history.[92] The made-up song can also serve as lullaby.[93]

The recurring decimal in lullaby is to calm and soothe the child to sleep has been described as playful and energizing.[94] For instance Nuoso mother's lullaby first stanza has the following words.

> Eagles in the sky
> Must stand sometimes
> Leopards of land
> Grow tired sometimes
> Sleep, Mama's son[95]

An example from Malaysia expresses the same sentiment:

> All children on earth are asleep
> Son, only you are lying awake
> Sleep now

> Those who have lulled their children to sleep
> Too fell Sleep
> The lullaby sung by the earth faded
> Only you lie yawning
> Sleep now…[96]

The lyrics can also communicate parents and singers' philosophies and outlook on life.[97] Honig categorises them into themes such religious and spiritual, tenderness, crabby and sorrowful, promises of treats and sweets, wonders for the child's future as well as other maternal feelings.[98] For the last category she identifies issues such as a mother's longings and preoccupations.[99]

Love Songs

Trutruca is also deployed by the Mapuches and Huilliches of Chile in performing love songs. The Chuuckese islanders of Micronesia used their nose flutes to play Engi, which speaks about unrequited love. There are also "older forms of love songs (Kéénun núkún) [that] exhibit expressive and ornate styles of melody."[100] The intimate nature of the nose flute Aagun make their soft reverberations to be "closely linked with clandestine, nocturnal practices outside of the public gaze."[101]

While males are expected to use music to target their love interest and women use it to indicate their availability, Zulus girls seize the bull by the horns in that they "may choose their own husbands; as an integral part of the process, they compose and sing love songs accompanied by their musical bow."[102] One common text of Arirang song from the central region of South Korea "tells of a woman waiting forlornly for her lover on the banks of a river"[103] A Zulu "sour grape" song sung during a wedding is attributed to an "old maid": "How fortunate I am to be unmarried – I can still follow my own inclination."[104]

Wars and Conflict

The Edos of Nigeria have Ugho, Esakpaide and Orogho war dance.[105] In the Brong Ahafo Region of Ghana a week is set aside by worshippers of the god, Ntoa to launch insults that would have been accumulated from ill feelings throughout the year. So, adherents let loose on authority figures and persons who have displayed anti-social and other misbehaviors during this period through the medium of songs.[106] Teasing songs among the Yupic Eskimos served a similar purpose as they were a gentle way of correcting misbehavior without endangering the glue that held the community together.[107] Hence, they employed humour, satire and parody to humiliate the offender thus ensuring that the person would no longer embark on such anti-social behavior.[108] It employed a special form involving repetition of stanza one three times, a verse and repetition of stanza twice.[109]

Then there are such other categories and examples: "Boasting songs such as ibiririmbo songs of the Hutu of Zaire, songs of contest such as the halo songs of the Ewe of Ghana, and judicial songs sung by people contesting cases."[110] Male social groups usually perform music that has to do with war and heroic deeds.[111] Among the Kuikuro of Brazil Kwambu songs involve antagonism between the sexes in that "women respond to the men insulting their vaginas by chanting against men's penises."[112] Similar to Kwambu, during Jamugikumalu performance "ritual jokes, often violent, are told by women and men who exchange sexual insults."[113] The battle of the sexes also plays out in the playing of the flute – Kagutu. While a few master flutist can play the instrument, women were forbidden from seeing the flutes and any woman who dared to break this taboo was "threatened with collective rape."[114]

Among the Santhal of India, incest and misbehaviour involving outsiders is named and shamed via the Bithala ritual

> The content of the songs tends to represent the deeply felt sentiments of the community. The songs are outpourings among groups of village men (some of whom are nude jesters) carrying sticks, drums, flutes and buffalo horns. The crowd drums, dances, and sings lewd songs as it approaches the house of the offender. In repeating and representing the sexual act in a gross and apparently crude and obscure manner, the elements of intimacy and fondness are removed. The sense of shame and guilt becomes so overwhelming that an individual would not dare to repeat the act in his/her lifetime.

The buffeting that indigenous culture has suffered has also inspired songs. An example is by Mandawuy Yunupingu of Yolngu northeast Arnhem Land in Australia.

> All the people in the world are dreaming
> (get up stand up)
> Some of us cry for the rights of survival now
> (get up stand up)
> Say c'mon c'mon, stand up for your rights
> While others don't give a damn
> They are all waiting for a perfect day
> You better get up and fight for your rights
> Don't be afraid of the move that you make
> You better listen to your tribal voice.[115]

Praise Songs

Praise singing is quite common all over Africa but there is considerable differences in terms of their delivery.[116] At social occasions featuring persons who have done well for themselves, you will find a musician lavishing praises on them as they are being sprayed with cash. Some go so far as to institutionalize these persons by recording songs about them and their exploits. There are professional praise singers who also described as "chroniclers and bards."[117]

The Zulu Izibongo has a "four-note, quasi-musical style" that makes the praise song stand out from those of other southern African tribes such as the Xhosa, Sotho and Venda with the singer having to "tune his voice to some melody when he recites his imaginative description."[118] An example is Izibongo zikaShaka.

> Shaka – I am afraid for thou art Shaka!
> Shaka – There was a king amongst the cattle tails!
> (i.e., A master of the cattle raid he was!)[119]

Izibongo lyrics are specially chosen based on imagery, sound and relevance.[120]

The Banyankore, another Bantu tribe from East Africa's praise song is rendered with "phenomenal rapidity and the overall intonation contour of each line is a gradually descending one, without the observance of fixed musical pitches."[121]

Travelling Songs

The Yupic Eskimos devised travelling songs that are deployed in their extensive travels which were intended to put food on the table as well as reinforce family and kinship ties. The travel songs thus relieved boredom and only communicated travel adventures:

> A common topic of travelling songs is the weather, including precise observation of wind direction and cloud formation. In one popular travelling song about the community of Tununeq, the southwest wind is referred to as though it possessed human qualities. In a song about the Nialruq hills, the singer sings of feeling warm inside as she arrives back in her home region.[122]

Education

The Yupic Eskimo bird and fish identification songs serve educational purposes. The former is used to teach children about different birds in the environment as well as their behavior. The language is rich enough to describe sex, age, colour marking and state of the birds through songs.[123] Examples of bird identification songs are "Loon go kiss your babies! So it will be calm tomorrow!", "Sucking eggs! Sucking eggs!", and "queter-r-r-r, queter-r-r-r" reflecting the cry emitted by the sandhill crane in flight.[124] The same posture applies to the latter as the sounds of sea food is mimicked so much so that a seal holes, the life-like sounds attracts the seals which are then captured for food.[125] Inability to accurately mimic the sound can be the difference between eating and going hungry.[126]

Conclusion

Music is ubiquitous and life would not be the same without it as it would reflect the stillness of the grave. No wonder music encompasses every aspect of our lives and is reflected in entertainment, religious and sacred occasions, funerals, education, travel, comforting and soothing children to sleep, love and the entirety of life. Indigenous communities have their own peculiar songs and themes but music also serve communication functions reflecting longings of the heart, philosophies of life, hope for the future etc.

Notes

1. Ekwueme, L.E.N. (1974). Concepts of African Musical Theory. *Journal of Black Studies, 5*(1), 35–64.
2. Dannemann, R. M. (1977). The musical traditions of the indigenous peoples of Chile. *The World of Music, 19*(3/4), 104–113.
3. Jähnichen, G. (2013). Field Note: Musical instruments used in rituals of the Alak in Laos. *Asian Ethnology, 72*(1), 119–142, p. 131.
4. López-Bertran, M., & Garcia-Ventura, A. (2012). Music, gender and rituals in the Ancient Mediterranean: revisiting the Punic evidence. *World Archaeology, 44*(3), 393–408.
5. Trehub, S.E., Becker, J., & Morley, I. (2015). Cross-cultural perspective on music and musicality. *Phils Trans R. Soc., 370* (1664), 1–9.
6. Boulton, L. (1974). The Laura Boulton Collection of world music and musical instruments. *College Music Symposium, 14*, 127–130.
7. Moulin, J. F. (2002). Kaputuhe: Exploring word-based performance on Marquesan musical instruments. *The Galpin Society Journal, 55*, 130–160. https://doi.org/10.2307/4149040
8. Phuthego, M. (1999). "Segaba", an African zither and its potential for music education. *Botswana Notes and Records, 31*, 119–128.

9. Muktupāvels, V. (2002). Musical Instruments in the Baltic Region: Historiography and traditions. *The World of Music*, *44*(3), 21–54.
10. Muktupāvels, V. (2002).
11. Nurse, G. T. (1972). Musical instrumentation among the San (Bushmen) of the Central Kalahari. *African Music*, *5*(2), 23–27.
12. Dannemann, R. M. (1977).
13. López-Bertran, M., & Garcia-Ventura, A. (2012).
14. Mok, R. T. (1978), p. 44.
15. López-Bertran, M., & Garcia-Ventura, A. (2012).
16. López-Bertran, M., & Garcia-Ventura, A. (2012).
17. López-Bertran, M., & Garcia-Ventura, A. (2012).
18. López-Bertran, M., & Garcia-Ventura, A. (2012).
19. López-Bertran, M., & Garcia-Ventura, A. (2012).
20. Muktupāvels, V. (2002), p. 23.
21. Muktupāvels, V. (2002).
22. López-Bertran, M., & Garcia-Ventura, A. (2012), pp. 401–402.
23. López-Bertran, M., & Garcia-Ventura, A. (2012).
24. Muktupāvels, V. (2002), p. 43.
25. López-Bertran, M., & Garcia-Ventura, A. (2012).
26. Dannemann, R. M. (1977), p. 105.
27. Dannemann, R. M. (1977).
28. Nketia, J. H. K. (1974). The musical heritage of Africa. *Daedalus*, *103*(2), 151–161.
29. Nketia, J. H. K. (1974), p. 153.
30. Johnston, T. F. (1989). Song Categories and musical style of the Yupik Eskimo. *Anthropos*, *84*(4/6), 423–431.
31. Muktupāvels, V. (2002).
32. Muktupāvels, V. (2002), p. 26.
33. Johnston, T. F. (1989) p. 424.
34. Johnston, T. F. (1989) p. 424.
35. Johnston, T. F. (1989).
36. Dannemann, R. M. (1977), p. 113.
37. Emielu, A. (2013). Ethnic and regional identities in Nigerian popular music: A special focus on the Edo. *African Music*, *9*(3), 92–110.
38. Nketia, J. H. K. (1974).
39. Nketia, J. H. K. (1974).
40. Jähnichen, G. (2013), p. 132.
41. Johnston, T. F. (1989) p. 428.
42. Johnston, T. F. (1989).
43. Johnston, T. F. (1989).
44. Johnston, T. F. (1989), p. 429.
45. Johnston, T. F. (1989).

46. Johnston, T. F. (1989).
47. Johnston, T. F. (1989).
48. Negro Folk Songs. (1976). *The Black Perspective in Music*, 4(2), 145–151. https://doi.org/10.2307/1214501
49. Muktupāvels, V. (2002), p. 23.
50. Muktupāvels, V. (2002).
51. Muktupāvels, V. (2002).
52. McCann, B. (2011). Bridging disciplinary divides in the study of Brazilian instrumental music. *Luso-Brazilian Review*, 48(1), 1–5.
53. Dannemann, R. M. (1977), p. 105.
54. Dannemann, R. M. (1977), p. 112.
55. Doubleday, V. (1999). The frame drum in the Middle East: Women, musical instruments and power. *Ethnomusicology*, 43(1), 101–134. https://doi.org/10.2307/852696
56. Doubleday, V. (1999), p. 106.
57. Ranade, A. D. (2003). Traditional musics and composition in the Indian Context. *The World of Music*, 45(2), 95–112.
58. Ranade, A. D. (2003), p. 100.
59. Jähnichen, G. (2013), p. 126.
60. Jähnichen, G. (2013), p. 131.
61. Keeling, R. (2012). Animal impersonation songs as an ancient musical system in North America, Northeast Asia, and Arctic Europe. *Ethnomusicology*, 56(2), 234–265. https://doi.org/10.5406/ethnomusicology.56.2.0234
62. Keeling, R. (2012).
63. Keeling, R. (2012), p. 239.
64. Dargie, D. (2013). Kavango music. *African Music*, 9(3), 122–150.
65. Nketia, J. H. K. (1974).
66. Nketia, J. H. K. (1974).
67. Johnston, T. F. (1989).
68. Keillor, E. (2002), p. 80.
69. López-Bertran, M., & Garcia-Ventura, A. (2012), p. 402.
70. López-Bertran, M., & Garcia-Ventura, A. (2012), p. 402.
71. López-Bertran, M., & Garcia-Ventura, A. (2012).
72. López-Bertran, M., & Garcia-Ventura, A. (2012), p. 402–403.
73. Dannemann, R. M. (1977), p. 113.
74. Doubleday, V. (1999).
75. Mu, Y. (1997). On musical instruments of the Li People of Hainan (China). *The World of Music*, 39(3), 91–112, p. 103.
76. Wolf, R. K. (2000). Mourning songs and human pasts among the Kotas of South India. *Asian Music*, 32(1), 141–183. https://doi.org/10.2307/834333, p. 146.

77. López-Bertran, M., & Garcia-Ventura, A. (2012).
78. Rycroft, D. (1962). Zulu and Xhosa praise-poetry and song. *African Music, 3*(1), 79–85.
79. López-Bertran, M., & Garcia-Ventura, A. (2012).
80. Wachsmann, K. P., & Kay, R. (1971).
81. Dannemann, R. M. (1977).
82. Dannemann, R. M. (1977), p. 108.
83. Ranade, A. D. (2003).
84. Mathur, N. (2008). Chanted narratives of indigenous people: Context and content. *Asian Ethnology, 67*(1), 103–121.
85. Diettrich, B. (2011), p. 237.
86. Diettrich, B. (2011).
87. Negro Folk Songs. (1976).
88. Johnston, T. F. (1989).
89. Johnston, T. F. (1989), p. 428.
90. Keillor, E. (2002). Amerindians at the rodeos and their music. *The World of Music, 44*(1), 75–94, p. 78.
91. Keillor, E. (2002), p. 79.
92. Johnston, T. F. (1989), p. 430.
93. Johnston, T. F. (1989).
94. Honig, A. S. (2005). The language of lullabies. *YC Young Children, 60*(5), 30–36.
95. Majia, J. (2018). Lullaby. *Mānoa, 30*(1), 18–19, p. 1.
96. Raman, P., & Sajeevan, T. P. (2018). A midnight lullaby. *Indian Literature, 62*(2 (304)), 159–160.
97. Honig, A. S. (2005).
98. Honig, A. S. (2005).
99. Honig, A. S. (2005).
100. Diettrich, B. (2011), p. 295.
101. Diettrich, B. (2011), p. 295.
102. Doubleday, V. (2008). Sounds of power: An overview of musical instruments and gender. *Ethnomusicology Forum, 17*(1), 3–39, p. 23.
103. Howard, K. (1999). Minyo in Korea: Songs of the people and songs for the people. *Asian Music, 30*(2), 1–37. https://doi.org/10.2307/834312, p. 8.
104. Rycroft, D. (1962), p. 83.
105. Emielu, A. (2013).
106. Nketia, J. H. K. (1974).
107. Johnston, T. F. (1989).
108. Johnston, T. F. (1989).
109. Johnston, T. F. (1989).
110. Nketia, J. H. K. (1974), p. 153.

111. Nketia, J. H. K. (1974).
112. Franchetto, B., & Montagnani, T. (2012). "When women lost kagutu flutes, to sing tolo was all they had left!" Gender relations among the kuikuro of central Brazil as revealed in ordeals of language and music. *Journal of Anthropological Research*, 68(3), 339–355.
113. Franchetto, B., & Montagnani, T. (2012), p. 345.
114. Franchetto, B., & Montagnani, T. (2012), p. 343.
115. Phipps, P. (2010). Performances of power: Indigenous cultural festivals as globally engaged cultural strategy. *Alternatives: Global, Local, Political*, 35(3), 217–240.
116. Rycroft, D. (1962).
117. Nketia, J. H. K. (1974), p. 153.
118. Rycroft, D. (1962), p. 79.
119. Rycroft, D. (1962), p. 80.
120. Rycroft, D. (1962).
121. Rycroft, D. (1962), p. 79.
122. Johnston, T. F. (1989), p. 427.
123. Johnston, T. F. (1989).
124. Johnston, T. F. (1989), p. 430.
125. Johnston, T. F. (1989).
126. Johnston, T. F. (1989).

CHAPTER 5

Iconographic Communication

Introduction

Iconographic communication involves an exploration of signs and symbols that through heavy use have acquired rich connotations and consequently convey powerful meanings that are clearly understood and are recognizable by members of a community. In fact, they give an inkling as to how communities came about.[1] More so as "identities are formed by signification processes spun around specific individuals or groups, where people in thought and action link somebody or something to a range of meanings representing characteristic traits and values for that person or collective."[2] Human beings are themselves symbolic animals who make sense of the world through deployment and use of symbols.[3] Symbols are images that have been invested with meaning. Kroeber makes a distinction between signs and symbols describing the former as natural even though it may be supplemented with learning unlike the latter which is wholly learnt but also subject to extensions to make them universally applicable.[4]

Types and Uses of Iconographic Communication

Signs themselves embrace words, statues, flags, gestures as well as paintings and drawings.[5] Based on society's history and experiences, signs and symbols become relevant but that does not mean that they communicate

© The Author(s), under exclusive license to Springer Nature Switzerland AG 2024
E. Akpabio, *Indigenous Communication*,
https://doi.org/10.1007/978-3-031-41766-5_5

a universal and monolithic message. For instance, among the so called "American Indians" are 300 distinct cultures in the United States.[6] The Brazilian Indians number about 200,000 and consists of 180 distinct language groups.[7] Signs and symbols can be used to emphasize a narrative that promotes a particular viewpoint.[8] They can and do communicate beyond their depictions and presence.

Hay et al. note that the statues, monuments, and plaques that line Prince Henry Gardens in Adelaide, Australia depict persons of British descent and does not accord any recognition to indigenous history.[9] They note that even attempts to right this injustice has resulted in pushing "indigeneity to the City's margins; to unsafe places..." away from the North Terrace which is the centre of South Australia's cultural and civic life.[10] In Seattle, you would not miss the ubiquity of Leschi a headman of the Nisqually people as a place name and who was executed by the authorities for his resistance to the treatise in the war of 1855–56.[11] This has been described as "articulating collective knowledge of indigenous dispossession and disavowing its political relevance" while at the same time proving "dispossession in the present but it also makes possible a direct challenge to settler colonial narratives that appropriate Native histories."[12] The starkness of the Leschi Park is such that it depicts "how Seattleites built an urban identity untroubled by the violence of settler colonialism by driving Native inhabitants from their homelands and replacing them with symbols lamenting Indians' unjust treatment."[13]

However there has been some pushback against consigning indigenous signs and symbols to the margins. What has informed this is pride in indigenous cultural norms as well as a conducive environment far removed from the past subjugation visited on anything indigenous. Conklin argues that

> It is equally clear that this shift responds not only to indigenous values and internal societal dynamics, but also to foreign ideas, aesthetics, and expectations about Indians. As some native South Americans have learned to speak the language of Western environmentalism and reframe their cosmological and ecological systems in terms of Western concepts like "respect for Mother Earth," "being close to nature," and "protecting biosphere diversity," so some also have learned to use Western visual codes to position themselves politically.

This is captured somewhat in the Australian state getting involved in the repatriation and reburial of the remains of the Indigenous Koori ancestors which were sitting in a museum after being dug up by the authorities of the day.[14] While the authorities felt it was fitting from a social justice perspective by righting the wrongs of the past, the community was somewhat ambivalent with a mix of emotions ranging from not wanting to identify with their tribal past to spiritual disturbances these might unleash amongst others.[15] Be that as it may, the episode itself points to the conducive environment alluded to above.

Signs and symbols are regarded as pictorial and ideographic in that they represent and symbolize ideas of objects and events. Iconographic communication can be classified into objectified and floral. Wilson in the latter category includes charcoal, white dove, kola nut, cow tail, white clay, egg, feather, calabash, beads, limb bones, drinking gourds, flag and in the former he identifies young unopened palm frond, Okono tree, Nsei, Nyama, Mimosa and plantain stems.[16] The objectics and floral as well as the local form of writing all point to the advances and sophistication of indigenous knowledge systems. These reflect the Akwa Ibom State of Nigeria perspective, but a global sweep reveals similar and different icons.

For instance, feathered ornaments are found among the Amazonian Indians of Brazil.[17] The Basubiya of Chobe District in Botswana have their canoes as a symbol. Among the Kayapơ of Brazil, nudity, penis sheath, lip plugs and body paint are examples. Australian Aborigines have their shell middens, eucalyptus smoke and rock engravings.[18] The Xavante of Brazil have their headdress, and ear plugs[19] while native Amazonians also have their beads, headdress, body paint and feathers.[20] Indigenous groups in Bolivia have their Pollera – big one-piece skirt – and whips.[21] The First Nations of Canada have their rock paintings, Indian heads, tomahawk, and teepees.[22] Maori of New Zealand have their *hei tiki*, a greenstone pendant signifying an ancestor, *tā moko* – facial tattoo as well as interlocking curvilinear *koru* designs amongst others.[23] The Nasa of Colombia have their stone carvings and water.[24] In Mexico, you have "the black pottery of San Bartolo, the weavings of Teotitlán, the ceramic skeletons of Capula, the lacquered boxes of Olinalá."[25] The Penan of Malaysia communicate with feathers, carving marks on the barks of trees, floral patterns as well as message sticks.[26] The Rawa speakers of Papua New Guinea have their shells.[27] *Ulu* or crescent-shaped knives are part and parcel of Inuit and Iñupiat women's daily lives in the Artic region.[28] The Twill-plaited baskets are associated with the Kaiabi of Brazil.[29] Rice (staff of life) and water buffaloes (virility, strength, prestige, status and power) are of huge significance for the Toraja of Indonesia.[30] The Bastar, Chhattisgarh of India are associated with bison horns and peacock feathers.[31]

Misuse of Indigenous Signs and Symbols

Indigenous icons and symbols have not remained stuck in the past. Like every facet of human endeavour, they have also adapted as circumstance warrants. It is said that "artefacts that are best suited for certain tasks survive and are subject to gradual modifications that improve their functionality."[32] This evolution of icons and symbols based on their acceptance by former adversaries and the pride of place that they occupy in indigenous communities have resulted in their appropriation by various entities. The positive valuations came about from indigenous communities contesting the narrative of former colonial overlords as well as their political and cultural empowerment.[33] However, this seeming acceptance of indigenous culture by dominant groups does little to address their alterity and marginal position in the scheme of things.[34]

Traditional Cultural Expressions (TCE) that embrace "words, images, symbols, music, performances or objects are increasingly being used to brand products, people, communities, corporations and disciplines" sometimes without obtaining the consent of such indigenous communities.[35] That TCEs communicate community membership, rank, responsibility and kinship relationship[36] does not factor into their misuse. In fact, the practice has assumed global dimensions. A few examples will drive home the point. In Canada and the United States for instance

> names of First Nations, such as Algonquin, Mohawk, Haida and Cherokee, as well as symbols such as Indian heads, tepees or tomahawks, are used as trademarks by many non-Aboriginal companies to market products ranging from firearms and axes to tobacco, gasoline and cars. In the United States, there are many examples of exploitation of Indian names and imagery, notably in relation to college or professional sports teams' names. It is estimated that more than 2,600 high school, college or professional teams have used Native American names and images as mascots, logos and team names.[37]

Activism against the implicit racism in the use of Indian nicknames and mascots by US colleges have resulted in changes to reflect the local history and interests of their various locations.[38] In New Zealand, Māori icons and symbols are deployed and used by corporates such as Ford, MacDonalds, Lego, Moontide, Paco Rabbane.[39]

Individuals are also involved in these appropriations:

many personalities have demonstrated a growing fascination with Māori culture. Celebrities such as rock star Robbie Williams and boxer Mike Tyson have exhibited Māori-style tattoos, and soccer player Eric Cantona appeared on the cover of British style magazine *GQ* with a painted moko on his face. In 1997, the Spice Girls caused offence when they performed a spontaneous *haka* with fans in Bali.[40]

There are also mass-produced imitation Māori products that are sold in New Zealand of all places that are a slap on the face of this community.[41] The Australian nation itself also appropriates Aboriginal culture to express their identity and sense of belonging.[42] In fact "many local governments, state organizations, churches and communities, groups participate in smoking ceremonies and welcoming rituals that effectively underwrite 'the idea that all Indigenous people embody the kind of Aboriginality that a segment of the nation longs to restore.'"[43]

Other misuse includes the *haka Ka Mate* a Māori TCE intended exclusively for men. However, a group of women enacted it to sell Fiat cars without obtaining permission.[44] Other recorded misuse of the *Haka* are

a mock performance by gingerbread men was featured in New Zealand's Bakery of the Year Awards; the Dutch brewer Heineken encouraged shoppers to perform "their" haka; an American high-school rugby team performed it in the Hollywood movie *Forever Strong*; in Japan, rival groups of men and women performed it in a television commercial for a soft drink by the Coca-Cola Company; and a haka was performed to the music of the song "Macarena" to parody the All Blacks, New Zealand's national rugby team.[45]

Native American symbols seem to be exclusively used by the US armed forces and it is argued that these reflect "both admiration and guilt" that "recognizes Indigenous fighting ability, while subordinating it to national control."[46]

Then there are spiritual implications of some of these appropriations which the impostors may be unaware of amongst other concerns.[47] The spiritual appropriations seem to continue the assault visited on indigenous people by colonialism by the scant disregard to what they value and hold sacred. A case in point is the Uluru – a massive rock in the centre of Australia – which is of spiritual significance to the Aboriginals which New Age religious adherents desecrated on August 16–17, 1987.[48] They had first tried to get the buy in from the Aboriginals, but they were put off by the "ritual apparatus relating to witchcraft."[49] Also rituals and festivals are now performed for the eyes of tourist thus losing their authenticity and ability to foster communal unity.[50]

Indigenous Forms of Writing and Communication

Examples of written, graphical, or drawn communication are the Khipu communication system of the Inka and the Yapana matrix from the Andes of Peru,[51] Cilka of the Mapuche of Chile, hieroglyphs of the Mi'kmaq Indians of Canada,[52] Nsibidi of Nigeria[53] and Liberia as well as the Mud cloth of Mali.[54] The indigenous civilizations in the Americas did not have phonetic symbols except for the lowland Maya rather the Aztec and Mixtec had pictographic books and elaborate cartographies.[55] Many indigenous groups in the Americas wrote on barks.[56]

Message Sticks

In addition to carving marks on trees in the rainforest to claim ownership, the Penan of Malaysia place sticks on the ground that communicate various messages. Documented messages include "please share wisely" which meant that only older sago stems were to be harvested making room for the young ones to mature or that only fruits that had fallen to the ground should be gathered.[57] Apart from its use in conserving forest resources, the sticks were also used for other purposes. There is a way twigs are arranged to show direction back to camp and for trading purposes.[58] A cleft stick with a mark along with a cake of tobacco meant it was for sale. A stick with leaves and feather communicates the availability of food as well as areas to be avoided because of the presence of dead bodies.[59]

Hindley has categorized these simulacra into three: Iconic, indexical, and numeric which are used to represent the number of people, days or distance.[60] He describes these as "efficient communication systems aimed at conveying succinct holistic messages."[61]

5 ICONOGRAPHIC COMMUNICATION   83

Iconic

Simulacrum	Icon	Index	Holistic message
Leaf cut into oblong shape Frond-centre of palm trimmed leaves stuck in ground	Empty plate	No food	Unsuccessful hunt. Unsuccessful hunt or no sago palm in this area.
Folded leaf containing sago, feathers, or bone	Full plate	Food	Food available + nature of food: sago, bird, meat.
Sago, feathers, bone or fruit		Game or fruit	
Rolled leaf			Food available.
Leaf pierced with leaf stalk	Barbecued meat	Game	Successful hunt.
Ladle leaf shape	Ladle	Liquid (soup)	Soup available.
Ladle leaf shape	Ladle	Liquid (water)	Gone to the river.
Long leaf stalk	Fishing rod	Fishing	Gone fishing.
Stick with frayed ends	Fork	Eating	Dead body when associated with no-through-way.
Y-shaped wood tied to bark			Dead body.
Knife-shaped stick	Parang	Stabbing	I will fight/kill you. Danger. Possibly unwelcome visitor in the camp.
Hook-shaped piece of wood			Going on a hunting trip.
Kelipui plant inserted at the top of the stick			Gone to visit another group.
Fibre tied in loops to the top of the stick			Several people have gone on a long journey.
Dart replica	Poison dart	Killing	Danger.
Bundle of vines	Medicinal herbs	Sickness	Someone is ill and needs help.
Grass wound into a circle	Manacle	Punishment	Pay a fine.
Two short shaved sticks of the same length	Sameness	Same tribe	Message only for Penan.
Two short shaved sticks of different-lengths	Differentness	Different tribe	Message concerns other ethnic groups.
Stick with sharpened end & spiral carving	Speediness		Hurry.
Piece of firewood			Urgent matter hurry.
Arrow shaped piece of wood	Arrow		Gone home.
Uprooted sapling	Family tree	Family	One family involved.

Indexical

Simulacrum	Holistic message
Top of sapling bent in direction of travel	Take this direction.
Shaved stick stuck in the ground pointing in a direction	Have gone in this direction. (May also indicate location of a fruiting tree).
Shaved stick without leaves at end of stick	Someone is not far ahead.
Shaved stick with leaves at end of stick	Someone is far ahead.
Shaved stick stuck in ground and bent so top half points to the ground	Have gone ahead. Make camp here and wait for us to return.
Two shaved sticks stuck in ground to form a V-shape	Party has split up.
A V-shape as above with a stick pointer placed horizontally between the shaved sticks	Leading group has returned in the direction indicated by horizontal pointer.
Arrow-shaped stick	Gone home.
Large leaves at base of trunk aligned in a certain direction	Take this direction.
Large leaves at base of trunk	Wait for us here.
Larger leaves in front of smaller leaves	Don't take this direction.
Barriers	No trespassing.

Numeric

Simulacrum	Icon/index	Holistic message
Short stick in front of long stick	Long stick represents distance completed & short stick distance to destination	Destination is not far ahead.
Long stick in front of short stick	Long stick represents distance to destination & short stick distance completed	Destination is still far ahead.
Two sticks of equal length	First stick represents distance completed & second stick distance to destination	You at the half-way point of the journey.
Length of rattan tied around stick	Unclear	The first party waited a long time.
Knots tied in rattan	Number of nights to destination	There are X number of night's rest before you reach your destination.
Knots tied in rattan	Number of nights to next meeting	There are X number of nights until the next meeting.

(continued)

(continued)

Simulacrum	Icon/index	Holistic message
Leaves left on branch accompanied by same number of knots tied in rattan	Number of nights to destination	There are X number of night's rest before you reach your destination.
Stick with circular notches		Party has got an enemy head, each notch represents one head.
Stick cut to a certain length accompanied by hair from pig's chin	Length of stick indicates quantity of pig fat	There is X amount of pig fat available.

Source: Hindley, P. (2017). Join Us for Lunch: Iconic, indexical, and numeric signposting used by the Penan for communicating in the rainforest. *Anthropos*, *112*(1), 75–93

The Khipu System

This consists of what has been described as complex and knotted cords that seem to encode 26 × 24 (the 24 colours) that equals 1536 distinct information units that covers everything from rituals, historic accounts, goods and services etc.[62] Its use was quite pronounced during the Inka (ca. 1400–1532 C.E.) and less so during Spanish colonialism and the twentieth century.[63] The system is said to be based on a binary and decimal system and it able to communicate complex and abundant information.[64] Its numerals are said to communicate non-quantitative information like a number on an international passport.[65] The inkas used the system to record quantitative information.[66] In fact

> *Khipus* were created and managed by specialised Inca accountants, called *khipucamayocs*. They were spun and tied using cotton and wool, or sometimes both, and were different colours according to the four natural cottons produced by the Incas – white, light, medium brown, and green – and the diverse pigments of alpaca and llama wool. Dyes were also used to increase the range of colours. A *khipu* consisted of one long 'primary cord' to which a series of pendent cords were attached.[67]

Translating the knots has been compared to the way a computer translates the eight-bit ASCII code into letters and words more so as its structure involved seven features

(1) raw material (cotton or wool), (2) colour ("red" and "dark" rainbows), (3) direction of spin and ply (Z/S or S/Z), (4) direction of attachment of

the pendant to the primary cord (front or back), (5) direction of knot (S or Z), (6) even or odd numbers, (7) decimal or non-decimal structure.[68]

The knots were also loose enough to allow for editing in that if goods were removed from an Inka storehouse the inventory could then be adjusted to reflect the change(s).[69] But studies are still being conducted to understand the full range of information in the colours, materials used and patterns of tying the knots.[70] But it has been surmised that they also contained songs, genealogies and historical data.[71]

Available evidence points to the system's ability to keep track of complex data. For instance, it was used to record persons who had played their role in the sacred irrigation canal cleaning festival:

> the multicolored cords on the khipu board recorded information not only about each person's attendance at the event, but also about the quality of the work, the use of specific ritual implements and special clothing, and even the degree of enthusiasm shown.[72]

Those found in tombs are said to contain "information pertaining to the history of the mummies and the social groups descended from them" as well as "a combined biennial calendar and census of the tribute payers in Chachapoya territory, around Laguna de los Condores, in late Prehispanic times."[73]

The Yapana Matrix, Cilka and Maya Scripts

A matrix which follows the accounting format of the Khipus is found among the Quechua of Peru and instead of knots, pebbles were the media of communication. The pebbles arranged on the floor allowed record keepers to keep tabs of various matters such as contributions to upkeep of communal properties.[74] Among the Potato Park community, the matrix consisted of chalk marks or coloured strings laid out on the floor which were used to register agricultural information such as potato varieties, uses etc. in addition to being deployed in storing other equally important information such as good, services, customary law and so on.[75]

Cilka in the Mapuche language refers to a space (wood, stone etc.) where information is stored.[76] Storage includes the social natural landscape to concrete that makes room for encoding, decoding and learning.[77]

The Maya scripts were present and deployed in Mexico, Guatemala, Belize, El Salvador, and Honduras from about the third century AD until the Spanish invasion in the sixteenth century AD.[78] It consisted of script combined with imagery which made it more accessible to the general population who had different languages and variable degree of literacy.[79] But this has not ensured uniformity in interpretations of the scripts. In fact, some of the figures and symbols used in depicting the supernatural are so extreme as to render interpretation impossible.[80]

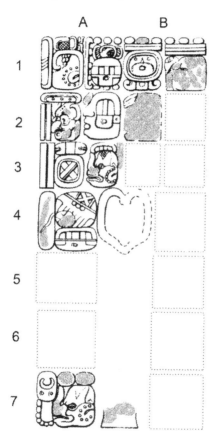

Source: Hudson, K. M., & Henderson, J. S. (2021). Script, image, and culture in the Maya world: A southeastern perspective. In P. J. Boyes, P. M. Steele, & N. E. Astoreca (Eds.), The Social and Cultural Contexts of Historic Writing Practices (pp. 231–248). Oxbow Books. https://doi.org/10.2307/j.ctv2npq9fw.17

NSIBIDI AND MUD CLOTH OF MALI

Nsibidi form of syllabic writing is present in Liberia, Cameroon and Nigeria and it is possible that there are connections between them in spite of Johnstone and Malcolm arguing to the contrary.[81] Macgregor became aware of it in old Calabar (present Cross River State, Nigeria) in 1905 when he claimed that the people were backward because they did not have a means of writing.[82] Thus began his journey of discovery about Nsibidi. The graphical scripts convey a myriad of information employing media such as human skin, masquerade paraphernalia, textile, walls of building, on the ground, calabashes, canoes, palm stems, stools, brassware etc.[83] While there are signs recording indigenous court proceedings, love and romance, labels, private messages and public notices, recording of goods and services, there were also signs restricted to only members of the Ekpe Society which made them off-limits to the general public.[84]

The example below tells the story of a bird feeding on a palm tree that then took flight when a man started to climb the tree:[85]

Dayrell, E. (1911). *Further Notes on 'Nsibidi signs with their meanings from the Ikom District, Southern Nigeria.* (Jul. – Dec., 1911), 521–540, p. 532

The mud cloth of Mali are made from locally-grown cotton and also contain a rich source of information.[86] The designs can include grasshoppers, diamonds, drums, trees, lines etc. that can and do communicate exploits at war to nobility amongst others.[87]

Conclusion

Indigenous signs and symbols have evolved from being derided and looked down upon to been accepted and even misappropriated and misused. The interests in the forms of iconographic communication makes them a work in progress as there is a lot to learn from these indigenous forms particularly the forms of writing to which a lot of scholarly attention has been devoted. But more work is still required to fully understand the length and breadth of these indigenous forms of communication so that these communities take their pride of place in the narrative about human progress and civilization. It is quite edifying to note that despite attempts to suppress and rubbish them they have survived to the present age.

Notes

1. Fornäs, J. (2012). Identifying symbols. In Signifying Europe (pp. 43–60). Intellect. https://doi.org/10.2307/j.ctv9hj915.6
2. Fornäs, J. (2012), p. 43.
3. José Luis L. Aranguren. (1974). Freedom, Symbols and communication. *The Annals of the American Academy of Political and Social Science*, 412, 11–20.
4. Kroeber, A. L. (1952). Sign and symbol in bee communications. *Proceedings of the National Academy of Sciences of the United States of America*, 38(9), 753–757.
5. Tigar, M. E. (1999). The power of myth: Justice, signs, and symbols in the criminal trial. *Litigation*, 26(1), 25–70.
6. Seppi, L. R. (2017). Chapter Nine: Indigenous activism: Art, identity, and the politics of the Quincentenary. Counterpoints, 515, 121–141. http://www.jstor.org/stable/45212256, p. 122.
7. Conklin, B. A., & Graham, L. R. (1995). The shifting middle ground: Amazonian Indians and eco-politics. *American Anthropologist*, 97(4), 695–710.
8. Hay, I., Hughes, A., & Tutton, M. (2004). Monuments, memory and marginalisation in Adelaide's Prince Henry Gardens. *Geografiska Annaler. Series B, Human Geography*, 86(3), 201–216.
9. Hay et al. (2004).
10. Hay et al. (2004), p. 201.
11. Blee, L. (2016). Seattle's Leschi memory and urban indigenous place names. *The Pacific Northwest Quarterly*, 107(4), 186–196.
12. Blee, L. (2016), p. 187.
13. Blee, L. (2016), p. 191.

14. Lambert-Pennington, K. (2007). What remains? Reconciling repatriation, Aboriginal culture, representation and the past. *Oceania, 77*(3), 313–336.
15. Lambert-Pennington, K. (2007).
16. Wilson, D. (2005). A taxonomy of traditional media in Africa. In K. Ansu-Kyeremeh (Ed.). *Indigenous communication in Africa: Concept, application and prospects* (pp, 39–61). Accra: Ghana Universities Press.
17. Conklin, B. A., & Graham, L. R. (1995).
18. Lambert-Pennington, K. (2007). What Remains? Reconciling repatriation, Aboriginal culture, representation and the past. *Oceania, 77*(3), 313–336. http
19. Conklin, B. A., & Graham, L. R. (1995).
20. Conklin, B. A. (1997). Body paint, feathers, and VCRs: Aesthetics and authenticity in Amazonian activism. *American Ethnologist, 24*(4), 711–737.
21. Postero, N. (2017). Race and Racism in the New Bolivia. In The Indigenous State: Race, Politics, and Performance in Plurinational Bolivia (pp. 116–136). University of California Press. http://www.jstor.org/stable/10.1525/j.ctt1pq34b0.11
22. Johnsson, D. Z. (2012). The branding of traditional cultural expressions: To whose benefit? In P. Drahos & S. Frankel (Eds.), Indigenous peoples' innovation: Intellectual property pathways to development (pp. 147–164). ANU Press.
23. Johnsson, D. Z. (2012).
24. Gnecco, C., & Hernández, C. (2008). History and Its discontents: Stone Statues, native histories, and archaeologists. Current Anthropology, 49(3), 439–466. https://doi.org/10.1086/588497
25. Carruthers, D. V. (2001). The Politics and Ecology of Indigenous Folk Art in Mexico. *Human Organization, 60*(4), 356–366, p. 357.
26. Hindley, P. (2017). Join Us for Lunch: Iconic, indexical, and numeric signposting used by the Penan for communicating in the rainforest. *Anthropos, 112*(1), 75–93.
27. Dalton, D. M. (1996). The Aesthetic of the Sublime: An Interpretation of Rawa Shell Valuable Symbolism. *American Ethnologist, 23*(2), 393–415.
28. Kambic, E. B. (2015). The changing lives of women's knives: "Ulus", travel, and transformation. *Historical Archaeology, 49*(3), 35–53.
29. Athayde, S., Silva-Lugo, J., Schmink, M., & Heckenberger, M. (2017). The same, but different: indigenous knowledge retention, erosion, and innovation in the Brazilian Amazon. Human Ecology, 45(4), 533–544.
30. Crystal, E. (1989). Myth, symbol and function of the Toraja house. *Traditional Dwellings and Settlements Review, 1*(1), 7–17.
31. Prévôt, N. (2014). The "Bison Horn" Muria: Making it "more tribal" for a folk dance competition in Bastar, Chhattisgarh. Asian Ethnology, 73(1/2), 201–231.

32. Fay, N., Garrod, S., & Roberts, L. (2008). The fitness and functionality of culturally evolved communication systems. *Philosophical Transactions: Biological Sciences, 363*(1509), 3553–3561, p. 3553
33. Gnecco, C., & Hernández, C. (2008).
34. Waldron, D., & Newton, J. (2012). Rethinking appropriation of the Indigenous: A critique of the Romanticist Approach. *Nova Religio: The Journal of Alternative and Emergent Religions, 16*(2), 64–85.
35. Johnsson, D. Z. (2012). The branding of Traditional Cultural Expressions: To whose benefit? In P. Drahos & S. Frankel (Eds.), *Indigenous peoples' innovation: Intellectual property pathways to development* (pp. 147–164). ANU Press.
36. Vézina, B. (2020). Introduction. In *Ensuring respect for indigenous cultures: A moral rights approach* (pp. 1–3). Centre for International Governance Innovation. http://www.jstor.org/stable/resrep25328.5
37. Johnsson, D. Z. (2012), p. 149.
38. Hofmann, S. (2005). The elimination of indigenous mascots, logos, and nicknames: Organizing on college campuses. *American Indian Quarterly, 29*(1/2), 156–177.
39. Johnsson, D. Z. (2012).
40. Johnsson, D. Z. (2012), p. 150.
41. Johnsson, D. Z. (2012).
42. Waldron, D., & Newton, J. (2012).
43. Waldron, D., & Newton, J. (2012), p. 69.
44. Vézina, B. (2020).
45. Vézina, B. (2020), pp. 1–2.
46. Poyer, L. (2022). "Martial myths" and native realities. In *War at the Margins: Indigenous Experiences in World War II* (pp. 90–100). University of Hawai'i Press. https://doi.org/10.2307/j.ctv2ngx5f5.10, p. 90.
47. Johnsson, D. Z. (2012).
48. Waldron, D., & Newton, J. (2012).
49. Waldron, D., & Newton, J. (2012), p. 65.
50. Bulilan, C. M. R. (2007). Experiencing cultural heritage and indigenous tourism in Banaue. Philippine *Quarterly of Culture and Society, 35*(1/2), 100–128.
51. International Institute for Environment and Development (IIED). (2006). Protecting Indigenous Knowledge against Biopiracy in the Andes. International Institute for Environment and Development. http://www.jstor.org/stable/resrep17953
52. Sarah Rivett. (2014). Learning to Write Algonquian Letters: The indigenous place of language philosophy in the Seventeenth-Century Atlantic World. *The William and Mary Quarterly, 71*(4), 549–588. https://doi.org/10.5309/willmaryquar.71.4.0549

CRYSTAL, E. (1989). MYTH, SYMBOL AND FUNCTION OF THE TORAJA HOUSE.
53. Johnstone, H.H., & Malcolm, LW.G. (1921). Short notes on the syllabic writing of the Eyap – Central Cameroons. *Journal of the Royal African Society, 20* (78), 127–129.
54. Imperato, P.J., & Shamir, M. (1970). Bokolanfini: Mud cloth of the Bamana of Mali. African Arts, 3(4), 32–41, +80.
55. Sparks, G. (2016). How 'bout them Sapotes?: Mendicant translations and Maya corrections in early indigenous theologies. *CR: The New Centennial Review, 16*(1), 213–244. https://doi.org/10.14321/crnewcentrevi.16.1.0213
56. Cáárcamo-Huechante, L. E. (2011). The long history of indigenous textual cultures: A response. *Textual Cultures, 6*(2), 142–146. https://doi.org/10.2979/textcult.6.2.142
57. Hindley, P. (2017), p. 76.
58. Hindley, P. (2017).
59. Hindley, P. (2017).
60. Hindley, P. (2017).
61. Hindley, P. (2017), p. 87.
62. International Institute for Environment and Development (IIED). (2006).
63. Hyland, S., Ware, G. A., & Clark, M. (2014). Knot direction in a Khipu/Alphabetic text from the Central Andes. *Latin American Antiquity, 25*(2), 189–197.
64. International Institute for Environment and Development (IIED). (2006).
65. Sillar, B., & Urton, G. (2005). Communicative technologies in the Ancient Andes: Decoding the Inka Khipu [Review of Signs of the Inka Khipu: Binary Coding in the Andean KnottedString Records]. *Current Anthropology, 46*(4), 690–691. https://doi.org/10.1086/432824
66. Urton, G. (1998a). From knots to narratives: Reconstructing the art of historical record keeping in the Andes from Spanish transcriptions of Inka Khipus. *Ethnohistory, 45*(3), 409–438. https://doi.org/10.2307/483319
67. International Institute for Environment and Development (IIED). (2006), pp. 10–11.
68. Sillar, B., & Urton, G. (2005), p. 690.
69. Sillar, B., & Urton, G. (2005).
70. Urton, G. (2005b). Khipu archives: Duplicate accounts and identity labels in the Inka knotted string records. Latin American Antiquity, 16(2), 147–167. https://doi.org/10.2307/30042809
71. Urton, G. (1998a).
72. Hyland, S., Ware, G. A., & Clark, M. (2014), p. 191.

73. Urton, G. (2001). A calendrical and demographic tomb text from Northern Peru. *Latin American Antiquity, 12*(2), 127–147. https://doi.org/10.2307/972052
74. International Institute for Environment and Development (IIED). (2006).
75. International Institute for Environment and Development (IIED). (2006).
76. -Huechante, L. E. (2011).
77. Huechante, L. E. (2011).
78. Hudson, K. M., & Henderson, J. S. (2021). Script, image, and culture in the Maya world: A southeastern perspective. In P. J. Boyes, P. M. Steele, & N. E. Astoreca (Eds.), The Social and Cultural Contexts of Historic Writing Practices (pp. 231–248). Oxbow Books. https://doi.org/10.2307/j.ctv2npq9fw.17
79. Hudson, K. M., & Henderson, J. S. (2021).
80. McDonald, J. A. (2016). Deciphering the symbols and symbolic meaning of the Maya world tree. *Ancient Mesoamerica, 27*(2), 333–359.
81. Johnstone, H.H., & Malcolm, LW.G. (1921). Short notes on the syllabic writing of the Eyap – Central Cameroons. *Journal of the Royal African Society, 20* (78), 127–129.
82. MacGregor, J.K. (1909). Notes on Nsibidi. *The Journal of the Royal Anthropological Institute of Great Britain and Ireland, 39*, 209–219.
83. Slogar, C. (2007). Early ceramics from Calabar, Nigeria: Towards a history of Nsibidi. *African Arts, 40*(1), Ceramic Arts in Africa (Spring, 2007), pp. 18–29
84. Slogar, C. (2007).
85. Dayrell, E. (1911). Further Notes on 'Nsibidi signs with their meanings from the Ikom District, Southern Nigeria. (Jul. – Dec., 1911), 521–540
86. Imperato, P.J., & Shamir, M. (1970). Bokolanfini: Mud cloth of the Bamana of Mali. *African Arts, 3*(4), 32–41, +80.
87. Imperato, P.J., & Shamir, M. (1970).

CHAPTER 6

Extra-mundane Communication

INTRODUCTION

Extra-mundane refers to those instances when communication goes beyond the realm of intra-personal, interpersonal and mass communication to embrace supernatural beings – ancestors, spirits, gods, the supreme God – or when they involve processes, elements or abilities that are superhuman as in witchcraft, reincarnation etc. More so as the supernatural is a natural part of the indigenous experience and worldview with the earth, the seen and unseen world perceived as intimately linked and connected. These features and elements have been collapsed in this chapter into a global outlook, bottom-up, and top-down as well as pointing out the syncretism of it all. The global outlook takes a sweep at indigenous religious practices across the globe, while bottom-up communication involves attempts by human beings to get the attention of supernatural forces for a variety of reasons. Top-down communication is actually the feedback component of the extra-mundane mode of communication in which the supernatural agent communicates his or her pleasure or displeasure, directs, gives guidance etc.

© The Author(s), under exclusive license to Springer Nature
Switzerland AG 2024
E. Akpabio, *Indigenous Communication*,
https://doi.org/10.1007/978-3-031-41766-5_6

Global Outlook

Extra mundane communication is present in every nook and cranny of the world. In Mesoamerican cultures particularly among the lowland Maya, there is the cosmic tree whose plant and animal elements communicate "a vital linkage between an aquatic underworld, the earth and its celestial realms."[1] The plant's basal stem is rooted in a watery substrate that is the underworld of the gods or the place of fear, the trunk ascends from the skull of an aquatic god known as the water lily monster with a square nose serpent and bird resting on its three branches.[2] There are similarities with the African worldview where there exists a reverence for the universe, creation, the living and the dead as well as supernatural forces. In the Andean region of South America, the Kotosh people had enclosed rooms with a central sunken space and a hearth for burning offerings.[3]

Animal offerings during the *Dharmāraj pūjā* in Goalpara, a multi-caste community in India, have Brahmanas providing the lead as they officiate and eat the sacrificial flesh availed on the last day of the festival.[4] The Sinhalese of Sri Lanka are said to practice four religions: "Buddhism; second, a cult of Hindu gods; third, a cult of planetary deities; and fourth, a cult of local hobgoblins."[5] The latter three cults involve healing rituals.[6] Among the Ifugao of The Philippines it is faunal sacrifices usually pigs, chicken and carabaos that are offered in order to connect the physical and the spirit worlds.[7]

Relics from the Indus Valley indicates that the world is administered by P*asupati*, the Lord of the Beats and the Mother Goddess.[8] In Andhrades, India, the worship of the seven sisters (*matrikas*) was quite prevalent.[9] This is contrasted with the Caddo Indians of the Hasinai confederacy in present day Texas who worshipped a "single omnipotent deity."[10] In the *Rgveda*, the oldest Sanskrit text, one finds the *vájra* a multipronged weapon that the god Indra uses to club his enemies to death; a precedent that kings and warriors are expected to follow.[11] The same text has 1028 poetic hymns directed at three gods: "The deified ritual fire *Agni;* the demiurge warrior god Indra; and *Soma*, who is the personification of the sacred beverage *sóma*."[12]

In Africa, this is manifested in ancestors, spirits and witchcraft. The first two can be manipulated through ceremonies and rituals while witchcraft attacks are usually encountered at the household level, and this becomes apparent when the witch confesses to their atrocities before passing on.[13] Among the Shona of Zimbabwe spirits are both the cause and cure of illnesses but they also acknowledge that witches can also be causal agents.[14] During the *Malambe* festival which is dedicated to the dead in Malawi, they cry for the dead and place *massa*, chicken and a calabash of water at the graves so that the dead can clean up after eating based on Machinga culture.[15] Gnawa *lila*, a possession trance ceremony in Morocco uses music to cure through spirit possession.[16]

Ancestors are seldom encountered by the average person in Equatorial Guinea, but they may appear to people in dreams wearing white or the shroud with which they were buried.[17] Ghost may linger a few days within the household because they care for the living but this can also result in taking along with the living to the land of the dead.[18] This may explain instances whereby people still talk about seeing a parent or loved still sitting in their favourite chair even after they have passed on. The Igbos of Nigeria believe in "one God", lesser deities, spirits and ancestors who all deserve to be worshipped.[19] The feeling seems to be as captured by a Sierra Leonean that "God is therefore regarded as an absentee Lord who, whilst wielding ultimate authority, relegates the details of everyday government to minor deities" and ancestors.[20]

In central Mexico, Ceramics were used for ritual and indigenous religious worship and they contained pictographic decorations for this purpose.[21] Kaluli séances are belligerent with growing voices which makes them fearful while Sora shamans speak in the voice of the dead threatening to afflict people with dreadful diseases.[22] The people of Kyrgyzstan attend funerals to get blessings from the soul of the dead (*arbak*) as well as obtain spiritual merits (*soopčuluk*).[23] People in central Himalaya have a healing ritual that involves trance, possession, animal sacrifice etc.[24] Giving of food by south Asians has been going on for over a millennium and is "central to ritual transactions."[25]

Diseases in Southern Africa can come about as a result of dreaming persistently about *shades* (who are invisible).[26] However, to

> have identified one's shade is to have a mystical helper who can come to your assistance. At other times the shades come in dreams and request beer or food offerings. If you do not satisfy these demands with appropriate responses, you will be stricken with disease.[27]

The Ngoma phenomenon in the African setting is also a prime example of a trilogy: the spirits, the sufferer and the healer. These work in harmony as emphasis is placed on "sufferer's acceptance of the condition and the calling as interpreted by the diviner or healer, and upon the relationship between the sufferer's song and spirit."[28] In other words, the sufferer seem to go through nose bleeding, headaches mental illness etc. which indicates their "call" and its acceptance opens the road to recovery.[29] Experiences from Cape Town South Africa to Dar es Salaam, Tanzania and Swaziland places premium on song, medicines and drumming to identify and propitiate the spirit as captured in this Lemba song: "That which was a 'stitch' of pain Has become the path to the priesthood."[30]

But the performances also serve other purposes such as tying an individual's life experiences into a coherent narrative, purification celebration for healers, celebration of novice *sangomas* (healers), to "wash the beads" or "throw out the darkness" following the death of a close kin etc. An instance of this requiem ngoma was performed at the Western Cape for a senior *sangoma* following the death of her mother and the disparate parts of the performance makes for interesting reading. Reference is made to her work environment "facing a white person", ancestors, Jesus (I love Jesus, He set free my soul) and various South African languages – Afrikaans, English, Xhosa, and Zulu. Thus a "poignant reminder of the cleavages and cosmopolitan diversity of South African society."[31]

In Ghana, dumping sites are the feeding places of witches and the stench from such sites pollute the soul.[32] The Giriama healers in Kenya are said to be less powerful than their Malindi Swahili counterparts because the latter "have the Quran."[33] Yet the Giriama making this assertion also has a Quran which she cannot read but cuts into talismanic strip or waves it around her client while also making supplication to the Giriama godhead *Mulungu* and the Muslim Allah.[34] This is similar to a Muslim Hausa woman from Nigeria who believes in spirits and asserts confidently that they "know everything…they are here in the compound, they are here in the town …everyone has his [sic] own."[35]

But the African experience has more complexities as the supreme God can be female, male or even androgynous. While the male role clearly springs to mind, there are also many African ethnic groups with a female supreme being. The Ijaw of Nigeria have four principal names for the Almighty God: *Temearu* (she who is the moulder of all); *Ayegba* (the foundress of the universe); *Woyingi* (our mother) and; *Oginarau* (she who dwells in heaven).[36] The Ashanti of Ghana have *Nyame*, the great mother who is associated with the moon, while their compatriots Akan have *Ngame* who is associated with the female cross that communicates creation of the revolving universe.[37] Among the Ibibios, the corresponding being is *Eka Abassi* (Mother of God) who is beyond all the other gods in the Ibibio pantheon.[38]

The supreme being as androgynous is found among the Batammaliba of Togo where *Kuiye* has both genitalia and is referred to as "The Sun, Our father and Our mother" and *Mwari*, the god of fertility from Zimbabwe.[39] The Ashanti of Ghana also have the female principle (the moon) and the male one (the sun) both involved in the creation of human beings.

Even though there are plenty of biblical injunctions against images

> anthropomorphic images of Yahweh appeared to have been made throughout the preexilic period, with Judahite practices being no less iconic than those of neighboring cultures. Religious observances in the First Temple period appear to have used many types of images, anthropomorphic and not, employed in processions and offered both libations and sacrifices. Even a quick survey demonstrates the range of evidence, including the finding of religious statues made of ivory, terra-cotta, and faience, as well as seals.[40]

Statues of gods were also present in the Graeco-Roman world even though the philosophers railed against them: "And they pray to these images just as if one were to have conversation with houses, having no idea of the nature of gods and heroes."[41] In Roman Britain there is a temple for the worship of the goddess *Sulis* with evidence pointing to public offering of sacrifices and libation and private ones involving coins and curse tablets.[42]

Other parts of the world have interesting stories to tell in this regard:

> The Persians, according to Herodotus, did not believe that the gods have the same nature as men and therefore rejected building images, altars, and temples. So too the Scythians used only a scimitar of iron as their image of Ares. Strabo depicted the rejection of statues as one of the many sensible traits of the Nabateans. Later Ammianus Marcellinus praised the Halani as not only tall and handsome but also as having no temples: according to him, they used only a naked sword fixed in the ground in their worship.[43]

In southern Italy there is *pizzica taranta* – a classical dance ritual that cures tarantism which is a disease brought on by the bite of a spider.[44] Its modern iteration has frenzied and suggestive movements that is emotionally draining but also with testimonies of healings.[45]

Effigy censers recovered from Petén, Guatamala could have represented a deity while the ones recovered in Tayasal must have been deposited by worshippers of *Nojpetén*.[46] Witches among enslaved people in the American south are described as "shape-shifting, body-leaving, nocturnal entities that 'ride' their hapless victims so much so that an informer said that he kept a bible under his pillow to ward off the attacks."[47] Other ways of dealing with the issue is pouring salt in one's surrounding as well as pouring salt and pepper on a corpse etc.[48] One riveting encounter makes for interesting reading:

> A notorious hag was discovered through the machinations of the husband of one of her alleged victims. He awaited the witch's nocturnal entry into his home and, upon perceiving his wife's struggles against an unseen entity, began wildly swinging an axe until he hit the spirit. After the strike, the man heard a "screech" and saw a cat exit through the window. He followed the cat's trail and found 'old Malinda Edmonde with three rib broke'.[49]

The Hawaiian precolonial state religion was known as *Aikapu* and was embodied in the image of *kū* carved from the breadfruit tree.[50] The grandmother features prominently in the Aztec and Mixtec ritual arts. She symbolizes the realm of force of nature encompassing creation, procreation, fertility, cleansing, spiritual and bodily strength.[51] This realm is under the sunlight but is concentrated in the steam bath (*temazcal*) and other sacred places.[52] This concentration implies violence hence she needs to be treated with respect and reverence as she gets easily offended.[53]

The dead in Europe may not turn into ancestors that are on the lookout for the living as we find in Africa but there are instances that show the veneration with which they are treated. There are for example monuments: "Etruscan tumuli, such as in the necropolis of Cerveteri (Italy)" and the "sarcophagus of Simpelveld in the Netherlands" that are houselike where the dead can "**dwell** (emphasis added) in comfort."[54] Severed heads and skulls from southern France while interpreted as war trophy "but the possibility of a parallel practice of ancestral veneration cannot be excluded."[55] In Siberia and the artic region wild animals offer themselves to be eaten, "so long as hunters respect their souls, thereby allowing them to be reincarnated in new flesh."[56]

Maya monuments, on the other hand, communicate the destiny of the dead. Inscription on the lid of the sarcophagus of Lord Pakal indicate that "the ruler is laid down in earth at the foot of the flourishing tree of rulership, amidst his ancestors who have turned into trees."[57] In Iraq, "shrines of highly revered religious men could also exert psychotherapeutic effects, as dead Imams are believed to be capable of offering blessings (*Baraka*) and conveying invocations to God."[58] A vessel from the Ñuu Dzaui archaeological site Cerro de las Minas (Huajuapan) contains a rich communication elements:

> the image of an elderly man, seated (as a ruler) on the *ñuu* sign (representing 'town', 'people' or 'nation'), holds a small gourd that probably contained ground *piciete;* as a consequence of consuming this hallucinogen, he is transforming into a powerful *nahual*: the fire serpent. As the vessel was placed at the foot of the buried person, i.e. facing the entrance/exit of the tomb, the total image suggests that the ruler is entering the trance world to meet his creators. At the same time, this would be the image for those who would enter the tomb to pay their respects and to seek counsel from the deceased. The vessel invites the approaching faithful to replicate the action: both would consume *piciete* and enter into a trance in order to meet and communicate with each other in the world beyond.[59]

The pig sacrifice among the Ifugao of Philippines also has communication properties. In addition to being the main means of exchange between the human and spirit world, a plethora of pig sacrifices communicates the elite status of the family undertaking this.[60] Carabao sacrifice, on the other hand, is meant to reverence ancestors while chicken is to thank the *bulul* or rice guardians for a good harvest.[61] Distributing the sacrifice (*bolwa*) communicated one's wealth and status and assisted in cementing kinship bonds and alliances.[62] The sacrifices also come into play in other aspects of Ifugao life and culture: Burial rituals (*bogwa*), weddings (*uyauy*), elderly ceremonies (*honga*), and prestige rites (*hagabi, ballihong, and kolot*).[63]

The Balinese of Papua New Guinea and Indonesia see the sea as polluted but regard the mountains as the "seat of the gods."[64] In contrast the Javanese and Tanga Islanders of Papua New Guinea see the sea as beyond human control and supernatural. In Kei Island of eastern Indonesia, the sea is the abode of their eighteen ancestors comprising males and females and collectively known as *wadar*.[65] For the indigenous people of Croker Island, Australia, the Rainbow Serpent rests on the seabed.[66] To the Wakuéna, a Northern Arawak-speaking people of the Upper Rio Negro region in Venezuela, Colombia, and Brazil, "the structure of human society are defined in relation to the life-giving and life-taking powers of mythic, patrilineal ancestors."[67]

Bottom-Up Communication

The way devotees go about getting their petition heard by the supernatural being they direct their supplications to, takes varied forms and involves diverse processes. The central focus of the *Dharmāraj pūjā* is to "coerce" the deity, *Dharmāraj*, to join the festival hence the loud shout by everyone present to "arouse" the deity.[68] There is also a lot of praise singing, drumming, animal sacrifice etc.[69] *Pasupati*, from evidence uncovered in the Indus Valley, is worshipped as the "protector" of cattle and plants while the Mother Goddess is venerated for offering protection from natural calamities and ill-health.[70] Still in Andhrades, India the worship of *matrikas* (the seven sisters) was intended to offer protection from evil spirits present in every village that were the causes of epidemics such as cholera, small pox and other afflictions such as barrenness.[71] The villages offered animals and foodstuffs to avert these evil and after their prayers have been answered they would embark on a festival, *jatara*.[72]

To curry the favour of ancestors in Equatorial Guinea, prayer and libation of "cold water" is used.[73] In the Nigerian context, local gin and in modern times, alcohol brands are also marketing themselves as being acceptable for use in pouring libation. In other words, the ancestors have moved with the times and brands from modern distilleries can also serve this role. The prayer and libation takes on a communal posture when

> women are miscarrying, crop yields seem to be down, injuries and accidents in the forest have increased. Sometimes it may be something dramatic such as a fire in the settlement, which is usually devastating and indiscriminate and is interpreted by the diviners as the wrath of the ancestors.[74]

This supplication to put an end to negative occurrences is also present in Taiwan where the demons there can be "bargained with."[75]

Igbo of South East Nigeria also through formulaic utterances can invoke and control the spirits.[76] They also call on ancestors, deities and spirits for help in times of crises and needs.[77] In Bastar, Chhattisgarh in India, there are *ghotuls* in which boys and girls engage in song and dance rehearsals that are "offerings to their gods."[78] The Sierra Mixe of Mexico offer miniature tortillas, dough rolls and poultry sacrifices at "the summit of a mountain called Zempoaltépetl to ask The One Who Makes Live (*yïkjujyky'äjtpï*; *-yïk*, causative, *jujyky'äjt* "living being," *i*, personifier) for his help" which may be bumper harvest to resolution of conflicts.[79] They also to have gods for various activities and endeavours that they consult for success and favour: Wind, fishing, hunting, war, peace, childbirth, water, planting etc.[80]

Kū, one of the major male deities in Hawaii is known as the god of war but it also the deity responsible for male generative power.[81] The Aztecc and Mixtec observe some symbolisms in their offerings which are in turn tied to the favours they are expecting

> the petitions (*pedimentos*) at sacred sites throughout the Ñuu Dzaui region express in material form (structures of stones, pine cones, etc.) the contents of what is prayed for (houses, good family life, children, cattle, cars, etc.). Similarly, by bloodletting in self-sacrifice people may be asking for life force; deposited weapons may express a wish for strength in battle as well as a desire for peace. The offering of jewels may indicate that the aim is to achieve good fortune, while imagery referring to dynastic history clarifies further that rulership and the legacy of the ancestors are involved.[82]

The Wola of Papua New Guinea recite spells and incantations as they go about the business of hunting. Analysis of these focus on "the successful setting of traps, including their construction, location (notably according to favoured food sources of animals), conduct of hunter, relevant behavioural traits of animals...."[83] The Tani tribes – Adi, Nyishi, Apatani, Tagin and Galo – in Arunachal Pradesh, India worship the Sun and Moon (*Donyi* and *Polo*) to derive benefits such as prosperity, fertility and avoidance of calamities.[84] The ritual involves:

> Candles and scented perfume [which] are used as ritual articles for burning on the altar in front of the images. After this the priest sprinkles sanctified water on the heads of the devotees. Then an experienced person will read or narrate the philosophy of *Donyi-Polo*. Either before or after prayer, the healing rope (*ridin*) is tied onto the wrist of the devotees by the priest, symbolizing the blessing of *Donyi-Polo*.[85]

In Mesoamerica, the Zapotecs of Yalalag conduct a ceremony to usher in the rains.[86] The sorcerers in the dead of the night visit a spring, offer offerings, construct a miniature dam and place stones and twigs at its edge to represent animals, trees and houses.[87] Then they proceed to describe the events that precede the rains, break the dam and pour water from a gourd while proclaiming "the rain is coming."[88] This is similar to deer hunting among the Huastec of northern Veracruz. They say a prayer accompanied with offerings of food and alcohol to the "owner of the animals" to make for a successful hunt before constructing a pen from which a "deer" would be allowed by the "owner" to escape into their hands.[89]

Ghana and South Africa also have a similar ritual. *Adevu* among the Ewe of Ghana is a performance in which someone plays the role of an animal by going on all fours and is then "symbolically killed" by other hunters as this "facilitates" the hunt.[90] The same process with the same expectation of a successful hunt called *Iguba* takes place in South Africa among Nguni speakers.

In the Republic of Benin, *Dangbe* the python deity is invoked for every necessity and difficulties including "excessive wet, dry or barren seasons", preservation of cattle and so on.[91] But their range and pantheons of gods seems to boggle the imagination and the quote below gives some inkling but these are by no means exhaustive

> Roof overhangs shield shrines from torrential seasonal rain. Also under the house eaves and near to the doorway are found shrines with bridged, twin vessels dedicated to the twin deity *Hoho* ... Inverted pots are used to cover shrines to the family deity or *Aiza*, which is located centrally within house compounds. At the foot of baobab trees and in free-standing shrines just beyond the house compound, *danzen*... or *dangbezen* ceramics can be found with small snake appliqués that indicate an affiliation with the serpent deity....[92]

Contained in the *Rgveda,* the oldest Sanskrit text is an offering of grain cakes, butter and meat (fat) during the Summer Solstice that is placed in the ritual fire so that the "smoke carries the essence of the offerings aloft to entice gods like Indra to the ritual ground."[93] Similarly, to curry the favour of the mercurial *Pomba Gira* among the Afro Brazilians she needs to be plied with gifts that gratify her vanity such as wine, cigarette, perfume and jewelry.[94]

Top-Down Communication

The results of the *Dharmāraj pūjā* in Goalpara include fertility, the entrance of the low caste *bhaktyās* into *Dharmāraj's* clan, holy/peace water used for anointing and curing etc.[95] Sinhalese of Sri Lanka credit their rituals with a number of benefits: fending off misfortunes and altering one's destiny for the better hence they propitiate or exorcise spirits to achieve these.[96] Buddhist practice is said to ensure "better karma" over and above "Celestial Master ritual idioms – 'petitions, talismans, seals, and registers'"[97] But Buddhism can also involve co-mingling:

> A seventeen year old novice of the Buddhist monkhood in a village near Matara ... was one day set upon by a female goblin or *succubus* and he became what people described as "sexually crazed." ...Occasionally he would look above him and moan, "Why did you do this to me?" apparently talking to the female goblin who had possessed him. It was quite unbecoming for a man in his condition to remain within celibate orders...The standard cure for sexual madness is a special kind of spirit cult called *yakuma* or "dance of the goblins." But monks who are sacred Buddhist specialists are ideally supposed to totally abstain from such profane ceremonies. So this is what the young monk did. He disrobed to lay status, returned to his natal village to undergo the ritual cure in the hands of a shaman, and then returned again to monastic orders, restored to "normal" and prepared to continue his sacred vocation.

This is similar to the Bicolanos of The Philippines usage of the image of Christ on a cross for barangay's saint known as the *Amang Hinulid* to heal "spirit-caused" illnesses.[98]

Among the Wakuéna, of Venezuela, Colombia, and Brazil there exist male ritual specialists known as *málikai líminali* who are able to exercise ancestral powers in handling crisis, curing diseases, foretelling the future and well as sanctioning anti-social behaviours.[99] Buddhism flowered in China in AD. 1127–1644 during the beginning of the Southern Sung to the end of the Ming dynasty to bring about "universal deliverance" as well as a "means of salvation."[100]

Ancestors in Africa usually take an interest in watching over the living and their favour and blessings is only withheld if "their descendants fail in their moral obligations to each other and to the ancestors."[101] Ancestral spirits which are forest-based in Equatorial Guinea deal more with individuals than the community as a whole.[102] They confer ambivalent benefits: they may favour a man over a woman or the other way round, confer artistic talent, confer untold wealth on an individual in exchange for a "regular supply of infant blood" and are the source of medicines which can be used for healing, protection, proving guilt or innocence etc.[103] An example of medicine is *nitie*. It takes the form of brass or iron rings with four knobs on them. Sometimes it is said that they may be found on the banks of rivers and streams. They are certainly not made by the people themselves. Paradoxically these metal objects are described as animals and can die prematurely if not cared for. It is important, for example, to keep it in a vessel of water, otherwise it will wander about at night.

In terms of their looks, ancestral spirit varies from large, hairy, and frightening so much so that the person encountering them comes away mentally disturbed; stunning beautiful like a mermaid or they make take the form of a leopard or snake.[104]

Ancestors in Fiji, in the same vein, are said to be bigger, more powerful and hardworking than the present crop of people in the country but their curses are also quite effective.[105] Villagers who have contacted are empowered to afflict their compatriots with poverty, lack of education, inability to get married or have children and sickness.[106]

To get the benefits of their miniature offerings the Sierra Mixe of Mexico also place miniature "receptors" such as a stone house, an enclosure, an anthropomorphic figurine to give direction in which the benefits should flow so that it does not go to persons who did not request such favours.[107] Such co-presence is also part of Yucatec Maya séances in which the shaman, the person seeking healing and the spirits whose help is being sought involves the enactment of ritual speech that brings about a spatio-temporal connection.[108]

But to be sure that the offerings have been received, the Sierra Mixe go through an intriguing process: The "ritual meals that follow it stage acceptance through human spokespeople who speak in the place of the silent nonhumans."[109] For the Efiks of South Nigeria, to determine if the spirits have accepted the revocation of a curse a mother places on her child a sacrifice of a hen is required

> She and the child go to the spot where the curse was spoken, and the mother turns the hen clockwise around her child's head. Next the mother rubs the hen on every part of the child's body while saying "All that I said should be revoked: voice enters; voice goes out." She then decapitates the hen and throws the carcass on the ground. The curse is revoked if the carcass lies on the left side after muscular contraction ceases, but if the carcass lies on the right side the curse is unrevoked.[110]

For the Arawakan-speaking Manchinery population in the Brazilian Amazon, the *ayahuasca* ceremony which involves the hallucinogen ayahuasca is used in rituals to obtain guidance, protection and knowledge from the forest spirits.[111]

In conducting healing, the Mesoamerican healer pours alcohol or water on the earth and smears the head and chest of the patient with the wet earth in the form of a cross.[112] In the same Aztecc and Mixtec tradition, the act of giving "are human *dzaha* to the divine powers and so integrate both parties in a strong community of confidence and faith."[113] For the Ifugao of The Philippines the faunal sacrifices ensures that the spirit realm intervenes to right wrong situations.[114] Among the Ibibios of Nigeria this can take the form of infertility and diseases which is made right by *Eka Abassi* (Mother of God).[115] The Inuit carried around miniaturized objects that would offer them protection.[116] Among the Shona of Zimbabwe consulting an indigenous medical practitioner (*n'anga*) helps in finding the root causes of sicknesses and bringing about the required healing.[117]

In the remote and poorer part of southern Italy, there is the *pizzica taranta* an annual ritual dance that is used to cure tarantism – a disease brought on by the bite of a spider.[118] The dance usually ended with a vision of St. Paul who grants the victim a temporary cure until the next year when they must embark on the same ritual.[119] The rituals were condemned in such strong words as being "a symbolic resolution of a neurotic crisis brought about by the harsh living conditions in the Italian countryside… a sign of the physical, psychological, and existential distress of the southern Italian peasantry, especially its women" and this ensured that it was killed it off.[120] But it has been revived as it is sad to alter "the consciousness of the participants, bringing purification, and the release of emotional blockages."[121]

In Croker Island, Australia, the indigenous people refrain from throwing meat into the sea in order not to arouse the Rainbow Serpent that is resting on the seabed as it would then unleash tidal waves, waterspouts and cyclones.[122] Korean shamans used bell and mirrors to cure illnesses as well as step on sharp blades to show how powerful they are.[123] During the Adevu performance among the Ewe of Ghana, people show of their powers (*ade-dzo*) by cutting themselves with sharp knives without drawing blood or coming to any harm.[124] They have, of course, being fortified with herbs to ensure that the knives have no effect.[125] In the same way, they are able to kill an animal by merely pointing at it after which it drops dead.[126]

When it comes to love and matters of the heart, *Pomba Gira* among the Afro Brazilians is able to come up with the love potion that would make one live happily ever after with the love of their life.[127] But to her adherents, most of whom are found in the poor and working-class neighbourhoods, she can also solve other life crises and problems.[128]

Conclusion

The syncretism that is apparent in this excursion is unmissable. Indigenous religious practices have not remained untouched by the goings-on around them. This statement about the Yoruba of Nigeria may not be too far from the truth as it seems people want to eat their cake and have it:

> Among the Yoruba it is not uncommon to find Christian, Muslim and Animist in the same family. Some say that this is a local tradition by which the family would sacrifice to the largest number of gods so as to have the greatest chance of good fortune.[129]

Same with Koreans who "honored their ancestors with Confucian rites, visited Buddhist temples to pray for health and wealth, and turned to shamans when they were in trouble."[130] In addition, the "shrine of mountain gods" (*sansingak*) and the "shrine of the Big Dipper" (*chilseonggak*) in Korean Buddhist temples demonstrate syncretism between Buddhism and popular beliefs.[131]

The highland Maya of Santiago, Guatemala have their *constumbre* that reveres the "earth lords, Jesu Cristo, saints, and ancestors, a year-bearer cult recognizing four sacred mountains as the seats of alternating mayors of the solar year, and the 260-day divining almanac or *Ch'olK'ij*."[132] In the same vein, urban Black South Africans Christians still perform rituals for success and health and would consult traditional healers and diviners when they face a crisis situation.[133] The folk-Buddhist sect in China recruited leaders from the ranks of fortune tellers etc.[134] Medieval Russian amulets had a cross added to the ancient symbolic bird form.[135] The Dalang Budiman from Indonesia offers some mantras before his performance to invoke "forces" and then acts out the story of Adam and Eve as well as the triumph of the "good" and "Islamic" over unbelievers.[136]

Similarly, *Espritismo* or Spiritism associated with African Diaspora and Caribbean culture also has the same elements. For instance, the altar in the home of its leader Don Miguel Flores has images of "Christ, the Virgin, and many saints...Buddhas and a camel, as well as a cluster of crouching all-black figures... the statue of an American Indian."[137]

There must be more globally than this excursion has unearthed given that both indigenous religious practices as well as Abrahamic and Eastern religions seem to have been affected in equal measure. These strange mixture rather than serve to strengthen the arguments of those who rail against indigeneity which we have laboured to show is real, speaks to the complexities of the world we live in and how people try to make sense of it all.

Notes

1. McDonald, J. A. (2016). Deciphering the symbols and symbolic meaning of the Maya world tree. *Ancient Mesoamerica, 27*(2), 333–359, p. 333.
2. McDonald, J. A. (2016).
3. Rosenfeld, S. A., & Bautista, S. L. (2017). An archaeology of rituals. In S. A. Rosenfeld & S. L. Bautista (Eds.), Rituals of the past: Prehispanic and colonial case studies in Andean Archaeology (pp. 3–20). University Press of Colorado.
4. Korom, F. J. (1999). "To be happy": Ritual, play, and leisure in the Bengali Dharmarāj pūjā. *International Journal of Hindu Studies, 3*(2), 113–164.
5. Ames, M. M. (1964). Buddha and the dancing goblins: A theory of magic and religion. *American Anthropologist, 66*(1), 75–82, p. 75.
6. Ames, M. M. (1964).
7. Von Rotz, M. P. (2018). Ifugao Identity: The retention of indigenous religion and rituals despite colonialism. *Philippine Quarterly of Culture and Society, 46*(1/2), 114–123.
8. Hymavathi, P. (1993). Religion and popular medicine in Medieval Andhra. *Social Scientist, 21*(1/2), 34–47. https://doi.org/10.2307/3517837
9. Hymavathi, P. (1993).
10. Barr, J. (2004). A diplomacy of gender: Rituals of first contact in the "Land of the Tejas." *The William and Mary Quarterly, 61*(3), 393–434. https://doi.org/10.2307/3491803, p. 403.
11. Whitaker, J. (2016). I boldly took the mace (Vájra) for might: Ritually weaponizing a warrior's body in Ancient India. *International Journal of Hindu Studies, 20*(1), 51–94.
12. Whitaker, J. (2016), p. 56.
13. Jedrej, M. C. (1986). Cosmology and symbolism on the Central Guinea Coast. *Anthropos, 81*(4/6), 497–515.

14. Shoko, T. (2011). Shona traditional religion and medical practices: methodological approaches to religious phenomena. *Africa Development / Afrique et Développement, 36*(2), 277–292.
15. Linden, I. (1974). Mponda mission diary, 1889–1891. Part III: A Portuguese mission in British Central Africa. *The International Journal of African Historical Studies, 7*(4), 688–728. https://doi.org/10.2307/216602
16. Becker, C. (2011). Hunters, Sufis, soldiers, and minstrels: The diaspora aesthetics of the Moroccan Gnawa. *RES: Anthropology and Aesthetics, 59/60*, 124–144.
17. Jedrej, M. C. (1986).
18. Jedrej, M. C. (1986).
19. Elechi, O. O., Saleh-Hanna, V., Affor, C., Agomoh, U., Agozino, B., Akporherhe, C., Anagaba, S. M., Eribo, O., Nagel, M., Odibo, I., Sudbury, J., & Ume, C. (2008). The Igbo indigenous justice system. In Colonial Systems of Control: Criminal Justice in Nigeria (pp. 395–416). University of Ottawa Press. https://doi.org/10.2307/j.ctt1ckph37.26
20. Parrinder, E. G. (1959), p. 136.
21. Sánchez, G. H. (2012). Ceramics, cultural continuity and social change. In Ceramics and the Spanish Conquest: Response and Continuity of Indigenous Pottery Technology in Central Mexico (pp. 207–225). Brill.
22. Tomlinson, M. (2004). Ritual, risk, and danger: Chain prayers in Fiji. *American Anthropologist, 106*(1), 6–16.
23. Quack, J., & Sax, W. S. (2010). Introduction: The efficacy of rituals. *Journal of Ritual Studies, 24*(1), 5–12, p. 7.
24. Quack, J., & Sax, W. S. (2010).
25. Weiss, R.S. (n.d). Giving to the poor: Ramalinga's transformation of Hindu charity. The emergence of modern Hinduism: Religion on the margins of colonialism. University of California Press.
26. Janzen, J. M. (1991). "Doing Ngoma": A dominant trope in African religion and healing. *Journal of Religion in Africa, 21*(4), 290–308. https://doi.org/10.2307/1581193
27. Janzen, J. M. (1991), p. 299.
28. Janzen, J. M. (1991), p. 300.
29. Janzen, J. M. (1991).
30. Janzen, J. M. (1991), p. 304.
31. Janzen, J. M. (1991), p. 293.
32. Atiemo, A. O. (2018). Dumping sites, witches and soul-pollution: A pastoral reflection on waste and the church in Ghana. *Worldviews, 22*(1), 84–103.

33. McIntosh, J. (2005). Baptismal essentialisms: Giriama code choice and the reification of ethnoreligious boundaries. *Journal of Linguistic Anthropology, 15*(2), 151–170, p. 151.
34. McIntosh, J. (2005).
35. Parrinder, E. G. (1959), p. 140.
36. Ebere, C. (2011). Beating the masculinity game: Evidence from African Traditional Religion. *CrossCurrents, 61*(4), 480–495, p. 485.
37. Ebere, C. (2011).
38. Ebere, C. (2011).
39. Ebere, C. (2011), p. 486.
40. Janowitz, N. (2007). Good Jews don't: Historical and philosophical constructions of idolatry. *History of Religions, 47*(2/3), 239–252. https://doi.org/10.1086/524212, pp. 240–241.
41. Janowitz, N. (2007), p. 244.
42. Revell, L. (2007). Religion and ritual in the Western Provinces. *Greece & Rome, 54*(2), 210–228.
43. Janowitz, N. (2007), p. 245.
44. Trulsson, Å. (2014). Liberating movements: Sensing and managing emotions in the Dance of the Spider. *Journal of Ritual Studies, 28*(2), 51–63.
45. Trulsson, Å. (2014).
46. Pugh, T. W., Sánchez, J. R., & Shiratori, Y. (2012). Contact and missionization at Tayasal, Petén, Guatemala. *Journal of Field Archaeology, 37*(1), 3–19.
47. Wells-Oghoghomeh, A. S. (2017). "She come like a nightmare": Hags, witches and the gendered trans-sense among the enslaved in the Lower South. *Journal of Africana Religions, 5*(2), 239–274. https://doi.org/10.5325/jafrireli.5.2.0239
48. Wells-Oghoghomeh, A. S. (2017).
49. Wells-Oghoghomeh, A. S. (2017). pp. 252–253.
50. Tengan, T. P. K. (2016). The Mana of Kū: Indigenous nationhood, masculinity and authority in Hawai'i. In T. P. K. Tengan & M. Tomlinson (Eds.), *New Mana: Transformations of a classic concept in Pacific languages and cultures* (pp. 55–76). ANU Press.
51. Jansen, M., & Jiménez, G. A. P. (2017). Synthesis: Heritage and spirit connection. In *Time and the ancestors: Aztec and Mixtec ritual art* (pp. 531–570). Brill.
52. Jansen, M., & Jiménez, G. A. P. (2017).
53. Jansen, M., & Jiménez, G. A. P. (2017).
54. Jansen, M., & Jiménez, G. A. P. (2017), p. 540.
55. Dietler, M. (1997). The Iron Age in Mediterranean France: Colonial encounters, entanglements, and transformations. *Journal of World Prehistory, 11*(3), 269–358, p. 321.

56. Vitebsky, P., & Alekseyev, A. (2015). Siberia. Annual Review of Anthropology, 44, 439–455, p. 446.
57. Jansen, M., & Jiménez, G. A. P. (2017), p. 540.
58. Rahim, T.A., Saeed, B.A., Farhan, H.M., & Aziz, R.R. (2014). Trends of indigenous healing among people with psychiatric disorders: Comparative Study of and Kurdish Ethnicities in Iraq. *Journal of Religion and Health*, 1(54), pp. 316–326, p. 317.
59. Jansen, M., & Jiménez, G. A. P. (2017), p. 541.
60. Von Rotz, M. P. (2018).
61. Von Rotz, M. P. (2018).
62. Von Rotz, M. P. (2018).
63. Von Rotz, M. P. (2018), p. 119.
64. Pannell, S. (2007). Of gods and monsters: Indigenous sea cosmologies, promiscuous geographies and the depths of local sovereignty. In P. Boomgaard (Ed.), *A World of Water: Rain, Rivers and Seas in Southeast Asian Histories* (pp. 71–102). Brill, p. 71.
65. Pannell, S. (2007), p. 71.
66. Pannell, S. (2007).
67. Hill, J. D. (1989). Ritual production of environmental history among the Arawakan Wakuénai of Venezuela. *Human Ecology*, 17(1), 1–25, p. 3.
68. Korom, F. J. (1999), p. 121.
69. Korom, F. J. (1999).
70. Hymavathi, P. (1993).
71. Hymavathi, P. (1993).
72. Hymavathi, P. (1993).
73. Jedrej, M. C. (1986), p. 501.
74. Jedrej, M. C. (1986), p. 501.
75. Tomlinson, M. (2004), p. 6.
76. Tomlinson, M. (2004).
77. Elechi, O. O., Saleh-Hanna, V., Affor, C., Agomoh, U., Agozino, B., Akporherhe, C., Anagaba, S. M., Eribo, O., Nagel, M., Odibo, I., Sudbury, J., & Ume, C. (2008).
78. Prévôt, N. (2014). The "Bison Horn" Muria: Making it "more tribal" for a folk dance competition in Bastar, Chhattisgarh. Asian Ethnology, 73(1/2), 201–231, p. 204.
79. Pitrou, P. (2016). Co-activity in Mesoamerica and in the Andes. *Journal of Anthropological Research*, Winter 72(4), 465–482, p. 467.
80. Pitrou, P. (2016).
81. Tengan, T. P. K. (2016).
82. Jansen, M., & Jiménez, G. A. P. (2017), p. 538.

83. Sillitoe, P. (2002). "Maggots in their ears": Hunting incantations and indigenous knowledge in development. *Journal of Ritual Studies, 16*(1), 64–77, p. 67.
84. Chaudhuri, S. K. (2013). The *Institutionalization of Tribal Religion*: Recasting the Donyi-Polo movement in Arunachal Pradesh. *Asian Ethnology, 72*(2), 259–277.
85. Chaudhuri, S. K. (2013), p. 267.
86. Dehouve, D. (2016).
87. Dehouve, D. (2016).
88. Dehouve, D. (2016), p. 507.
89. Dehouve, D. (2016), p. 507.
90. Thackeray, J. F., Apoh, W., & Gavua, K. (2014). Adevu and Chiwara rituals in West Africa compared to hunting rituals and rock art in South Africa. *The South African Archaeological Bulletin, 69*(199), 113–115, p. 113.
91. Norman, N. L. (2009). Powerful pots, humbling holes, and regional ritual processes: Towards an archaeology of Huedan Vodun, ca. 1650–1727. *The African Archaeological Review, 26*(3), 187–218, p. 192.
92. Norman, N. L. (2009).
93. Whitaker, J. (2016), p. 56.
94. Hayes, K. E. (2008).
95. Korom, F. J. (1999).
96. Ames, M. M. (1964).
97. Campany, R. F. (2012). Religious repertoires and contestation: A case study based on Buddhist miracle tales. *History of Religions, 52*(2), 99–141. https://doi.org/10.1086/667205 . p. 115.
98. Von Rotz, M. P. (2018), p. 117.
99. Hill, J. D. (1989).
100. Overmyer, D. L. (1972). Folk-Buddhist Religion: Creation and eschatology in Medieval China. *History of Religions, 12*(1), 42–70, p. 43.
101. Jedrej, M. C. (1986), p. 501.
102. Jedrej, M. C. (1986).
103. Jedrej, M. C. (1986), p. 501.
104. Jedrej, M. C. (1986).
105. Tomlinson, M. (2004).
106. Tomlinson, M. (2004).
107. Pitrou, P. (2016), p. 467.
108. Pitrou, P. (2016).
109. Pitrou, P. (2016), p. 467.
110. Simmons, D.C. (1956). Efik divinations, ordeals and omens. *Southwestern Journal of Anthropology, 12*(2), 223–228, p. 226.

111. Virtanen, P. K. (2006). The urban Manchinery youth and social capital in Western Amazonian contemporary rituals. *Anthropos, 101*(1), 159–167.
112. Jansen, M., & Jiménez, G. A. P. (2017).
113. Jansen, M., & Jiménez, G. A. P. (2017), p. 538.
114. Von Rotz, M. P. (2018).
115. Ebere, C. (2011).
116. Dehouve, D. (2016). A play on dimensions. *Journal of Anthropological Research, 72*(4), pp. 504–529.
117. Shoko, T. (2011).
118. Trulsson, Å. (2014).
119. Trulsson, Å. (2014).
120. Trulsson, Å. (2014), p. 52.
121. Trulsson, Å. (2014), p. 52.
122. Pannell, S. (2007).
123. Kim, C. (2016). The concept of "Korean religion" and religious studies in Korea. Journal of Korean Religions, 1(1/2), Problematizing "Korean Religions" pp. 23–41.
124. Thackeray, J. F., Apoh, W., & Gavua, K. (2014).
125. Thackeray, J. F., Apoh, W., & Gavua, K. (2014).
126. Thackeray, J. F., Apoh, W., & Gavua, K. (2014).
127. Hayes, K. E. (2008). Wicked women and femmes fatales: Gender, power, and Pomba Gira in Brazil. *History of Religions, 48*(1), 1–21. https://doi.org/10.1086/592152
128. Hayes, K. E. (2008).
129. Parrinder, E. G. (1959). Islam and West African indigenous religion. *Numen, 6*(2), 130–141. https://doi.org/10.2307/3269310, p. 133.
130. Baker, D. (2010). A slippery, changing concept: How Korean new religions define religion. Journal of Korean Religions, 1(1/2), 57–91, p. 58.
131. Kim, D. (2010), p. 25.
132. Cook, G., & Offit, T. (2008). Pluralism and transculturation in indigenous Maya religion. *Ethnology, 47*(1), 45–59, p. 45.
133. du Toit, B. M. (1980). Religion, ritual, and healing among urban Black South Africans. *Urban Anthropology, 9*(1), 21–49.
134. Overmyer, D. L. (1972).
135. Biddick, K., Clarke, J. R., Eisenman, S. F., Okoye, I. S., & Pohl, F. K. (1996). Aesthetics, ethnicity, and the history of art. *The Art Bulletin, 78*(4), 594–621. https://doi.org/10.2307/3046210
136. Harnish, D. (2003). Worlds of Wayang Sasak: Music, performance, and negotiations of religion and modernity. Asian Music, 34(2), 91–120, p. 91.
137. Bettelheim, J. (2005). Caribbean Espiritismo (Spiritist) altars: The Indian and the Congo. *The Art Bulletin, 87*(2), 312–330, p. 312.

CHAPTER 7

Visual Communication

This chapter examines the cues supplied by one's physical appearance, clothing, hairdo, tribal marks, tattoos, incisions and other marks on the body. The skin can be encoded to convey messages such as a "person's rank, authority, ethnicity, group membership, gender, and ritual condition."[1] The communication function includes being an unfailing tell-tale sign of one's ethnic origin, but they also convey social relations, spirituality, beauty and creativity as well as indicate lineage and family membership with the accompanying duties, status and obligations. Colours and the significance attached to them across various cultures in the context of tattoos, scarification and body art in general are also explored.

CLOTHES

Clothes among indigenous people ranged from the barest minimum to the elaborate with rich communication properties. They, like every other thing indigenous, were derided but the climate of acceptance has made them symbols of identity and status.[2] Bark cloth, for instance is associated with commoners while its raffia counterpart demonstrates prestige and royalty.[3] In the Kuba kingdom in the present-day Democratic Republic of Congo a deceased woman was dressed in raffia so that her family and ethnic group can "recognize" her.[4] For the Edo people of Nigeria, the *eyeon* – an ankle-length, full-length wrapper – was worn by title holders.[5] In

© The Author(s), under exclusive license to Springer Nature Switzerland AG 2024
E. Akpabio, *Indigenous Communication*,
https://doi.org/10.1007/978-3-031-41766-5_7

Ecuador, the ponchos, straight skirts and shawls are regarded as marks of Indianness.[6] The Emberá of Panama are known for their loincloth (men) and *parumas* – rectangular piece of cloth used by women as a skirt.[7]

In pre-Inca Ecuador, men wore a loin cloth while women put on a wrapped skirt accessorized with a mantle or cloak.[8] Those of the nobility wore tunics (*unku*) while standard bearers or other higher nobles had *tocapu* – bands of decorative motifs – crosscutting the tunic into two or three zones. They have been refereed to as "king's robes" serving as "woven signifiers of the vastness of the inca empire" as well as demonstrating the diversity of the people they ruled over.[9] More so when contrasted with the average inca who wore plain tunics "usually limited to a standardized single motif like the stepped red, white and black checkerboard."[10] The Australian Aboriginals in the southern colder and higher regions wore possum fur cloaks that were slung over their shoulders and fastened at the front.[11]

The Wari' of Western Brazil wore no clothing but expressed modesty in discreet postures but with intrusion from outsiders' intent on starring at the "naked savages" they opted to cover their nakedness in relation to their dealings with outsiders.[12] Indigenous groups also adopted Western ways such as minimal clothing to be on the same footing with others that they are forced to interact with daily.[13] For the Aboriginals of Australia, clothing was forced upon them to the end of colonizing and subduing them.[14] The first encounters between the Aboriginals (Eora) and settlers (Derewalgal) were quite revealing. The latter were surprised to see people walk about "perfectly naked" while the former was also quite curious about the clothes so much so that they touched and felt the "Coat, Waistcoat, and even the Shirt and on seeing one of the Gentlemen pull off his Hat, they all set up a loud hoop."[15] It must have seem to then that there were layers of skin as they do not have a word for nakedness in their language.[16] The hoop accompanying the pulling off of the hat was to them pulling off a layer of skin to reveal hair underneath it.[17]

To the Berewalgal, this lack of clothing was savagery at best and a sign of deprivation, so "giving these poor creatures clothing was thus an act of kindness and charity."[18] But is it true that the Eora were undressed? This is a matter of perspective as the Aboriginals

> dressed their bodies in many complex and distinctive ways. ... In the Sydney region, each of the more than 30 groups of Aboriginal people dressed their bodies in distinctive ways. Men and women were marked by with cicatrices

(raised scars) in distinctive patterns on their chests and arms. They painted their bodies with clay: white for corroborées, red for war, contests and mourning. Men everywhere wore long beards, but the different groups were distinguished by their hairstyles. Those from the Botany Bay area gummed their hair in dreadlocks, which to the Berewalgal looked like 'the thrums of a mop'; other groups adorned their hair with the teeth and the tails of animals. Men and women sometimes wore multi stranded necklaces made of dried reeds, or cascades of kangaroo teeth. Initiated Eora men of the coastal Sydney region were also marked by a missing front tooth, while women had lost the top two joints of the little finger of their left hands. Many had pierced septums, for wearing small bones or sticks.

The Eora warriors did have string waistbands that held their weapons while the prepubescent girls wore *barin* or aprons.[19]

Clearly these "layers of skin" in a gendered Eora society made communication quite difficult as they could not tell if these "pale creatures" were male of female more so as they wore no beards and their genitals were hidden from sight.[20] Contrast these with the Eora men who walked around with their genitals quite visible for all to see unlike the women who expressed modesty while seated with one leg bent and the other covering the genitals.[21] When a sailor was thus asked to remove his trousers, this elicited a whoop: "They are men."[22]

The Awá of Ecuador have adopted a similar posture of wearing clothing as this allows them to be left alone and hence retain their cultural practices.[23] Could this also be the reason why the Bostwana chiefs dress in complete suits apart from the Animal skin in their ensemble? But the Himbas of Namibia have retained theirs and ignore the stares and disapproval of other tribes. But the interest from a tourists' perspective remains. In fact, they seem to never have enough of the people and their way of life.

But even skin and hair colour etc. also have communication properties. An analysis of a painting from Rome featuring a Black bath servant at the entrance of the caldarium is to warn bathers about the heat "because the Romans believed that the Aethiops's black skin came from being burned by the sun."[24] In terms of the ideal good looks both the Black person as well as "tall, blond and red-headed Germans" would not qualify.[25] Rather a good looking person "would be of the Caucasian race, of medium stature, with an olive complexion and wavy brown hair."[26] Clearly, the blond blued-eyed boy/girl would have their time, but not at this time. Same with their equivalent *yellow bone* (person with light complexion) in the African setting.

In the same vein, the oversize phallus that have come to be associated with Africans and people of African descent was "unbecomingness" to the Romans.[27] How things have changed in these days when size is all that matters. But this feature of the Black man offered protection against the evil eye – that is an envious look that could spell tragedy to the person to which it was directed.[28] It was said to be ubiquitous so much so that

> a person could encounter the envious evil eye anywhere but, was particularly susceptible in baths and at passageway spaces, such as doorways. People wore amulets on their persons, and artists frequently put symbolic images on floors or walls of dangerous, liminal spaces. These apotropaia in mosaic and fresco included the representation of the evil eye itself attacked by spears, scorpions, dogs, and the like, as well as images of the erect phallus, sometimes in conjunction with the vagina. In the first instance the image enacts direct aggression against the evil eye; in the second it invokes male and female fertility, the life force, for protection from death.[29]

Accessories

Various kinds of accessories used to adorn the body are also; present among indigenous people. *Meo* armbands of the Atoin Meto- culture are classified as sacred garments that provide the wearer protection in conflict, warfare and especially during headhunting.[30] The scarlet forehead fringe called *maskaypacha* in pre-Inca Ecuador communicated ultimate political authority.[31] Indians in the now present-day Virginia in the United States adorned themselves with copper beads.[32] Chukché men had bones inserted in their lips and sides of their mouth as well as adorned themselves with nephrite.

The Makonde of Mozambique have the *Ndona* or lip plug which is regarded as one feature that makes the tribe stand out.[33] Even though it is associated more with women in this matrilineal society, but men also did have the plug based on the insistence of their love interests who would not want to be seen with someone that "looks like a monkey" – san lip plug.[34] It is also a sign of beauty and tribal identity.[35] Their compatriots, Makua, have a nose button worn on the left side of the nose. For the Makua, piercing the lips and ears at puberty communicates "a social move from a modest position to a more responsible one."[36] The Edo tattoos (*Iwu*) also played a similar role but unlike the lip plug, it is mandatory for both sexes as no man would marry a woman without them ... The community called a mother's children *omo iwu* ("children of the tattoo") when necessary to distinguish them from more distant blood relations such as a grandchild. The tattoos were thus transformative, signaling a change in jural status (unmarried/married, youth/adult).[37]

Pierced ears among Mozambicans are for aesthetic reasons but it is much more in the case of some other tribes such

> the older Shangaans of Gazaland, northwest of Lourengo Marques, [who] have a large slit in the lower ear lobe, while the Chopi, north of Lourengo Marques, have a triangular-shaped cut made with a knife and awl. The triangle has its base near the opening of the ear and its apex towards the tip of the lobe. The slit is gradually distended by inserting successively larger reeds until, eventually, the handle of a drinking gourd can be pushed through. Rings of metal or wood are subsequently worn. Noblemen in the Makua tribe have a single perforation in the left earlobe and a series of small holes all around the rim of the right ear; into each are inserted small stalks of grass, spikes of wood or wire rings.[38]

Makondes also shape their incisors teeth into points.[39] This is done at initiation rites as a mark of beauty for girls and a test of courage for boys.[40]

The Emberá of Panama adorned their bodies with the juice of the jagua fruit as well as necklaces and beads.[41]

Colours

Colours also communicate a myriad of information. The Berewagal red-coated soldiers was an intimidating tactics in relations with the Eora – Aboriginal Australians. This is because the red colour in body paint for the later was a sign of "anger, revenge, fighting and mourning" in addition to conveying warnings and alarm.[42] So, predictably, the Eora avoided the soldiers or anyone in red garb. For native Americans from the Mississippi Valley, accomplishments in war were communicated by tattoos in blue, red and black lines on their stomach.[43] The more tattoos native American men featured on their anatomy, the more valorous they were.[44]

A blue dye obtained from burning some trees was used by the Māori in their tattoos and apart from the aesthetics the tattoos also communicated dignity and bravery.[45] In "Upper Egypt", women punctured their lips "to give them a dark bluish tinge."[46] Black was the colour preferred by Indians in the now present-day Virginia and this was used to paint serpents and other animals on the breasts, hand, faces and legs of women.[47] Three blue marks on Mojave woman's chin communicated that she was married in what is now the United States.[48] Other native American tribes used other colours. For instance, the now present day Alaska, Kutchin women tattooed their chin with a black pigment while Chukché men had a black or red cross painted on their cheeks.[49] Tattoos in black ink was a marker of a commoner in Samoa.[50] Black pigment was deployed in Maori tattoos.[51]

In Mozambique, the Makua and Lomwe come up with tattoos that are blue or grayish in colour on the cheeks and foreheads that communication status and rank. But to achieve these, the process involves puncturing

> (1) the skin … with needles ritually purified in fire, and caustic substances such as the acid from the fruit of the cashew nut are rubbed in to raise scars; (2) the scarring can be made with a special stiletto, also purified and rubbed in ashes, to obtain high and low relief patterns; (3) irritating materials are inserted under the skin by means of hooks and fine needles dusted in ashes in patterns of circles, rectangles, triangles, crosses or fish spines in black or dark blue.[52]

The Makua and Makonde women also have a face and neck paint made from crushing the roots of a special plant which is then mixed with water.[53] This makes for an attractive complexion as well offers protection from the sun.[54] White dots are also deployed by Makonde witchdoctors to paint their bodies when they conduct puberty rites.[55]

While leadership position in the Hagen society of Papua New Guinea is ephemeral with leaders going and coming not so with gender as this is a permanent position hence girls are tattooed on the face with charcoal and blue dye.[56] In Tamil, green is the preferred colours deployed in tattoos.[57] Haitians tattoos of demons (*çemis*) was executed in black colour.[58] Black colour is predominant in the masks of the Malinke and Bambara of Mali and the reason for this is twofold: They are hung on the rafters of kitchens and blacksmiths char their surface with a hot knife or blade.[59]

Body Art

Body art embraces tattoos, scarification, body paint and other means of decorating the body whether for aesthetic, ritual or other purposes. The word tattoo itself is of Tahitian origin (from *tatu* meaning to mark the skin) and was introduced into the English language by Captain Cook upon his return from a trip to the South Seas.[60] Inuit tattoos was associated with women for millennia before the first Europeans set foot in the Artic region.[61] There seems to be no evidence of tattooing or body art before 7000 BC, but it might have existed in Paleolithic times.[62] This is because it was a means of dressing for the unclothe globally and wearing of clothes made it fall into disuse.[63]

Apart from being a means of adornment it also had ceremonial uses such as initiation rites.[64] Tattoos also functioned as status markers.[65] It is speculated that after realizing that pots could be decorated that human beings came to the realization that they could also make changes to their bodies.[66] And there is usually some legend or myth informing whether it is males or females that should have tattoos. For instance, *Tila* the goddess of the tattoo artist in Fiji instructed those that were to introduce it to Samoa to sing "tattoo the women but not the men" but while on the long journey they got it mixed up ("tattoo the men but not the women") hence men in the Samoan society where the only ones with tattoos.[67]

Ötzi, the iceman who died about 5000 years ago in the Italian Alps is the most famous tattooed man.[68] His well-preserved remains had more than 50 tattoos made up of lines and crosses into which charcoal had been inserted.[69] The conclusion was that the tattoos were more therapeutic than aesthetics and were made to ensure his health and wellbeing.[70] Tattoos in ancient Egypt seem to have been the exclusive preserve of women with evidence of actual tattoos on thighs and abdomen of women thus serving an erotic and sexual function.[71] The Ainu of Japan had intricate face and arm tattoos; a tradition that goes back thousands of years to the Jōmon people who also had the etchings in the same parts of the body.[72] The tattoos on the chin of women was intended to imitate the beards worn by men.[73] Lapitas, who are the ancestors of today's Pacific people, are believed to be originators of the Polynesian tattoos that have become world famous.[74]

Even back then views about tattoos were not uniformly the same. In the Graeco-Roman world it had negative connotations and were reserved for slaves, criminals, enemies and prisoners of war.[75] But to the Thracians, Scythians, Dacians, Gauls, Picts, Celts, and Britons, they were a thing of pride.[76] Tattoos were associated more with "of the lower class criminals in Europe" who spotted geometrical, pictorial, dot or streak designs.[77] But one or two odd nobleman also had tattoos.[78] Not so in Britain as tattoos were associated with the upper classes and was an emblem of cultural superiority.[79]

The same sentiment is found among the Maoris of New Zealand as the painful tattoos consisting of curved lines covering the face indicated dignity as well as that the wearer was a warrior. For Eskimo women, tattoos on the chin distinguished between classes with the lower-class spotting "one vertical line in the centre, and one parallel to it on either side" while the upper classes had "two vertical lines from each corner of the mouth."[80] It is unclear what the tattoos on the chin and face of Chukché women stood for.[81]

Tattoos on the lips and chin of Maori women communicated that they were married much like the wedding ring.[82] Motu women from Papua New Guinea had tattoos on their chin.[83] Their compatriots, Maisin women spotted "curvilinear tattoos that covered their entire faces like veils" and marked the transition from childhood to adolescence.[84] The Moche of Peru's tattoos communicated identity and life force and were administered in moments of life-crisis rituals such as initiation etc. as well as serving an aesthetic purpose[85] Shamans, in these communities, also spotted tattoos of various animals thus communicating their ability to shapeshift when they are in s state of trance.[86] Heavily tattooed figurines from the western Mexican states of Jalisco, Nayarit, and parts of Colima are believed to communicate life force or polished speech based on classic Maya society philosophy since they are found around the mouth.[87]

Adherents of what has come to be known as Southeastern Ceremonial Complex in scattered settlements across what is now the United States featured tattoos which were seen as central to the religion.[88] This is because

> they played a role in celebrating the perpetuation of life …. For warriors, facial tattoos were snares for capturing the soul of someone they killed in battle. Capturing those enemy souls through permanent tattoos helped extend not only their own lives, but helped ease the passage of their dead relatives.[89]

The practice in Europe also had magical and medicinal purposes so much so that Simon Forman, a medical astrologer was able to alter his destiny in 1609 by tattooing "cosmological symbols on his own body, at precise astrologically calculated moments."[90]

The Nagas of India also had tattoos on the face called *Ak* that has "four continuous lines carried across the forehead, round and underneath the eyes up to the nose, back over the cheeks, and round the corners of the mouth to the chin... two fine lines mark out the nose."[91] The diverse Yoruba facial scarification communicated clan membership.[92] But they also have aesthetic, class and spiritual connotations.[93] Some other Naga tribes do not tattoo the face rather it is placed on shoulders, breasts, thighs, back and wrists. Inuit women had perpendicular lines on their chins and eyes. In Egypt, the women in the *fellahs* as well as those labouring in the cities had tattoos on their chin, forehead, breast, hands, and legs.

The Ibaloi of The Philippines tattooing practices were like that of the native Americans. After successful head-hunting expeditions, Ibaloi warriors would etch omen animals such snakes, lizards, centipedes and scorpions on their bodies.[94] In fact, encountering any of these animals before an expedition could be the difference between success and failure.[95] Still on issues of good fortune, children in Mecca were given three incisions on each cheek to ward off the evil eye.[96] Apart from animals, Ibaloi tattoos also featured circles on wrists which are interpreted to be solar discs as well as zigzag lines which are thought to communicate lighting or rice fields.[97]

The Chopi and Shangaan of Mozambique have elaborate designs that also have rich communication properties. Chopi marks running from the eye to under the chin communicates tear drop and is considered sacred while those running from the eye to the ears and from the corner of the mouth to the ear lobes are also sacred and represent saliva tracks.[98] Other designs include cock comb above the right eye and triangular dots on the cheeks and forehead.[99] There are also tattoos and scars for specific situations such as when someone commits adultery,[100] mourning, initiation and illnesses. Medicines are rubbed into the incisions in the case of illness.[101] Those of their compatriots, the Makonde, contain animals, insects, reptiles; plants like the palm tree as well as "chevrons, angles, zigzag and straight lines with an occasional circle, diamond or dot."[102] The diamond or dot plays the same role as a period in a sentence![103] They go to all this trouble to self-identify as a Makonde but it must also be conceded that tattoos in the pubic area is intended to attract a husband as well as being erotic and magical.[104]

Throughout Polynesia, tattoos which involve inserting ink or other colouring into the skin via a needle or other sharp objects served as markers of status.[105] The upper class spotted tattoos of stripes and small bands while those of lower status where usually black in colour from the waist to the knee.[106] There were also distinctions even among the upper classes: "Triangles down the back of a man's leg proclaimed rank. And two variations of a pattern known as *aso tali tu* served to distinguish a chief and a 'talking man' from all others of high rank."[107] Maori chiefs had more tattoos to distinguish them from the average person while slaves spotted one called *papa* on their backs.[108] The Arioi people also had tattoos to distinguish between the seven classes in their society.[109] In the Marquesas Island tattoos in addition to communicating class also indicated tribal belonging.[110] Hawaiians used tattoos to differentiate between slaves and citizens. The former spotted, "a round spot in the middle of the forehead, a curved line over the nose, and curved lines resembling parentheses outside the eyes."[111]

Congolese scarification also known as *tatouage* involved "incisions that bled and healed over, creating permanent patterns."[112] The result was that Congolese faces and chests featured "graphic pattern, from 'curved wavy lines' to 'ledges, squares, circles, ... knots,' and 'rosettes,' from thin rows of lines and points from 'temple to temple' to 'glossy tubercules' 'as large as hens' eggs.'"[113] A similar practice is found in Australia where the scarification is usually on the back, shoulder and breasts so much so that one example on the shoulders of an aboriginal was described as resembling "a great tassel, like a footman's shoulder-knot."[114]

In Mozambique. Tattoos and scarification speaks volumes. It is

> done with great ceremony at an important juncture of a child's development, usually connected with initiation rites. It is also performed as a member of the tribe assumes a more important political rank or passes from one social level to another, while at other times it has been used to mark slaves. Scarifications are also sometimes made during illnesses with medicines rubbed into them by *curandeiros* or witchdoctors.[115]

Chiefs and important men spot a straight line; higher status women have parallel lines on the face and breast while commoners have more complex designs such as "spider shapes or a labyrinth of curves and rectangles."[116] Persons in Mozambique featuring the impregnated tattoos found on the back and shoulder blades were slaves while members of secret societies, musicians and dancers spot straight or perpendicular lines around their chin and mouth.[117] In North America, African Americans ha\d the marks of their owners inscribed on their bodies during the slave era, "country marks" that indicated where they were from in Africa as well as marks communicating "scars from diseases, accidents or beatings."[118]

Tattoos were also deployed by authority figures in various jurisdictions in several ways:

> made by slave owners in ancient Greece and Rome ... and in the southern United States ..., Nazi concentration camp markings, and tattoos made as punishment in south Asia, Europe, Russia ... and colonial East India ... and in convict transports to Australia.[119]

In the same vein, Chinese tattoos covered the entire body and was used as a form of punishment.[120] Tattoos in Europe also served other purposes: To identify one's occupation, religion personal mementos as well as to communicate patriotism and loyalty.[121]

Edo people from Nigeria spotted a tattoo – *Iwu* – as a means of clan identification.[122] The "scarification (deliberate incisions that leave deep scars) and cicatrization (the intentional formation of keloids)" they engaged in was for medicinal purposes but they also served as distinguishing marks of various person and their place in society.[123] The Māori moko, in the same vein "was literally carved in skin in grooves up to a depth of 6 mm" thus giving it a three dimensional appearance.[124] It could cover the whole body or parts of it and it communicated accomplishment and rank.

Tattoos were also quite widespread among native Americans with some tribes spotting more and some less.[125] The tattoos mostly featured mainly flora and fauna, animals, the sun and moon.[126] They communicated bravery for the men and beauty for women.[127] Syrian Christians tattooed themselves with the sign of the cross, the Malabar of India had a bird representing the Holy Ghost tattooed on their forearms while Myanmar tattoos were said to be artistic, complex and varied.[128] Tattoos of demons (*zemis*) were found on the naked bodies of West Indians according to the Spanish.[129] Haitians were also observed to have tattoos of demons (*çemis*).[130]

In fact, by the fifteenth century there were already records of tattooed women in Myanmar.[131] The Chin women's tattoos which was black in colour contrasted sharply with their light complexion and was subject to various interpretation. Indigenous sources said they were ornamental, but the British colonialists felt that the "facial tattoos protected the women of the hill tribes by making them so unattractive that the Burmese kings would not wish to abduct them."[132] The men from Myanmar referred to the Chin's women tattoos as "dog face" but it seems that the purpose was to stamp the women as tribal property hence undermining the authority of the Myanmar indigenous rulers.[133] However, the hill tribes had a fondness for tattooed women in addition to their fierce independence stance from Myanmar.[134] For men, tattoos communicated a criminal past and royal punishment.[135]

Body paint, unlike tattoos, are not permanent. In Papua New Guinea this plays out rather interestingly. The paint and feathers used to cement the status of a leader are temporary so that when someone else take his place the markers of status can be easily transferred.[136] English women applied paste and patches to their faces.[137] Throughout Europe tattoos and body paint "were variously used to mark outlaw status and nobility, insiders and outsiders, soldiers and slaves."[138] Recorded about Nicagarua were practices such as blackening the teeth and the use of body paint.[139] Teeth blackening was also quite common in Melanesia and Micronesia and these communicated maturity, sexual attraction and beauty.[140]

Conclusion

While indigenous clothing, accessories, body art in general have experienced a revival, they have also been impacted by colonialists and encounters with other cultures as this excursion has demonstrated. An interesting example is the modern Aymara woman that "may put on a hat that is German in origin, a shawl that can be traced back to the Philippines (*the manton de Manila*), and a multi-layered woolen Spanish skirt (*pollera*)."[141] These, in turn, communicate her language, ethnic group and birthplace.[142] We have equally come a long way from the dark age of equating body modification with self-harm that requires psychiatric intervention.[143] The modern iteration manifested in plastic surgery has taken on a life of its own but, sadly, the art form is dying off apart from tattoos that have become quite popular. The 1960s have been identified as the period in which tattoos became part of popular culture.[144] However, indigenous forms of body art have rich communication properties from clan identification to aesthetics and spiritual purposes. Like most things indigenous, the condemnation by various groups have succeeded in killing them off except where concerted efforts have been deployed to revive and modernize them.

Notes

1. Steiner, C.B. (1990). Body personal and body politic. Adornment and leadership in cross-cultural perspective. *Anthropos, 4./6*, 431–445, p. 431.
2. Beaule, C. D. (2018). Cambios en la vestimenta indígena en el altiplano andino bajo el colonialismo español/Indigenous clothing changes in the Andean highlands under Spanish colonialism. *Estudios Atacameños, 59*, 7–26.
3. Beaule, C. D. (2018).
4. Beaule, C. D. (2018), p. 10.
5. Nevadomsky, J., & Aisien, E. (1995). The clothing of political identity: Costume and scarification in the Benin kingdom. *African Arts, 28*(1), 62–73.
6. Radcliffe, S. A. (1997). The geographies of indigenous self-representation in Ecuador: Hybridity, Gender and Resistance. *Revista Europea de Estudios Latinoamericanos y Del Caribe/European Review of Latin American and Caribbean Studies, 63*, 9–27.
7. Theodossopoulos, D. (2012). Indigenous attire, exoticization, and social change: dressing and undressing among the Emberá of Panama. *The Journal of the Royal Anthropological Institute, 18*(3), 591–612.
8. Beaule, C. D. (2018).
9. Beaule, C. D. (2018), p. 20.
10. Beaule, C. D. (2018), p. 21.
11. Conklin, B.A. (1997). Body Paint, Feathers, and VCRs: Aesthetics and authenticity in Amazonian activism. *American Ethnologist, 24*(4), 1–36.
12. Conklin, B.A. (1997), p. 716.
13. Conklin, B.A. (1997).
14. Karskens, G. (2011). Red coat, blue jacket, black skin: Aboriginal men and clothing in early New South Wales. *Aboriginal History, 35*, 1–36.
15. Karskens, G. (2011), p. 10.
16. Karskens, G. (2011).
17. Karskens, G. (2011).
18. Karskens, G. (2011), p. 10.
19. Conklin, B.A. (1997).
20. Karskens, G. (2011), p. 11.
21. Karskens, G. (2011).
22. Karskens, G. (2011), p. 11.
23. Conklin, B.A. (1997).
24. Cammann, S. (1957). Ancient symbols in modern Afghanistan. *Ars Orientalis, 2*, 5–34.
25. Biddick, K., Clarke, J. R., Eisenman, S. F., Okoye, I. S., & Pohl, F. K. (1996), p. 602.

26. Biddick, K., Clarke, J. R., Eisenman, S. F., Okoye, I. S., & Pohl, F. K. (1996), p. 602.
27. Biddick, K., Clarke, J. R., Eisenman, S. F., Okoye, I. S., & Pohl, F. K. (1996), p. 602.
28. Biddick, K., Clarke, J. R., Eisenman, S. F., Okoye, I. S., & Pohl, F. K. (1996).
29. Biddick, K., Clarke, J. R., Eisenman, S. F., Okoye, I. S., & Pohl, F. K. (1996), p. 602.
30. Beaule, C. D. (2018).
31. Beaule, C. D. (2018).
32. Buckland, A. W. (1888).
33. Buckland, A. W. (1888).
    Schneider, B. (1973). Body decoration in Mozambique. *African Arts*, 6(2), 26–92. https://doi.org/10.2307/3334776
34. Buckland, A. W. (1888).
    Schneider, B. (1973), p. 30.
35. Schneider, B. (1973).
36. Schneider, B. (1973), p. 30.
37. Nevadomsky, J., & Aisien, E. (1995), p. 68.
38. Schneider, B. (1973), p. 30.
39. Schneider, B. (1973).
40. Schneider, B. (1973).
41. Theodossopoulos, D. (2012).
42. Conklin, B.A. (1997), p. 11.
43. Balvay, A. (2008).
44. Balvay, A. (2008).
45. Buckland, A. W. (1888).
46. Buckland, A. W. (1888), p. 325.
47. Buckland, A. W. (1888).
48. Buckland, A. W. (1888).
49. Buckland, A. W. (1888).
50. Steiner, C.B. (1990).
51. Steiner, C.B. (1990).
52. Schneider, B. (1973), p. 26.
53. Schneider, B. (1973).
54. Schneider, B. (1973).
55. Schneider, B. (1973).
56. Steiner, C.B. (1990).
57. Rao, C. H.
58. Sinclair, A. T. (1909). Tattooing of the North American Indians. *American Anthropologist*, 11(3), 362–400.

59. Imperato, P. J. (1980). Bambara and Malinke Ton masquerades. *African Arts, 13*(4), 47–87. https://doi.org/10.2307/3335784
60. Steiner, C.B. (1990).
61. Jelinski, J. (2018). "If only it makes them pretty". *Collections arctiques/Arctic Collections, 42* (1), 211–242.
62. Lobell, J. A., & Powell, E. A. (2013). Ancient tattoos. *Archaeology, 66*(6), 41–46.
63. Buckland, A. W. (1888). On tattooing. *The Journal of the Anthropological Institute of Great Britain and Ireland, 17*, 318–328. https://doi.org/10.2307/2842170
64. Buckland, A. W. (1888).
65. Schneider, B. (1973).
66. Lobell, J. A., & Powell, E. A. (2013).
67. Buckland, A. W. (1888).
68. Lobell, J. A., & Powell, E. A. (2013).
69. Lobell, J. A., & Powell, E. A. (2013).
70. Lobell, J. A., & Powell, E. A. (2013).
71. Lobell, J. A., & Powell, E. A. (2013).
72. Lobell, J. A., & Powell, E. A. (2013).
73. Buckland, A. W. (1888).
74. Lobell, J. A., & Powell, E. A. (2013).
75. Lobell, J. A., & Powell, E. A. (2013).
76. Lobell, J. A., & Powell, E. A. (2013).
77. Rao, C. H. (1942). Note on tattooing in India and Burma. *Anthropos, 37/40*(1/3), 175–179, p. 176.
78. Schildkrout, E. (2004). Inscribing the body. *Annual Review of Anthropology, 33*, 319–344.
79. Jelinski, J. (2018). "If only it makes them pretty". *Collections arctiques/Arctic Collections, 42* (1), 211–242.
80. Buckland, A. W. (1888), pp. 324–325.
81. Buckland, A. W. (1888).
82. Buckland, A. W. (1888).
83. Buckland, A. W. (1888).
84. Barker, J., & Tletjen, A. M. (1990). Women's facial tattooing among the Maisin of Oro Province, Papua New Guinea: The Changing Significance of an Ancient Custom. *Oceania, 60*(3), 217–234, p. 217.
85. Lobell, J. A., & Powell, E. A. (2013).
86. Lobell, J. A., & Powell, E. A. (2013).
87. Lobell, J. A., & Powell, E. A. (2013).
88. Lobell, J. A., & Powell, E. A. (2013).
89. Lobell, J. A., & Powell, E. A. (2013), p. 46.
90. Schildkrout, E. (2004), p. 325.

91. Buckland, A. W. (1888), p. 322.
92. Orie, Ọlanikẹ Ọla. (2011). The structure and function of Yoruba Facial Scarification. *Anthropological Linguistics, 53*(1), 15–33.
93. Ojo, O. (2008). Beyond diversity: Women, scarification, and Yoruba Identity. *History in Africa, 35*, 347–374.
94. Lobell, J. A., & Powell, E. A. (2013).
95. Lobell, J. A., & Powell, E. A. (2013).
96. Rao, C. H. (1942).
97. Lobell, J. A., & Powell, E. A. (2013).
98. Schneider, B. (1973).
99. Schneider, B. (1973).
100. Schneider, B. (1973).
101. Schneider, B. (1973).
102. Schneider, B. (1973), p. 27.
103. Schneider, B. (1973).
104. Schneider, B. (1973).
105. Steiner, C.B. (1990).
106. Steiner, C.B. (1990).
107. Steiner, C.B. (1990), p. 433.
108. Steiner, C.B. (1990).
109. Steiner, C.B. (1990).
110. Steiner, C.B. (1990).
111. Steiner, C.B. (1990), p. 433.
112. Silverman, D. L. (2012). Art nouveau, art of darkness: African lineages of Belgian modernism, Part II. *West 86th: A Journal of Decorative Arts, Design History, and Material Culture, 19*(2), 175–195. https://doi.org/10.1086/668060, p. 176.
113. Silverman, D. L. (2012), p. 177.
114. Buckland, A. W. (1888), p. 319.
115. Schneider, B. (1973), p. 26.
116. Schneider, B. (1973), p. 26.
117. Schneider, B. (1973).
118. Schildkrout, E. (2004), p. 323.
119. Schildkrout, E. (2004), p. 323.
120. Schildkrout, E. (2004).
121. Schildkrout, E. (2004).
122. Nevadomsky, J., & Aisien, E. (1995).
123. Nevadomsky, J., & Aisien, E. (1995), p. 65.
124. Ellis, N. (2014). "Ki tō ringa kingā rākau ā te pākehā?" Drawings and signatures of "Moko" by Māori in the early 19th Century. *The Journal of the Polynesian Society, 123*(1), 29–66.

125. Balvay, A. (2008). Tattooing and its role in French-Native American relations in the Eighteenth Century. *French Colonial History, 9*, 1–14.
126. Balvay, A. (2008).
127. Balvay, A. (2008).
128. Rao, C. H. (1942).
129. Sinclair, A. T. (1909).
130. Sinclair, A. T. (1909).
131. Jelinski, J. (2018).
132. Jelinski, J. (2018), p. 37.
133. Jelinski, J. (2018), p. 38.
134. Jelinski, J. (2018).
135. Jelinski, J. (2018).
136. Steiner, C.B. (1990).
137. Schildkrout, E. (2004).
138. Schildkrout, E. (2004), p. 325.
139. Sinclair, A. T. (1909).
140. Zumbroich, T. (2015). "We blacken our teeth with oko to make them firm": Teeth blackening in Oceania. *Anthropologica, 57*(2), 539–555.
141. Beaule, C. D. (2018), p. 13.
142. Beaule, C. D. (2018).
143. Pitts, V. (2004). Debating body projects: Reading "Tattooed" [Review of Tattooed: The sociogenesis of a body art, by M. Atkinson]. *Health, 8*(3), 380–386.
144. Schildkrout, E. (2004).

CHAPTER 8

Institutional Communication

INTRODUCTION

This chapter discussed indigenous institutions that ensure smooth running and harmonious relationships such as the traditional ruler, secret societies, age grades, kinship and family, masquerade and marriage. The institutions are revered for reasons which include powers – spiritual and temporal – which they possess. They could order physical sanctions on offenders or non-conformists and even invoke the wrath of deities to ensure compliance with their directives.

MARRIAGE

Like in other parts of Africa, the Limba of Sierra Leone weddings involve families who make the arrangements. According to Ottenberg,[1] the father of the bride would have identified her husband usually someone much older at about six years of age. The wedding takes place when she is between 15 and 18 years while the husband will be in his late twenties and above. He is expected to work on the farm of his future in-laws as well as supply them with food, jewelry, clothes as well as the bride price. Days before the wedding the girls invites friends and family members by giving out kola nuts. This is referred to as *asangani*; literally saying goodbye. The husband also invites friends and family with gifts of kola nuts. There is a

© The Author(s), under exclusive license to Springer Nature Switzerland AG 2024
E. Akpabio, *Indigenous Communication*,
https://doi.org/10.1007/978-3-031-41766-5_8

lot of singing and dancing during the wedding itself which takes days of preparation.

The Wawa of Cameroon marriage involved marriage by exchanging sisters or through compensation. This means that

> in the first case, focus was on the equity of the transaction. Ideally, both women should give birth to the same number of children. If one marriage was sterile, one had to be broken and the children taken back to the woman's father. If both marriages were successful, the fathers kept their rights over their children and their offspring. In the case of a marriage by matrimonial compensation, the husband only acquired rights in *uxorem* (over his wife) but not in *genetricem* (over her children). The wife's father kept the custody on his daughter's children, and would collect the highest part of their matrimonial compensation (which consisted of 3 to 10 hoes).[2]

Families are equally very much involved in marriages in India and marriage seems to be front and centre so much so that among Hindus an individual is not trusted to go it all alone.[3] Anyone that decides to marry for love without involving the lineage and caste is regarded as going against tradition and embarking on a dangerous path. This is because marriage is "an act of choosing kinsmen."[4] While the life of males do not change much when they get married, but the act itself has tremendous social and spiritual significance. It means that the married man has moved from being a "useless" member of society to someone in good standing.[5] This is because he is now able to beget a son that will pay off the debts he owes his ancestors, light his cremation pyre thus saving him from hell reserved for those with no sons.[6] In addition, the married state "propels a man into the second, and the most important of the four asrama-s or stages of life" thus saving him and his ancestors from "perdition".[7] In fact, the man is so transformed by marriage that he temporarily become a deity: King to the lower caste and divinity to the Brahmins.[8]

But what of the Indian woman, what does she gain from the married state? Since her husband takes on the role of a god temporarily, she equally become a goddess hence the couple do not take their bath until three days after in which they wash away their divinity.[9] She also enjoys two privileges on her wedding day and then never again: "She eats food with her husband (normally the wife eats after her husband), and she perform the *homam* sacrifice with him."[10] Marriage among the Heian in Japan also marginalized women with a man having many wives leaving women wondering what to do with themselves.[11] But they were also quite complex involving different categories:

> boshokon, in which the mother's! wife's residence is central; tsumadoikon, the husband visiting the wife; mukotorikon, adopting a son-in-law; shoseikon, inviting the husband into the wife's residence-basically the same as boshokon; yometorikon, the husband taking the wife into his family; and dokyo, living together.[12]

In Java, Indonesia families are also central in the marriage arrangements. They make arrangements for the ceremony including contacting prominent persons to give speeches, refreshment, rituals and entertainment.[13]

Masquerade

The Afikpo of South East Nigeria's masquerade, ɉkumkpa enacts events in the environment to encourage redress.[14] For instance if a girl is refusing suitors, the male masquerade will role play her while others take on the role of the rejected suitors. The underlying communication in this enactment

> reiterates ... maleness and the supposed dominance of men, which, in fact, is one raison d'étre for the men's secret society. Culturally, the act is a statement of the important value that a girl should marry at adolescence and not be too choosy or remain defiant of her 'natural' role as wife and mother, although a man may marry at a later age. Also, the act says that women should neither be too independent minded nor refrain from marrying because of greed or other reasons.[15]

The age grades (*ton*) of the Malinke and Bambara of Mali have something similar to the ɉkumkpa called *koteba*. *Koteba* involves the use of mask and headdress whose enactment conveys expected appropriate behaviour. So, in addition to entertainment they rail in their performance against drunkenness, philandry, dishonesty etc.[16]

The French version – *mommeries* – involved participants in costumes engaged in mime and dance for entertainment and escape while communicating the sophistication and wealth of the country.[17] The masked assembly was a popular form of entertainment in eighteenth century

London that was open to anyone willing to pay the entrance fee and don a costume.[18] The costumes embraced

> the classic black mask and domino, ... foreign or exotic "fancy dress," transvestite costumes, ecclesiastical parodies (of nuns or priests), picturesque occupational costumes (of shepherds, milkmaids, and the like), as well as costumes representing animals, supernatural beings, and literary, historical, and allegorical personages.[19]

And it seems the anonymity allowed for so much excess that it was labelled the "promiscuous assembly".[20] But this did not dampen interest in the spectacle so much so that it became the "emblem of modernity itself, the very signature of fashion, spectacle, and surreptitious excitement."[21] It also allowed for expression of sexual freedom and liberty that had no place in the stiff British society.[22]

But the European masking tradition itself is traceable to Italy also had religious origins before it veered off into secular entertainment and excess with growing urbanization.[23] According to this view

> masking originated in Italy where the term maschera gained currency in the thirteenth century with the Carnival of Venice (Italian: Carnevale di Venezia) ... Masking evolved and expanded from Venice to France (French: mascarade) around 1393, and subsequently to other European countries, including Great Britain.[24]

The seventeenth century Swedish masquerades also served to entertain the sovereign and make for peace among the foreign ambassadors.[25]

The hunters' masquerades in Burkina Faso also serves an entertainment purpose such as twirling, dancing, imitating a warthog searching for food etc.[26] But it serves other purposes such as paying homage to important persons, fostering good relations among hunters and the community as well as honouring colleagues who have passed on.[27] The positives displayed by the hunters' association contrasts sharply with their perception in the past of being able to turn humans into animals for hunting, manifesting powers akin to sorcery by manipulating material and energy to heal or cause harm as well as other negative perception of the vocation.[28] The rebranding has helped as their skill is now utilized in securing lives and property as well as maintaining order.[29]

The Wawa of Cameroon's masquerades had taboos as well as uses in the funerary rites of a deceased male. The taboos included that the masks could not be touched after sexual intercourse, women and children could not see them, a chicken had to be sacrificed before wearing it, they were not allowed to be soiled etc. failing which the transgressor would be struck dead.[30] According to Gausset,[31] in terms of the funerary rites, the deceased person came back as a masquerade a few days after the burial and danced in his compound while everyone was in a mourning mood. A few months later, the same masquerade came back and this time it went into a specially prepared place in the forest called *Mbarai* and, in addition to other activities, this was meant to find out if the deceased person was killed by witchcraft. This entailed curses on witches and any suspected witch was to come and lick the mask of the deceased. If no one died after this ceremony, then the deceased died of natural courses.

The last ceremony called *purpubi* takes place during the dry season one or two years after his passing and the masquerade would again come into the compound and a lot of dancing will take place even involving the widows. Afterwards, the masquerade will depart for the *Mbarai* where a test would be conducted to determine if the widows have had sexual intercourse after his passing. If everything is in order, a lot more dancing and merriment will ensue, and this finalizes the mourning period. The purpose of this is "to remember the dead in order to forget them and to be forgotten (left in peace) by them" hence "the mourning ceremony reaffirms the distinction between the world of the living and that of the dead, and helps the soul of the deceased in its difficult transition between the two."[32]

Similarly, the Igbo of Nigeria's Odo masquerade "honors the dead by helping them to return in masked form to their families and communities."[33] But there is more to the Odo masquerade when they appear than this intermingling of the dead with the living. In the towns of Ikolo and Aku, they take charge of the initiation of boys into the masquerade society, conduct the Odo festival as well as control non-Odo masquerades.[34] Their appearance in the community is seen as a welcome development as the dead come with blessings for the living.[35] Since men are central in the appearance and activities of the masquerade it serves to reinforce their position over women in society.[36]

Masquerades in Freetown, Sierra Leone are the public face of the otherwise secret societies – *Agugu, Hunters and Odelays*.[37] In the same vein, masquerades in Ghana serve as the public face of the *Sakrobundi* cult. But the masquerades are also quite effective in literal witch-hunt. The Abron look down on the Gbain in all other areas but utilize their masquerades to root out witches in their community since they are too afraid of their own witches.[38] *Simma* and *Sikilen* masquerades perform in honour of deceased important members of the community in Gokja and Wa in Ghana.[39]

To summarize, in the African contexts, masquerades' roles and functions were law enforcement, support for justice administration, ensuring social conformity, and fighting crimes "in order to maintain balance and a more peaceful order in a world fraught with disorder and chaos."[40] They have been described in terms such as "individuals turned spirit forces" and "masked figures as omnipotent spirits."[41] In fact female masquerades – *agod* and *ekuake* –which are a rarity in the African context are present among the Ejagham of South-south Nigeria in which women wore a wooden headdress. The function of the masquerades includes "obtaining a public voice, gaining access to the ancestral and spiritual realm, and presenting a public identity that constructs notions of femininity and masculinity."[42]

Kinship and Age Grades

The Bambara and Malinke of Mali basic social and economic set up is the extended family.[43] According to Imperato,[44] the extended families make up a village (*dugu*) consisting of about 600 persons and headed by a chief (*dugu-tigui*). Groups of villages in turn make up a *kafo* or *dyamana* headed by a *kafo-tigui* who was selected by heads of extended families (*li-tigui*). The Wawa of Cameroon's kinship setup is patrilineal but with very strong matrilineal alliances.[45] This translates to strong links with maternal grandparents who are often heavily involved in upbringings of children.[46]

The Arab because of their nomadic nature practiced "Bedouin tribalism" in which people lived in tightknit patriarchal kinship groups made up of a few households called *hayy*.[47] Members of the *hayy* constitutes a larger kinship group – *qawn* – while a large groups of clans constitute the largest kinship group or tribe – *quabíla*. In the same vein, in the scattered settlements of the Australian Aboriginals the tribe consisted of local groups in varying locations.[48] This meant that the "number, size, composition and interrelations of local sub-groups within a tribe varied with the ecological region, with the seasons, with current disputes and so on."[49] But this did not stop them from displaying varied categories or groupings based on kin and descent that are regarded as remarkable in that a tribe of no more than 1,200 members, for instance, could be so complexly organized as to include at the same time patrilineal moieties and patrilineal clans, matrilineal moieties and matrilineal clans, endogamous moieties of grouped generation levels, sub-sections and, for good measure, age grades .... In addition, there were tribes with small patrilineal or matrilineal clans only, others with clans and phratries, some with moieties and clans, some that were simply cognatic or bilateral, and so on. When the distribution of these tribes is plotted on maps, it is clear that the several kinds of social groupings were not haphazardly interdigitated; their spread was not merely random. Rather, they tended to be assembled into large, continuous collocations which in some places merged.[50]

The age grades in this arrangement based on imitation and shared religious experience did not confer leadership on any group including elders.[51] Among the Australian Aboriginals there were clear demarcation of roles. The patrilineal groups engaged in sacred functions such as initiation and totemism while the matrilineal groups' role was more secular such as birth, marriage, mourning and avenging deaths.[52]

According to Imperato,[53] the Bambara and Malinke of Mali's age grade system caters for both males and females. Boys and girls were subdivided into three groups: Six to nine years (*bilakoro-dogoma*); 10–12 years (*bilakoro-dogoma*) and; 13–15 years (*bilakoro-koroba*). After circumcision, the 13–15 years cohort moved into the village *ton* – a group set up to achieve common goals that consists of all the circumcised men and excised women. In the same vein, the oldest group in the *ton* moved out to join the elders. Each age grade is called a *flan-bolo*. Each *ton* elects a leader who is able to get everyone to work together but male and female roles differ:

> The boys and girls of each *flan-bolo* are paired off into couples known as *flani* (twins), with the *flan-mousso* (girl) performing domestic chores for her *flan-tye*, carrying food and water out to the field when he is working there with the other *ton* members; the boy is responsible for guarding the girl's virginity and suffers physical punishment and public shame if he fails to do so. This relationship is finally ended when one marries.[54]

In addition, the male *ton* members were part of the fighting force as local law enforcement to maintain law and order. Each *ton* also engaged in community service involving food production and civil engineering.

Among the Masaai of Kenya and Tanzania, age grades are based on communal initiation which usually occurs between the ages of 15–20 years.[55] Once circumcised the men become known as warriors.

Chieftaincy and Leadership

The colonialists and their successors have done much damage to leadership in the indigenous community context based on various misconceptions and missteps in a new environment that they had no clue about. The British for instance were of the view that

> Africa's population was neatly divided into tribes-an assumption so basic to British thought that even anthropologists have only recently begun to struggle free of it ... The typical tribal leader was assumed to be a hereditary ruler with extensive, diffuse authority, whose ties to his people were ultimately religious; thus rulers could claim not only obedience but also allegiance. If the polity were large and the rule authoritarian, the tribal leader might be referred to in English as a king, but if small, a chief.[56]

However, the situation on the ground was far from this simplistic assumption. In Papua New Guinea, for instance, anyone can take on the mantle of leadership and there were no divine rights for the "big man". He falls from grace when his authority is "undermined and cracked, his social and material base collapses beneath him and his faction disperses, to rally around one or other of his rivals, who is thus raised by his fall."[57] Among the Malinke and Bambara, anyone with leadership abilities can take on the role as long as he is able to get everyone on the same page in executing the functions of the age grade.[58] Among the Lango of Uganda, clan-based leadership was based on charisma and the ability to be successful in war.[59]

In Fiji, the British colonialists through a blending of traditional and modern leadership styles created the Great Council of Chiefs (GCC) which then met and ceded their islands to the new colonial overlords.[60] The GCC was made up of high-ranking hereditary chiefs as well as many officers who were charged with administration of the rural areas.[61] This would soon change to accommodate other persons which made it more of a "chiefly" council that a council of chiefs.[62] In Melanesia, the colonialists came up with chiefs where there were none in order to execute the African type of indirect rule.[63] Same for the Tonga people of Zambia and Zimbabwe in which the British created new chiefdoms for this amorphous community.[64]

The same disruptions that involved welding together disparate groups and the ensuing divide and rule can be detected wherever the colonialists of every hue and cry set their foot. The idea was to put in place chiefs that were strong enough to control their people but weak enough to be under the control of the colonialists.[65] In Lesotho, the ruling clan (Bakhoena) could exercise centralized authority because of threats of external aggression.[66] But this would soon change. Moshoeshoe 1 grip was pried off by Afrikaners settlers who noted a weakness in his leadership style. Subordinate chiefs were

> patriarchs in their own domain, and bound to the hierarchy primarily as the guarantor of their local status. But that status depended increasingly on their ability to ensure access to land, and scope for the acquisition of wealth in the form of livestock. Accordingly, the Afrikaners attempted to minimize the geographical reach of Moshoeshoe's polity by offering autonomous territories to individual chiefs, within which they would be acknowledged ruler but part of a broader Afrikaner state, and so free from settler harassment. This modification of principle emphasised collective residence and land use as a group, rather than possession of the land itself, as markers of geographical space. ... Moshoeshoe's model served as a basis for uniting people in defence of indigenous principles of social order. In practice however, it encouraged expansion through the subordinate chiefs in service of their overlord. By appealing to the patriarchal status of individual chiefs and capitalising on the segmentary character of chiefdoms the colonists subverted this dynamic. Moshoeshoe's model offered little to counter colonists' offers of land and autonomous status to chiefs, or to prevent further modifications of those principles by others.[67]

But Cameroon was a different kettle of fish. Major chiefs were ritually installed thus conferring on them some level of immortality so much so that they occupied "an intermediary position in the monistic hierarchy at the apex of which was the supreme Being."[68] But their powers were not absolute as checks and balances were provided by the descent groups heads, ritual specialists, council and title holders.[69]

In KwaZulu-Natal, South Africa the chiefs' (Amakhosi) power came from "patronage, ritual and symbolic power" that enabled them to weld together the disparate groups they ruled over.[70] This meant that they distributed tribute usually cattle, resolved conflicts, allocated land and determined land use as well played social and ritual roles in tribal life.[71] In Botswana, there was no centralized paramount chief rather the eight major tribes – Bakgatla, Bakwena, Bamalete, Bangwaketse, Barolong, Bamangwato Batawana and Batlokwa – were ruled by hereditary chiefs.[72]

In the Arab world, there was no central political authority but each group was headed by a *sayyid* or *shaykh* elected by tribal elders or prominent families.[73] The *shaykh* was advised by the council of elders (*majlis*) made up of heads of prominent families and spokespersons of the clans within the tribe.[74] Elders also play a prominent role in conflict resolution between clans in Somali Regional State of Ethiopia.[75] This takes the form of paying compensation in the form of camels and even marriages to cement the bonds between the clans.[76]

Among the Australian Aboriginals, the scattered nature of settlements did not allow for centralized leadership.[77] It seems that roles were clearly demarcated so much so that tribes people knew what to do based on the socialization process in cases of threats, crises etc.[78] Since there "existed interlocking sets of clearly formulated, publicly accepted and religious sanctioned norms covering all manner of activities, there was little need or room for chiefs or headmen."[79]

Secret Societies

Secret societies exist to assist members make sense of the complexities of the world we live in.[80] African Americans after the slavery era flocked to church benevolent groups and secret societies so as to be on the lookout for each other and assist in coping with life's exigencies.[81] Secret societies have a global presence, and their symbols, rites and signs seem also to be universal.[82] For instance by the period of the US civil war, African Americans did not have secret societies dedicated to their group rather they sought to "associate themselves with Europe's most distinguished secret orders and with the only American order which permitted them."[83] Examples of secret societies include the global Freemasons, the American Klu Klux Klan and Black Hand as well as the Italian Secret Societies that fought under Garibaldi for independence. But power and prestige also rank high in terms of raison dētre of secret societies.[84]

The Triad Society, a quasi-religious entity has been identified as the progenitor of all Chinese Secret societies and its motto was "obey heaven and act righteously."[85] While the beginning of fraternal secret societies in the US has been traced to 1869 when the Ancient Order of Workmen began to make assessments for the payment of heirs of deceased members. This advantage to be gained fueled more secret societies more so given the "magnetism of secret rituals and the popular prejudice against old-line insurance companies, fanned by the failure of some sixty of them in the 1870s."[86] In the same vein, secret societies had particular appeal to recently freed slaves given their "pomp and splendor with its colorful regalia and resounding titles, the camaraderie and heightened sense of importance which comes with a shared secret."[87]

The secret rites of Chinese secret societies are threefold and tied to human evolution: "The end of man's allotted span in this mundane world; a period of initiation and purification to prepare him for the otherworld which lies beyond; and, finally, rebirth into the mundane world whence he came."[88] The Chinese secret society in Singapore has lodges, an initiation ceremony and is intended to be on the lookout for its members.[89] The initiation of new members is long and convoluted but it ends with a call upon Buddhist and Taoist gods, angels, spirits, the five ancestors, the five tiger generals and the four ancient worthies with this invocation:

> This night we pledge that the, brethren in the whole universe, shall be as from one womb, as begotten by one Father, and nourished by one Mother; that we will obey Heaven and work righteousness; – that our faithful hearts shall never change. If august Heaven grants that the "Beng" be restored, then happiness will return to our land.[90]

The interest in members' welfare as well as nationalist bent in the Chinese secret society in Singapore is also present in the Egyptian secret society *Jam'iyyat al-Ittihad al-Islami* (The Society of Islamic Union). Its objectives were to help fellow Muslims, observe sharia law and preserve secrecy, which is to be expected.[91] The society underwent some changes including in names – *Jam'iyyat alTadamun* (The Society of Solidarity), and in 1908, *Jam'iyyat al-Tadamun alAkhaw* as well as objectives – freeing Egypt from the claws of the British colonialists as well as gaining political power.[92]

In Freetown, Sierra Leone there are the exclusive secret societies – *Agugu* and Hunters Club -as well as *Odelays* which are open to all comers and assists in giving members a sense of belonging.[93]

Conclusion

Institutions that make for good order in society have been the focus of this chapter and they played their role before the colonialists came along to displace, replace and change them. Indigenous forms of leadership have seen more interventions that the other institutions. For good or worse need not detain us here. Interestingly, the institutions seem to have a global spread particularly secret societies and masquerades and have the same roles and function across the board which speaks to commonalities among human beings despite all the othering taking place in our world today. The communication component of the masquerades clearly points to democratization as upper and lower classes were able to mix freely in London as the masks they wore gave everyone the required anonymity to mix freely. The democratization of communication is also apparent in the female Ejagham masquerades in a male dominated field in the African continent. Even though the repertoire of communication media we have today was not present, the kinship and family descent groups still could tell their roles and enacted same given the socialization process they had undergone. This speaks to effective communication with the little that was available. Compared to the way we are drowning in information today; it is worth researching if we are anyway as effective. But the narrowcasting of secret society based on closed membership could qualify as an outlier but their ability to provide a welcoming environment and sense of belonging made for strong brand equity especially given their popular appeal.

Notes

1. Ottenberg, S. (1989). The dancing bride: art and indigenous psychology in Limba weddings. *Man*, *24*(1), 57–78. https://doi.org/10.2307/2802547
2. Gausset, Q. (2001). Masks and identity. The significance of masquerades in the symbolic cycle linking the living, the dead, and the Bush Spirits among the Wawa (Cameroon). *Anthropos*, *96*(1), 193–200, p. 194.
3. Harman, W. (1987). The Hindu marriage as soteriological event. *International Journal of Sociology of the Family*, *17*(2), 169–182.
4. Harman, W. (1987), p. 170.
5. Harman, W. (1987).
6. Harman, W. (1987).
7. Harman, W. (1987), p. 171.
8. Harman, W. (1987).

9. Harman, W. (1987).
10. Harman, W. (1987), p. 174.
11. Haruko, W., & Gay, S. (1984). Marriage and property in premodern Japan from the perspective of women's history. *Journal of Japanese Studies, 10*(1), 73–99. https://doi.org/10.2307/132182
12. Haruko, W., & Gay, S. (1984), p. 83.
13. Hull, T.J., & Hull, V.J. (1987). Changing marriage behavior in Java: The role of timing of consummation. Southeast Asian Journal of Social Science, 1987, 15(1), Social and Political change in contemporary Indonesia, 104–119, p. 106.
14. Ottenberg, S. (1973). Afikpo masquerades: Audience and performers. *African Arts, 6*(4), 33–95. https://doi.org/10.2307/3334798
15. Ottenberg, S. (1973), p. 35.
16. Imperato, P. J. (1980). Bambara and Malinke Ton masquerades. *African Arts, 13*(4), 47–87. https://doi.org/10.2307/3335784
17. Croizat-Glazer, Y. (2013).
18. Castle, T. (1984). The carnivalization of eighteenth-century English narrative. *PMLA, 99*(5), 903–916. https://doi.org/10.2307/462143
19. Castle, T. (1984), p. 904.
20. Castle, T. (1984), p. 904.
21. Castle, T. (1984), p. 905.
22. Castle, T. (1983). Eros and liberty at the English masquerade, 1710–90. *Eighteenth-Century Studies, 17*(2), 156–176.
23. Njoku, R. C. (2020). On origins of masking: History, memory, and ritual observances. In West African masking traditions and diaspora masquerade carnivals: History, memory, and transnationalism (NED-New edition, pp. 20–42). Boydell & Brewer.
24. Njoku, R. C. (2020), p. 22.
25. Fielden, F. J. (1921). Court masquerades in Sweden in the Seventeenth Century. I. *The Modern Language Review, 16*(1), 47–58.
26. Gadliardi, S.E. (2013). Masquerades as the public face: Art of contemporary hunters' associations in Western Burkina Faso. *African Arts, 46*(4), 46–59
27. Gadliardi, S.E. (2013).
28. Gadliardi, S.E. (2013).
29. Gadliardi, S.E. (2013).
30. Gausset, Q. (2001).
31. Gausset, Q. (2001).
32. Gausset, Q. (2001), p. 197.
33. Reed, B., & Hufbauer, B. (2005). Ancestors and commemoration in Igbo Odo masquerades. *RES: Anthropology and Aesthetics, 47,* 135–152, p. 135.
34. Reed, B., & Hufbauer, B. (2005).

35. Reed, B., & Hufbauer, B. (2005).
36. Reed, B., & Hufbauer, B. (2005).
37. King, N. (2016). Freetown's Yoruba-modelled secret societies as transnational and transethnic mechanisms for social integration. In J. Knörr & C. Kohl (Eds.), *The Upper Guinea Coast in Global Perspective* (pp. 58–74). Berghahn Books. https://doi.org/10.2307/j.ctt1kk66c1.7
38. Bravmann, R. A. (1979). Gur and Manding Masquerades in Ghana. *African Arts, 13*(1), 44–98. https://doi.org/10.2307/3335609
39. Bravmann, R. A. (1979).
40. Njoku, R. C. (2020), p. 21.
41. Ottenberg, S. (1982). Illusion, communication, and psychology in West African masquerades. *Ethos, 10*(2), 149–185, p. 150.
42. Carlson, A., & Mark, P. (1998). Women's masquerade issue. *African Arts, 31*(3), 11–87. https://doi.org/10.2307/3337571, p. 12.
43. Imperato, P. J. (1980).
44. Imperato, P. J. (1980).
45. Gausset, Q. (2001). Masks and identity. The significance of masquerades in the symbolic cycle linking the living, the dead, and the Bush Spirits among the Wawa (Cameroon). *Anthropos, 96*(1), 193–200.
46. Gausset, Q. (2001).
47. Kirazli, S. (2011). Conflict and conflict resolution in the pre-Islamic Arab society. *Islamic Studies, 50*(1), 25–53, p. 32.
48. MeggitT, M. J. (1964). Indigenous forms of government among the Australian Aborigines. *Bijdragen Tot de Taal-, Land- En Volkenkunde, 120*(1), 163–180.
49. MeggitT, M. J. (1964), p. 170.
50. MeggitT, M. J. (1964), p. 171.
51. MeggitT, M. J. (1964).
52. MeggitT, M. J. (1964).
53. Imperato, P. J. (1980).
54. Imperato, P. J. (1980), p. 50.
55. Coast, E. (2006). Maasai marriage: A comparative study of Kenya and Tanzania. *Journal of Comparative Family Studies, 37*(3), 399–419.
56. Gartrell, B. (1983). British Administrators, Colonial Chiefs, and the Comfort of Tradition: An Example from Uganda. *African Studies Review, 26*(1), 1–24. https://doi.org/10.2307/524608, p. 3.
57. Steiner, C.B. (1990). Body personal and body politic. Adornment and leadership in cross-cultural perspective. *Anthropos, 4./6*, 431–445, p. 435.
58. Imperato, P. J. (1980).
59. Gartrell, B. (1983).

60. Norton, R. (n.d.). The changing role of the Great Council of Chiefs. In J. Fraenkel, S. Firth and B. V. Lal. *The 2006 military takeover in Fiji.* ANU Press.
61. Norton, R. (n.d.).
62. Norton, R. (n.d.), p. 99.
63. White, G. M. (1992). The discourse of chiefs: Notes on a Melanesian society. *The Contemporary Pacific,* 4(1), 73–108.
64. Kaoma, K. J. (2016). African religion and colonial rebellion: The contestation of power in colonial Zimbabwe's Chimurenga of 1896–1897. *Journal for the Study of Religion,* 29(1), 57–84.
65. Kaoma, K. J. (2016).
66. Coplan, D. B., & Quinlan, T. (1997). A chief by the people: Nation versus state in Lesotho. *Africa: Journal of the International African Institute,* 67(1), 27–60. https://doi.org/10.2307/1161269
67. Coplan, D. B., & Quinlan, T. (1997), p. 33.
68. Chem-Langhee, B. (1983). The Origin of the Southern Cameroons House of Chiefs. *The International Journal of African Historical Studies,* 16(4), 653–673. https://doi.org/10.2307/218271
69. Chem-Langhee, B. (1983).
70. Beall, J., Mkhize, S., & Vawda, S. (2005). Emergent democracy and "resurgent" tradition: Institutions, chieftaincy and transition in KwaZulu-Natal. *Journal of Southern African Studies,* 31(4), 755–771.
71. Beall, J., Mkhize, S., & Vawda, S. (2005).
72. Proctor, J. H. (1968). The House of Chiefs and the political development of Botswana. *The Journal of Modern African Studies,* 6(1), 59–79.
73. Kirazli, S. (2011).
74. Kirazli, S. (2011).
75. Bouh, A. M., & Mammo, Y. (2008). Indigenous conflict management and resolution mechanisms on rangelands in Somali Regional State, Ethiopia. *Nomadic Peoples,* 12(1), 109–121.
76. Bouh, A. M., & Mammo, Y. (2008).
77. MeggitT, M. J. (1964).
78. MeggitT, M. J. (1964).
79. MeggitT, M. J. (1964), p. 175.
80. Comber, L. (1956). Chinese secret societies in Malaya; an Introduction. *Journal of the Malayan Branch of the Royal Asiatic Society,* 29(1 (173)), 146–162.
81. Palmer, E. N. (1944). Negro Secret Societies. *Social Forces,* 23(2), 207–212. https://doi.org/10.2307/2572146
82. Comber, L. (1956).
83. Palmer, E. N. (1944), p. 209.

84. Papista, M. L. (1963). Secret societies. *The Clearing House, 38*(4), 230–230.
85. Comber, L. (1956), p. 147.
86. Palmer, E. N. (1944), p. 209.
87. Palmer, E. N. (1944), p. 209.
88. Comber, L. (1956), p. 146.
89. Pickering, W. A. (1879). "Chinese secret societies." *Journal of the Straits Branch of the Royal Asiatic Society, 3*, 1–18.
90. Pickering, W. A. (1879), p. 17.
91. Tauber, E. (2006). Egyptian secret societies, 1911. *Middle Eastern Studies, 42*(4), 603–623.
92. Tauber, E. (2006).
93. King, N. (2016).

CHAPTER 9

Venue-oriented Communication

These are sites in which indigenous communication, particularly as opposed to other forms take place. Of course, communication is a continuing activity that is not limited to any site. However, this postulation is important because it differentiates communication processes in this mode from others. Two points worth considering also are the structure of the communication process and its accessibility. Ansu-kyeremeh[1] categorises conversations and communication in this mode into "structured and unstructured": Structured when information is conveyed based on the direction of an authority figure such as chiefs, paramount rulers etc. and unstructured when it is informal involving the active involvement of all participants with no restriction whatsoever. As regards accessibility Doob[2] identifies geographic and social categories and these may either be facilitating or restricting factors. While geographic deals with physical movement to sites where communication takes place; social deals with level of participation based on age, sex, and other demographic factors. It involves habitation patterns where the mores, values, and way of life of each community are communicated to new members through the words and deeds of older members in the home environment. Markets, whose primary purpose is buying and selling of goods but that also exhibit communication function is within the ambit of this chapter.

© The Author(s), under exclusive license to Springer Nature Switzerland AG 2024
E. Akpabio, *Indigenous Communication*,
https://doi.org/10.1007/978-3-031-41766-5_9

Settlement Patterns

A number of considerations informs settlement patterns such as water supply, soil fertility, minerals, building materials, safety, trade routes, kinship, political allegiance, cultural preservation etc.[3] Natural resources and mineral deposits and the ability to exploit them is also a consideration. Indigenous people's relationship with the territories they occupy is usually also informed by sacred or ceremonial sites, sporadic cultivation, seasonal gatherings, hunting and fishing as well as natural resources.[4] In some instances safety was of paramount importance. For instance, large and fertile portions of Madagascar during the pirate area were not inhabited as people preferred to stay in fortified villages.[5] The strategic location of the Malay-Indonesian Archipelago, on the other hand, made for a thriving commercial trading enterprises with the straits serving as a convenient stop for traders while waiting for the changing winds to the east and the west.[6]

Tarapaya in Chile was a thriving agricultural community situated at the confluence of Totora and Tarapaya rivers. In the instance of Potosi in Bolivia, it was founded in 1545 by miners to exploit the silver in Cerro Rico.[7] When the deposit was exhausted the settlement's population reduced considerably but picked up in the 1570s when Viceroy Toledo promoted the use of mercury amalgamation to process lower grade silver.[8] As a consequence, Potosi was a thriving multicultural city with about 160,000 inhabitants despite the fact that its location was unfavourable: Highland with an elevation of 4000 m, cold and arid.[9]

Tarapaya located at an elevation of 3300 m was almost a ghost town after mining companies dredged its rivers thus destroying the floodplains that sustained agriculture, but its attraction are the other natural resources it possesses:

> The thermal springs located in 2 small basins 80 m (260 ft.) above and 1 km (0.6 mi.) to the north of the village. The upper basin contains a small, circular lake, while in the adjacent lower basin two hot springs feed a rectangular, concrete-lined swimming pool. These springs also provide water to two recreational complexes located adjacent to the river below.[10]

The lake was enlarged and made circular by Mayta Capac, the Inka who were the first conquerors of Tarapaya hence the rectangular pool at the lower basin is referred as the Inka bath.[11]

The Nasa of Colombia offer an interesting example. After being relocated from Tierradentro in the Andes of Southwestern Colombia after a devastating earthquake to Santa Leticia, a small frontier town between the provinces of Cauca and Huila that lies outside current Nasa territory they came to a realization that this was part of their history all along.[12] Apart from the relocation being embarked upon after approval by *the'walas* (shamans) based on "sensorial survey"

> In 1995, a year after the Juan Tama settlement had been established, [there was] confirmation of the mythical boundaries of the new area based upon Nasa social memory. Although the area was devoid of indigenous peoples in the eyes of Westerners until a decade ago, it is widely believed that this de facto extension of the pre-1994 Nasa *resguardos* [reservation] is a redrawing of the preconquest boundaries of Nasa territory ... The *the'walas*, elders, political officials (the governor and members of the *cabildo*, the corporate governing body), and members of the community walked the territory, finding similarities with their heartland in Tierradentro and recognizing points of reference mentioned in myths (notably a waterfall located to the west).[13]

These along with stone statues at La Candelaria confirmed the new settlement as Nasa ancestral land.

But the story of the Aboriginals of Australia offers no such reclamation of ancestral land. This is because the settlers did irreparable damage such that

> dreaming sites marked by mountain peaks, rock outcrops, and water holes were often now on the other side of the boundary fences. The raised-earth circles (*bora* ground) which had been used for initiation rites were liable to be bisected by roads or crossed by telegraph lines. Sacred carved trees were cut down.[14]

The indigenous communities in Canada suffered the same fate as they were deprived of their land, political and governing powers thus doing untold damage to their economy and livelihood.[15] This becomes starker because "the relation between indigenous peoples and their territories expresses itself in certain forms of sociability, agency, and autonomy."[16] So whether it is violence perpetuated by the colonialists in Canada or armed groups in Columbia the same sticky end is the result. American Indians settlements have shone through all attempts by Europeans to silence and erase them. It emerged that they "fix their towns commonly on the Edges of great Rivers for the Sake of the rich Lawns to sow their Corn in. The intermediate ground they reserve for their Hunting."[17]

Choices of settlements by the competing colonial powers was intended to give them military and economic advantages as they sought to undo each other in acquisition of oversea territories. Take an example of the Augusta Roatán Island in Hondura:

> The deep waters and protective features of New Port Royal Harbor attracted Governor Trelawney and Hodgson to the southeast side of Roatán Island. This location provided the colonists with the benefits of a highly defendable harbor protected by land and coral reefs that restricted access to only one entrance into the harbor. Water depth allowed for large ships to be accommodated for repairs, to restock resources, and to use as a stopping point from which to defend English shipping through the Bay of Honduras. A permanent settlement in the Bay Island was meant to be a type of "general head-quarters, or base camp" for English colonists and shipping routes in the Bay of Honduras and a "starting-point for illicit trade with the Spaniards, and perhaps a post from which men-of-war or customs authorities could enforce the laws of navigation and drive the Dutch out of the logwood trade."[18]

The Inca had Adobe and checkerboard designs of houses and streets respectively which has deep spiritual undertones.[19] This is because they represented "terraced mountainsides and agricultural fields, which were part of Kay Pacha (earthly realm of ploughed fields, stepped terraces, towns and cities), as opposed to Hanan Pacha (the celestial world) and Urku Pacha (the underworld)."[20] In the same vein the ancient city of Adranon next to The Simeto river by Mount Etna was founded close to temple of the indigenous god Adranos.[21] But the Greek model of having settlements around deities is not peculiar to Adranon as Hellenized towns such as Inessa and Morgantina contained sanctuaries of the Sicel Palici gods.[22]

Raupa which was a *pa* of the Ngati Tamatera tribe in New Zealand was crisscrossed by rivers rich in resources that sustained the people.[23]

> The river brought fish including mullet, kahawai, eels, lamprey and whitebait to the pa. The wetlands of the vast swamp were a rich habitat for duck and other waterbirds. Above the water-table the natural levees and other higher ground provided rich soil for food crops, notably *kumara* but probably also the newly introduced potato, sweet corn, melon and other

vegetables... *Harakeke* (flax) which was valued for making items from the finest cloaks to the most everyday food baskets and other mundane items, and *raupo* for thatching and other purposes, were available in great abundance. Timber trees for the construction of houses and *pa* defences and for fashioning a vast range of objects both aesthetic and utilitarian were available at hand or in the ranges nearby.[24]

The Ngati Tamatera tribe could harvest the valued timber for houses, canoe etc. while the nearby hill had stone materials such as obisidian, chert, *kokowai* and oven stones were available on the bed of the Ohinemuri River. They could also feed fat on pigeons, tui, kaka, kiwis, and other birds.

In sub-Saharan Africa, indigenous settlements employed building materials that best responds to the weather pattern ranging from coastal humid rain forest, woodland savannah, grassland savannah to semiarid desert.[25] In the rain forest belt where is not much change in temperature throughout the year, buildings needed to have proper ventilation hence you have "Bamboo walls simulating openwork screens" as well as raised foundations to make the most of the ocean breeze.[26] This creative solution was copied by the colonial overlords:

> Early British and French colonial settlers and administrators, recognizing the merit of indigenous solutions to climatic comfort, emulated them by raising their expatriate mansions high above the ground and by developing a wall system composed of louvered doors and screened verandahs. Many examples can still be seen in Abidjan, Accra, Lagos, and Dakar.[27]

In contrast to the rectangular structures found at the coast, circular desert houses were intended to provide refuge to the extremes of heat and cold as the seasons change. So, the earthen houses with insulating walls captured the heat of midday to make them comfortable to sleep in during the cold nights.[28] The deployment technical knowledge was outstanding in that it concentrated "thermal radiation in a central, enclosed, interior space" which also played out in very little ventilation given the harsh environment.[29] The dwellings also responds to the moderated lighting from the sun enabled by the thick forest in the coastal areas while the sun's intensity in the savannah is moderated by the curved surfaces and rough earthen walls converting the rays into "softly graded shade and shadow."[30]

But much more that responding to the vagaries of the weather the indigenous dwellings in West Africa have rich communication properties:

The plan of a West African compound will reveal to the careful observer not only the size of the occupant group as a whole, but the precise hierarchical and jurisdictional relationships which exist among its members, male and female, young and old. The distribution of cooking spaces will reveal the relationships between wife (wives) and husband, between children and parents, defining areas of responsibility and territoriality as well as ownership of or jurisdiction over crops and livestock. The disposition of room units will reflect not only the relationships between residents but their relationship as a whole to the extended homestead which they farm.[31]

The fluid nature of the arrangements accommodates new members such as through marriage as the compound expands and decreases as member pass on, leave to get married or decide to relocate such as leaving parts of the dwelling to decay and crumble back into the earth hence "the personal spaces will realign themselves to accommodate the changing human relationship."[32]

Almost the same settlement patterns could be observed of the Aboriginals of Australia as their environment consisted of "coastal, riverine, tropical forest, plains/savannah and desert."[33] And these played a role in terms of population density.[34] A more sedentary lifestyle was observable in the riverine areas with the abundance of sea food while their coastal colleagues placed a lot more emphasis on hunting of games.[35] The jungles and rainforest of northeastern Australia supported the hunter and gatherer lifestyle while the desert made for a migratory lifestyle in search of sustenance.[36] However, no matter the terrain, to the Aboriginals, the land they occupied also occupied them as custodians of tribal patrimony for the forces that provided their daily sustenance.[37]

Ahupua'as which are pie-shaped land arrangement among the Hawaiian and Polynesian settings made the inhabitants self-sufficient because of "the interrelated economic activities of forest gatherers, farmland taro cultivators, and coastal fishing."[38] Terraces in Konso in southern Ethiopia, south Shewa in central Ethiopia and Harangue Plateau in eastern Ethiopia are used "to protect soil from erosion, for water conservation, and in the creation of agricultural fields." In response to their peculiar topography.[39] In addition they were guidelines for maintenance of sacred forest, woodlots, trees in the homestead and farms which along with manuring, crop rotation, fallowing and tree plantations made them at peace with their environment.[40] The Orang Asli of Malaysia live in or close to forests that provide their means of sustenance.[41]

The Orissa coastal plain in India has a settlement pattern that is linear intersecting roads and river levees as well as coastal sand ridges with a higher density recorded along canals and waterways.[42] The streets are oriented towards oriented towards a temple or water tank with the caste system playing a prominent role.[43] Water was also a consideration in terms of settlement patterns of the Emberá who resided in rainforest ecosystem of Columbia and Panama.[44] But in the twentieth century they have literally moved through the Darién rivers system of Panama sharing a border with Columbia "in search of marriage partners, new hunting or fishing grounds, and land suitable for slash-and-burn cultivation."[45]

The Awas Tingni – and indigenous Manyanga community of Nicaragua's land claim includes their hitherto traditional agricultural, fishing and hunting areas.[46] Jiyeh and Chimm in the Lebanese coast came about as a result of access to sea and land transportation systems as well as agricultural terrain.[47] The Amerindians were able to inhabit swathes of Quebec specifically regions surrounding Lake Mistassini, e.g., the Abitibi and the Saguenay following glacial melts and afforestation in the Archaic period (8000–3000 BP).[48]

Markets

Markets can be categorized into periodic and daily with the former associated with rural areas and the latter with large and well populated urban centres.[49] African markets are avenues for social interaction and can also communicate civic engagement as well as breakdown.[50] The markets were usually located in intersections: Forest and savannah; agricultural and fishing settlements; and between different ethnic groups thus facilitating exchange of various goods.[51] The communication component of markets is clear from the Aba Women riot when "women used the marketplace as a means of passing messages between markets to galvanize mass action."[52] But markets also play the role of globalization from below as petty traders in the borders of the Caucasus and Central Asia crisscross the border as they go about their business.[53]

Periodic markets are features of East Africa and regular markets are said to be new inventions.[54] Social and demographic profiles of traders are diverse however some are worth a mention such as more females and older persons (Ghana) and a majority come from families where one parent was a trader thus continuing the family tradition (Ghana and Nigeria).[55] In Kerala, India the men go out fishing and the women sell the fish.[56] The fishers belong to the lowest rung of the caste system marked by poverty, low literacy rate and poor access to water, sanitation and other social services. In Uganda there are fulltime traders but those in periodic markets engage with this part-time because of the precarious nature of their involvement and look out for other sources of making ends meet.[57] Traders can also be divided up into fixed and mobile categories although the former can take up the role of the latter if circumstances such as low sales and other economic vagaries so dictate.[58]

According to Porter et al.,[59] the myriad ethnic groups in Nigeria and the resulting tensions and conflicts are also registered in markets where they assemble for the purpose of buying and selling. But the markets also make for integration as persons from various ethnic groups look out for each other when there is a crisis based on their long-standing business relationships which can include extension of credit facility, providing a home away from home for traders from other ethnic groups that have travelled long distances etc.[60] But there is more as markets help

> to survive economic crunches, social, family, and personal challenges. Furthermore, the older women traders assist the younger ones to care for their children within the market environment. They encourage nursing trader mothers to breastfeed their children adequately and offer pieces of advice on treatment options, depending on the knowledge base of the "adviser".[61]

In addition the rowdy and unorganized atmosphere that pervades the informal markets also possesses communication properties. Even though stalls are usually properly demarcated traders still go ahead and place goods for sale in every available space thus signifying the rowdy environment that the subaltern classes inhabit outside of the market space.[62] The only deterrent is if the practice is frowned upon by others.[63] But there is some order in this disorder in that even though the demarcations assists buyers to locate wares, traders still go ahead and shout out their goods using terms of endearments to "confuse" buyers and ensure that the bargaining process does not detract from profitability.[64]

Local Chinese markets also have their own story but the similarity with the Nigerian informal market is uncanny. There exists manipulation of weights and measures, hoarding and monopolies, benefitting from price differentials in neighboring markets, adulteration of goods, creation of artificial shortages, buying of goods outside of the traditional perimeters of the market and haggling.[65] The markets in England were also disorganized and rowdy so much that injuries and death resulted from the animal and wares put up for sale on the streets.[66] Hawkers in the early London markets were said to sell dubious goods and as taking business away from traders who had paid for their shops but they were increasingly tolerated because of their ability to widely distribute goods beyond the confines of the markets.[67] These are precisely the reasons that have informed governments wading in to protect consumers and ensure ethical and legal practice globally.[68]

Quito in Ecuador still exhibit some of these features with a

> considerable number of traders who operate on public land, particularly in the streets, squares, parks and municipal markets. Some are itinerant hawkers who walk from door to door offering their merchandise, and a few drive lorries and pick-up trucks to deliver fresh foodstuffs to houses and to sell from their vehicles while parked near well-frequented road junctions. The majority, however, trade in or around markets designated or permitted by the Municipal Council.[69]

Just like Nigerian markets, the ones in Quito are also large and congested but they diverge from their Nigerian counterparts because they are active only for a few hours during the day.[70] They cater for the lower segment of the market as affluence shoppers prefer the comfortable environment of the shops to the stifling and chaotic environment of markets.[71]

Oje market in Ibadan, southwest Nigeria offers a good case study because of some of it unique features. It is under the guardianship of the Delesolu family who are both the original owners of the market as well as the de facto managers even though there are elected men and women charged with this responsibility.[72] There is an indigenous court presided over by senior Delesolu family members that handle

> transactional space disagreements, petty theft, rumor mongering and backbiting among the traders, and spousal and partner disloyalties. The court is utilized by many of the traders who go in for consultation and settlement. The court venue is also a meeting place for different groups of traders who deliberate on affairs of their traders' groups. In addition, the court settles disputes among members of the Delesolu family. The decisions of the court are respected and accepted as final.

That is a market supreme court right there!

The Poncho market in Otavalo, Norther Ecuador involved trade by barter and apart from when the market is in session it was just an empty space but on market days people would sit around in twos and threes bargaining away.[73] But much more than being empty spaces when markets are not in session, the springing up of markets can have huge transformational effects. Sapon market in Abeokuta, southwest Nigeria started life as a hospitality spot for travelers but soon grew from being a resting place to a market as wares were brought for sale weekly and not too long after stalls sprang up and food production to cater for the new development equally picked up to supply various players with provision.[74] In the same vein markets in in the 1670s London multiplied to cater for the increasing population and new settlements so much so that 30 different markets could be counted.[75] They were "venues where city and country shook hands."[76]

The markets in Yorubaland have been described as "foci of communications."[77] But they are by no means the only markets were communication and information dissemination are a key element of the interactions. The Irish market in Poyntznpass was an opportunity for neighbors to get all the latest news and gossips.[78] But in the midst of all these endless going and coming on market days were activities such as

> small boys earned an odd "tanner" keeping restless cattle together; dealers stood around spittingon their hands to seal a bargain or "splitting the difference" aided and abetted by "tanglers" who earned a pound if a deal was made and nothing if the parties couldn't agree. There was a special atmosphere in the village on a Fair Day. There was bustle and business, banter and bargaining, giving opportunity for shrewd judgment and great entertainment for the non-involved.[79]

Same also applied to the early London markets as they were "the centre for community interchange … the principal focus of community identity … where all classes … could mingle cheek by jowl."[80]

Markets in northern Nigeria served the usual economic roles but there were also political and information dissemination purposes.[81] The communication function is based on the fact that "information necessary for both daily and longer-term decision making originates in rural markets; this is especially significant in the context of the farmer's commitment of scarce resources to specific production programs."[82]

The border markets in the Caucasus and Central Asia connect Europe and Asia, and Russia and Iran in a marketing embrace marked by vibrancy so much so that "besides tourists and commuters, you will meet Iranian truck and Georgian minibus drivers, Armenian fruit and vegetable retailers, Turkish businessmen – and, invisible to the eyes of ordinary travelers, smugglers of drugs and weapons."[83]

Conclusion

The communication function in settlements is clear from the ties between indigenous people and the lands they occupy as these have deep spiritual and sentimental values. The Nasa of Columbia's example is instructive in that the mores and culture in their cultural capital served to confirm that their "new" location was actually ancestral land. Let's bear in mind that settlers have often forcibly removed the indigenous inhabitants to the periphery to take away their patrimony hence this example shows how deep the communication of ancestral origins are that years after these indigenous people could still locate landmarks present in their mores and myths of origins. Markets also exhibit communication functions in a variety of ways including differentiating between various classes. As societies "develop" they seem to move away from informal markets towards a preference for better and well organized forms of shopping hence the malls springing up in almost all capitals around the world. But are we not missing out? Some regret that markets are gone in the West.

> The fair has gone from the village streets and while the inhabitants may not have regretted its passing, one of our oldest social gatherings has come to an end. For a saleyard is not a fair. It lacks the atmosphere, the cut and thrust of the real thing that had its beginnings at the dawn of our history.[84]

The haggling and atmosphere in informal markets seem ingrained in us and doing away with it completely may cause irreparable harm based on the roles they play.

Notes

1. Ansu-Kyeremeh, K. (1998). Indigenous communication systems.: A conceptual framework. In K. Ansu-Kyeremeh (Ed.). Perspectives on indigenous communication in Africa: Theory and application (vol. 2). Legon, Ghana: School of Communication Studies Printing Press., p. 85.

2. Doob, L. (1966). Communication in Africa: A search for boundaries. New Haven, Connecticut, CT: Yale University Press.
3. Wilson, T.H. (1982). Spatial analysis and settlement patterns on the East African coast. *Studies in History, Trade and Society in the East African Coast, 28*, 201–219.
4. Inter-American Commission on Human Rights. (2010). Indigenous and tribal peoples' rights over their ancestral lands and natural resources: norms and jurisprudence of the inter-American human rights system. *American Indian Law Review, 35*(2), 263–496.
5. Bialuschewski, A. (2005). Pirates, slavers, and the indigenous population in Madagascar, c. 1690–1715. *The International Journal of African Historical Studies, 38*(3), 401–425.
6. Hussin, N. (2012). Trading networks of Malay merchants and traders in the Straits of Melaka from 1780 to 1830. Special Focus: Trade and Finance in the Malay World: Indigenous History Revisited. *Asian Journal of Social Sciences, 40*(1), 51–82.
7. Van Buren, M. (1999). Tarapaya: An elite Spanish residence near Colonial Potosí in comparative perspective. *Historical Archaeology, 33*(2), 108–122.
8. Van Buren, M. (1999).
9. Van Buren, M. (1999).
10. Van Buren, M. (1999), p 110.
11. Van Buren, M. (1999), p. 111.
12. Gnecco, C., & Hernández, C. (2008). History and Its discontents: Stone Statues, native histories, and archaeologists. Current Anthropology, 49(3), 439–466. https://doi.org/10.1086/588497
13. Gnecco, C., & Hernández, C. (2008) pp. 440 & 442.
14. Byrne, D. (1996). Deep nation: Australia's acquisition of an indigenous past. *Aboriginal History, 20*, 82–107, p. 86.
15. Ojha, A. (2003). Trail of tears: Looking at indigenous history of Canada (17th to 19th centuries). *Proceedings of the Indian History Congress, 64*, 1272–1280.
16. Tovar-Restrepo, M., & Irazábal, C. (2014). Indigenous women and violence in Colombia: Agency, autonomy, and territoriality. Latin American Perspectives, 41(1), 39–58, p. 43.
17. Anderson, C. (2016). Rediscovering Native North America: Settlements, maps, and empires in the eastern woodlands. *Early American Studies, 14*(3), 478–505, p. 500.
18. Mihok, L. D., & Wells, E. C. (2014). Miskitu labor and English royalization at Augusta, Roatán Island, Honduras. *International Journal of Historical Archaeology, 18*(1), 100–121, p. 107.
19. Beaule, C. D. (2018). Cambios en la vestimenta indígena en el altiplano andino bajo el colonialismo español/Indigenous clothing changes in the

Andean highlands under Spanish colonialism. *Estudios Atacameños, 59*, 7–26, p. 18.
20. Beaule, C. D. (2018), p. 18.
21. Pratolongo, V. (2014). The Greeks and the indigenous populations of eastern Sicily in the classical era. *Mediterranean Archaeology, 27*, 85–90.
22. Pratolongo, V. (2014).
23. Prickett, N. (1990). Archaeological excavations at Raupa: The 1987 season. *Records of the Auckland Institute and Museum, 27*, 73–153, p. 76.
24. Prickett, N. (1990), p. 76.
25. Prussin, L. (1974). An Introduction to Indigenous African Architecture. Journal of the Society of Architectural Historians, 33(3), 183–205. https://doi.org/10.2307/988854
26. Prussin, L. (1974), p. 185.
27. Prussin, L. (1974), p. 186.
28. Prussin, L. (1974).
29. Prussin, L. (1974), p. 186.
30. Prussin, L. (1974), p. 187.
31. Prussin, L. (1974), p. 191.
32. Prussin, L. (1974), p. 191.
33. Meggitt, M. J. (1964). Indigenous forms of government among the Australian Aborigines. *Bijdragen Tot de Taal-, Land- En Volkenkunde, 120*(1), 163–180, p. 165.
34. Meggitt, M. J. (1964), p. 165.
35. Meggitt, M. J. (1964).
36. Meggitt, M. J. (1964).
37. Meggitt, M. J. (1964).
38. Grim, J. A. (1997). Indigenous traditions and ecological ethics in "Earth's Insights." *Worldviews, 1*(2), 139–149.
39. Engdawork, A., & Bork, H.-R. (2014). Long-term indigenous soil conservation technology in the Chencha Area, southern Ethiopia: Origin, characteristics, and sustainability. *Ambio, 43*(7), 932–942.
40. Engdawork, A., & Bork, H.-R. (2014).
41. Aiken, S. R., & Leigh, C. H. (2011). In the way of development: Indigenous land-rights issues in Malaysia. *Geographical Review, 101*(4), 471–496.
42. Singh, S. P. (1994). Vulnerability of settlements to cyclones on the northeast coast of India. *Ekistics, 61*(366/367), 193–197.
43. Singh, S. P. (1994).
44. Theodossopoulos, D. (2012). Indigenous attire, exoticization, and social change: dressing and undressing among the Emberá of Panama. *The Journal of the Royal Anthropological Institute, 18*(3), 591–612.
45. Theodossopoulos, D. (2012), p. 593.

46. Stocks, A. (2005). Too much for too few: problems of indigenous land rights in Latin America. *Annual Review of Anthropology, 34*, 85–104.
47. Waliszewski, T., & Gwiazda, M. (2015). Porphyreon through the Ages: The fading archaeological heritage of the Lebanese Coast. *Journal of Eastern Mediterranean Archaeology & Heritage Studies, 3*(4), 330–348.
48. King, G., & Muller, T. (2018). Taming the waterways: The Europeanization of Southern Québec's Riverside Landscapes during the 16th–18th Centuries. *Journal of the North Atlantic, 34*, 1–38.
49. Bromley, R. J. (1974). The organization of Quito's urban markets: Towards a reinterpretation of periodic central places. *Transactions of the Institute of British Geographers, 62*, 45–70. https://doi.org/10.2307/621515
50. Porter, G., Lyon, F., Adamu, F., & Obafemi, L. (2010). Conflict and cooperation in market spaces: Learning from the operation of local networks of civic engagement in African market trade. *Human Organization, 69*(1), 31–42.
51. Hodder, B. W. (1965). Some comments on the origins of traditional markets in Africa South of the Sahara. *Transactions of the Institute of British Geographers, 36*, 97–105. https://doi.org/10.2307/621456
52. Porter, G., Lyon, F., Adamu, F., & Obafemi, L. (2010), p. 36.
53. Fehlings, S. (2018). Informal trade and globalization in the Caucasus and Post-Soviet Eurasia. In M. Stephan-Emmrich & P. Schröder (Eds.), Mobilities, boundaries, and travelling ideas: Rethinking translocality beyond Central Asia and the Caucasus (1st ed., pp. 229–262). Open Book Publishers.
54. Good, C. M. (1975). Periodic markets and traveling traders in Uganda. *Geographical Review, 65*(1), 49–72. https://doi.org/10.2307/213833
55. Resnick, D. (2020). *The politics and governance of informal food retail in urban Africa*. International Food Policy Research Institute.
56. Hapke, H. M. (2001). Petty traders, gender, and development in a south Indian fishery. *Economic Geography, 77*(3), 225–249. https://doi.org/10.2307/3594073
57. Good, C. M. (1975).
58. Bromley, R. J. (1974).
59. Porter, G., Lyon, F., Adamu, F., & Obafemi, L. (2010).
60. Porter, G., Lyon, F., Adamu, F., & Obafemi, L. (2010).
61. Omobowale, M.O., & Omobowale, A.O. (2019). Oju and inu. *Journal of Black Studies, 50*(4), 401–420. p. 402.
62. Omobowale, M.O., & Omobowale, A.O. (2019).
63. Omobowale, M.O., & Omobowale, A.O. (2019).
64. Omobowale, M.O., & Omobowale, A.O. (2019), p. 408.

65. Solinger, D. J. (1979). State versus merchant: commerce in the countryside in the early People's Republic of China. *Comparative Studies in Society and History, 21*(2), 168–194.
66. University of Southampton, & Great Britain. Royal Commission on Market Rights and Tolls. (1891). Market rights and tolls : volume X [Documents]. HMSO.
67. Smith, C. (2002).
68. Solinger, D. J. (1979).
69. Bromley, R. J. (1974). The organization of Quito's urban markets: Towards a reinterpretation of periodic central places. *Transactions of the Institute of British Geographers, 62,* 45–70. https://doi.org/10.2307/621515, p. 50.
70. Bromley, R. J. (1974).
71. Bromley, R. J. (1974).
72. Omobowale, M.O., & Omobowale, A.O. (2019).
73. Korovkin, T. (1998). Commodity production and ethnic culture: Otavalo, Northern Ecuador. *Economic Development and Cultural Change, 47*(1), 125–154. https://doi.org/10.1086/452389
74. Hodder, B. W. (1965).
75. Smith, C. (2002). The wholesale and retail markets of London, 1660–1840. *The Economic History Review, 55*(1), 31–50.
76. Smith, C. (2002), p. 33.
77. Hodder, B. W. (1965), p. 99.
78. Lennon, J. (1988). Fairs and assemblies in Ireland: "Before I Forget". *Journal of the Poyntzpass and District Local History Society, 2,* 55–62.
79. Lennon, J. (1988), p. 55.
80. Smith, C. (2002), p. 34.
81. Scott, E. P. (1972). The spatial structure of rural northern Nigeria: Farmers, periodic markets, and villages. *Economic Geography, 48*(3), 316–332. https://doi.org/10.2307/142911
82. Scott, E. P. (1972), p. 316.
83. Fehlings, S. (2018), p. 230.
84. Lennon, J. (1988), p. 55.

CHAPTER 10

Taxonomic Communication

Universally, names provide a symbolic system of identification so that we can tell one person, ethnic and racial group from the other. The system is "historically constructed, socially maintained, and based on shared assumptions and expectations of members of a particular community."[1] Names are not meant only for identification as they communicate lots of information about their owners, his or her family and communal values. They are markers of family connections.[2] Names have been deployed to effect social and political changes as well as to assert indigenous identity.[3] They have been described as *aide de memoirs* that are capable of unleashing powerful emotions.[4] Names can reflect various circumstances surrounding the coming into being of a people, their location, special or unique features, identification with animals (totems), their particular behaviour, strengths or skills amongst others. People group may not have the privilege of naming themselves but are named by their neighbours or distant persons as the colonial experience demonstrated hence a number of tribal and group names are based on the principle of nickname, terms of greeting, or salutation.[5] In some instances their names reflect their subaltern status.[6] Place names can also give an indication of cultural inclusivity or exclusivity.[7] They, in addition, are "channels for locating, analysing and comprehending the world."[8] Personal names can give an indication of the political and economic context, attitude of parents or even be a brief adage. It is key to understanding a person's character and behaviour and

© The Author(s), under exclusive license to Springer Nature Switzerland AG 2024
E. Akpabio, *Indigenous Communication*,
https://doi.org/10.1007/978-3-031-41766-5_10

this is especially true of nicknames and praise names.[9] African names in particular have been singled out for their rich meanings and complex linguistic forms.[10] Be that as it may any study of naming does reveal a lot about the cultural attitudes.[11]

Personal Names

Personal names are informed by a variety of factors. In Oceania, personal names reflects one's place in the procreational chain as well as geography, time of and circumstances surrounding their birth.[12] The Irish add O (grandson) or Mac (son) to their names linking themselves to their ancestors from the tenth to eleventh centuries or from 850 to 1290.[13] English names have been impacted by a variety of influences such as Christianity, classical and vernacular sources as well as literary coinages and borrowings from other languages.[14] Anglo-Saxon naming tradition consists of a forename and surname with the latter being the family name.[15] However, in India the naming practice is village name, father's name and personal name in that order.[16] In the West where individuality is highly prized, names "literally 'personifies' the individual by encapsulating the essence of that person for those who know them or know about them. Speaking or writing a name conjures up an "image, a history, a sense of personal taste and style.""[17]

Israeli personal names by contrast have been categorized into theophoric names, hypocoristic theophoric names, and others.[18] The first takes the form of a sentence with God or divine appellatives such as Yahweh, Kemosh and Quas while the second refers to abbreviated theophoric names which makes it unclear what the theophoric element was.[19] The last category has no religious reference and may embrace flora and fauna or "substitute names, i.e., names that designate the name-bearer as a substitute for a deceased relative (e.g., *Mnḥm, Tnḥm*)."[20]

Abazas, a small autochthonous Caucasian people living in the Karacaj Cerkes Republic of the Russian Federation, have a two-name system consisting of a surname and a "postposed" first name.[21] But this rule does not tell the entire story as

> some people, beside their official first name, have several other given names, up to five or even six. For example, one woman had Fat'ima as an official name, P'ap'a – the name used by her mother, Śjaśja – the name given to her by the relatives of her husband, Carica – the name given by the wife of her

husband's brother, and Gwagwana – the name given by her aunt ... Typically, different names are used by different circles of peoples surrounding a person: family, friends, work, etc.

Then the Russian Federation came up with their own naming system: First name, father's name and surname.[22] This is very much like the Ibibio of south-south Nigeria who also have the same system. Example is my name: Eno Ime Akpabio. This reflects my name, my father's name and surname. The Abazas however adapted this Russian Federation three-name system to their purposes by using the surname + patronymic (= X his-son) + first name structure.[23] In this tradition also the use of the first names of one's spouse in public is forbidden in favour of substitutes such as "the children's father", "your daughter in law" etc.[24]

In the same vein, the Dene Tha of northern Canada practice teknonymy with names such as father or mother of but their neighbors – Kaska's – naming practice is pseudo teknonymy with persons given the same names (father of, mother of) as children but not renamed after their children when they attain adulthood.[25] Other interesting naming practices among them include the use of kinship terms instead of personal names thus emphasizing kinship bonds and the corresponding obligations,[26] Descriptors such as "the one who was foolish", "the older one" are also used to reference individuals when personal names are not known.[27] Names of individuals used in "curing" are usually kept secret and individuals can be given other names based on their actions, interpersonal relationships and specific incidences.[28] This is also recorded in China with persons given other names in adulthood or posthumously that "impart information about them especially their distinctive moral or physical characteristics."[29]

The Yorubas of southwest Nigeria's naming practices reflects experiences and their worldview in addition to factoring in the "lexical, syntactic, semantic and pragmatic rules of the Yoruba language."[30] The Balinese of Indonesia give names that have no meaning and that are not related to their cultural context so much so that these names have been described as "arbitrarily coined nonsense syllables"[31] that foster "genealogical amnesia."[32] European names fall in the middle of these extremes – Yoruba and Bali in that

> there is usually a clearly recognizable inventory of personal names some of which may indicate familial connections or membership in some particular

group. But the linguistic and cultural implications of European personal names do not in any way approximate those of the Yoruba.

North American Indian and Australian personal names are taken from clan animals thus tying individuals firmly to the apron strings of their clans.[33] American names reflect a relationship between surnames, family structure and descent lines.[34] Personal names in Western Europe during the Middle Ages were derived from two-name stocks: German and Christian.[35] The former because of the great migration and the latter derived from the Bible and saints.[36]

The Yoruba naming system while signifying the place of communalism and cultural capital also serve as communication function: "an open diary by providing a system through which information is symbolically stored and retrieved." Igbo names communicate the gender binary: *Chukwu* for males and *Chi* for females based on *Chi* the Igbo personal life force.[37] But the binary also applies to other names example are market-day names in the table below:

Market day	Male name	Gloss	Female name
Èke	Òkeèke	'Male/Female of Eke'	Mgbeèke
Orìe	Òkorìe	'Male/Female of Orie'	Mgborìe
Àfò	Òkaàfò	'Male/Female of Afo'	Mgbaàfò
Nkwọ	Òkoñkwọ	'Male/Female of Nkwo'	Mgbọkwọ

Source: Onụkawa, M. C. (2000). The Chi concept in Igbo gender naming. *Africa: Journal of the International African Institute, 70*(1), 107–117

Zulu names also reflect circumstance at the time of the child's birth and fathers and grandfather were the name givers.[38]

In Britain, naming generally solidifies patriarchy in that

> whilst not obligatory, the Anglo-Saxon convention is for a surname which is patronymic, that is, children take the surname of their father, who had the name from his father and so on. This means that the process of naming a child embodies male generational continuities. The strength of the patriarchal preference is also reflected in the conventional custom for a woman to change her surname to her husbands on marriage – thus also expressing her links to a new kin network.[39]

And this was also imported into the colonies hence here we are! It is said that when a woman adopts her husband's name it puts her in an inferior position.[40] But the practice goes way back. In classical Rome, women were given a single name which was usually the feminized form of the ancestral name used by their fathers.[41] In the same vein, most documents were written by men for men thus marginalizing women whose names rarely made it into the narratives.[42]

Iceland stands out from the Euro-American practice of patrilineal surnames as they do not have surnames in line with an old Norse tradition.[43] Icelanders are known by their first name which communicates their persona while the second name is usually "a patronym (matronyms, however, are increasingly used, either on their own with the patronym). 'Jonsson' (or 'Jonsdottir'), for example, simply indicates that the person in question is the son (or daughter) of a man named 'Jon.'"[44] Moreover, couples rarely change their names when they get married.[45]

Major considerations play a role in the Yoruba naming practice: The home, circumstance of birth, the family's occupation, religious affiliation etc. Hence a name like Ìgè- indicates that the child was born leg first; Ajèwọlè means born at a prosperous time while Odeyemi references a hunting family. The Omani naming system also has these considerations. In addition they carefully select names to reflect favourable attributes as well as future expectations and wishes for their children.[46] Omani names also communicate prestige and social status. Thus a child named *adi:b* (well behaved) is expected to well, be well behaved. In the same vein, a woman named *gami:l-ah* (beautiful) is expected to take care of herself and appear presentable at all times in line with her name.

As a consequence, in Oman women are under more pressure to reflect their names in their actions and speech hence

> women devote more attention to maintaining their prestige, revealing their noble social status, and boasting about the pedigree of their family in social settings than men do. Therefore, it seems inevitable that women should feel obliged not to disgrace their names and to carefully project their names' positive attributes and qualities to their interlocutors. They can do so by acting in conformity with the meanings of their names, and this, in turn, reflects the women's social status and prestige.[47]

More so as adult women in Muscat, Oman deploy derogatory names derived from their interlocutor's personal names to express their exasperation and because these involve derogatory or taboo words in Arabic, they are regarded as a grave insult.[48]

This effect of names on people and their destinies have informed changes in first and last names. For instance Muhammad Ali after winning the heavyweight boxing belt changed his name from Cassius Clay to severe "the genealogical connection to the slavery which past generations of his family endured."[49] Among the Inuit of Canada and Greenland, names also have deep spiritual significance. Their names create their personality, and more names means more personal essences.[50] The names contain personality traits that are intergenerationally transmitted and reincarnated in succeeding generations.[51] Slave owners also understood this principle as they punished slaves who tried to hold onto their indigenous names preferring that they take names given by their owners thus deforming them and tearing them away from their former environment.[52]

The Bimanese an indigenous ethnic group in Indonesia that inhabit the eastern part of Sumbawa Island in West Nusa Tenggara province's naming system has three components: An arbitrary label, names of relatives and a title. The first and second usually are almost always derived from Arabic, Islamic or Indonesian history while examples of the respect form include *Heko* for someone named *Ishaq* and *Lamu* for *Halimah*, Tannese names, on the other hand, link the bearers to the tribe but also confer property rights.[53]

In Egypt several names are proposed for a child by its parents, but the name chosen is the one on the candle that outlast all the other candles with the other names.[54] This is usually done a week after the birth of the child in the presence of family members and relatives with the idea being that the candle that burns out last is a good omen signifying longevity.[55] The superstition goes even further in that to protect the child from the evil eye parents also adopt "reverse gender reference" such that

> the birth of a male is especially disguised as he is awarded gender-ambiguous names such as *intisa:r* "victory" and *ʔismat* "protection". Moreover, the sex of a child is hidden "beyond birth into childhood and even into young adulthood" … by circumlocution, which involves announcing the arrival of a baby boy by such vague phrases as *ti-trabba fi ʔizz-ak* "may she be raised in prosperity".[56]

Arabic naming practices in rural areas and among the Bedouin also reflect the same attempt to shield the newborn from harm. So, parents blessed with a very good looking boy would give him an ugly name in Arabic translating into donkey, envelope, thunder etc. However, if the baby becomes sickly or cries too much that is the cue for changing the name because the child by these actions is dissatisfied with the given name.[57] Omanis also follow the latter practice of making changes to the name given at birth.[58]

Omanis are not alone in changing names even though states insist on a formal name from birth to death. Nicknames are an example. They may start life as a means of differentiating persons with similar names, but they may go onto to locate such persons in particular social spaces.[59] They may go on to become family names passed on from generation to generation.[60] The only snag is that if the nicknames were given to put down and denigrate persons they also impact

> the life and persona of the individuals to whom they are attached. Like other names, they depend on a social contract without which they would have no force or ontological weight. In extreme cases, the persona is severely injured as a result of a nickname. The wounds inflicted in the process may not be highly visible, although sometimes people clearly "lose face" but nevertheless they are just as serious as physical violence. Indeed this *is* (emphasis authors) physical violence in a very real sense, with lasting and damaging embodied results.[61]

Iroquoians embracing Mohawk, Oneida, Onondaga, Cayuga, Seneca, Huron-Wyandot Tuscarora and Cherokee nations revere names alluding to luck as it conferred favours on the bearer now and in the hereafter.[62] Several personal names were given to individuals beside their main name to guard against mentioning a person's name whether deceased or alive as this was considered sacrilegious.[63] The personal names were derived from geographic features, the heavens, flora and fauna, water, the atmosphere etc.[64] Native Hawaiian names were also derived from object, artifact, personality traits, in commemoration of an event and they were not gendered or hereditary.[65]

First sons in Kuwait are named after their grandfathers thus cementing family relationships as central to their naming system.[66] Thus, the naming scheme is for example "/,ubaah/ is the son of /saalim/, /saalim/ is the son of /subaah/."[67] The total name is rarely used except for remonstration purposes when a mother deploys it: "/Khalid Mustafa Al-Wazzan, where have you been? if she wants to scold him for arriving home late."[68] Names in this tradition can reflect family occupation, communicate circumstance at birth, sheikhs or ruling class; indicate that the bearer is

Kuwaiti of Bedouin origin, is a former slave, identify females in urban areas, indicate thanksgiving and offers of praise.[69] People are also named after the prophet of Islam, geographical features etc.[70]

Tamil personal names do not follow the norm. They usually take this format:

Sequence:	First	Second	Third
Name Type:	Initial(s)	Given Name(s)	Caste Name
Status:	Optional	Obligatory	Optional
Examples:	K.	Muthiah	Chettiyar
		Shankaran	Pillai
	M.K.	John Joseph	
		Nalini	

Source: Britto, F. (1986). Personal names in Tamil Society. *Anthropological Linguistics*, 28(3), 349–365

Individuals have one or more given names, but no last name and they can choose to use or not use their caste names. The babble in naming among Tamils is captured here: "Tamils moving in international circles are also likely to have one name in their birth certificate, another in their school record, and still another in their visa or business documents."[71]

Tribal and Ethnic Names

Just like personal names, there are a number of considerations that inform tribal names. In Hungary, for instance, clans of noblemen and court commoners took the names of their ancestors "from the time of St. Stephen."[72] But not so the conquered tribes as these were named after the tribal identity of conquerors.[73] This must have served to erase identity and patrimony. This is precisely the case in Adelaide Plains, Australia as colonialism has done a lot of damage in this regard. This is because 160 years after the colonialist came on board and generations after the last Kaurna speakers passed on nothing is certain anymore as regards the origins and meaning of indigenous place names.[74]

The saving grace in the Australian example is that there are a few surviving relics. Example is *Witongga* in Fulham which means reedbed based on the abundance of reeds in the area more so as the word for reed is *wito*.[75] The Kaurna word for Morphett Vale is *Parnanga* which combines *parna* – autumn star – with the location *ngga*. This is especially significant from the purview of Kaurna cosmology as "it is likely that *Parnanga* is the place from where the Ancestral Being Pama ascended into the heavens, or where he or she performed some other feat."[76]

Still in Australia, the appropriation of indigenous names for place names have been categorized into pragmatic and imperialistic categories. For the latter the argument is that after decimating the Aboriginals and their culture, the colonial overlords appropriate indigenous names for their own gain while denying their complicity in the genocidal behaviours they enacted. The pragmatic one has been described in terms such as "colonial historical identification" and "Anglo-indigenous historical identification" in which the naming claims the land for the British crown while acknowledging the Aboriginals in a few instances.[77]

Menchari located in low Bartsham in Bhutan got its name thus:

> A long time ago *mithun* (a local species of domesticated free-range cow) belonging to a rich household in Yangkhar, a village located in central Bartsham, went missing. After a long and futile search, the owner traced the *mithun's* footprints down the Yangkhar Zor (Yangkhar hillock) toward Zongthung Shong (Zongthung stream). The footprints led him farther across the Zongthung stream through the lush green forests of rhododendrons and oak and then to the drier areas of towering chirr pines. The owner had almost given up hope of finding the *mithun* in an area with no source of water, when he just found him sitting calmly in a little clearing on a hillock. The owner wondered how the *mithun* quenched his thirst in such a dry area. When the owner looked around a bit, he was surprised to find a spring at the side of the hillock. Since then, the name of this place came to be known as Menchari. Menchari means *mithun*, and *ri* means water in Sharchop.[78]

Tribal identity and a people's history also inform placenames as the case of the Arapaho of Colorado aptly demonstrates.[79] The Arapaho place names have been categorized into "descriptive, based on resemblances, or associated with human use of or action in the landscape."[80] Examples in the descriptive categories include beniiΘoonóó (steep/canyon-deep river, Frasier River, Middle Park area, Colo) and beniisotoyóó (hairy/fuzzy-mountain-II 'pine ridge' Shadow Mountain, Echo Mountain, and Lookout Mountain RMNP).[81] BeiΘe'eēéno ('head mountains' Mount Alice and the peak west of there, RMNP) is an example of names with human resemblance while baanes-do-Xokoy yah (fort where-square-II 'square forts' hills south of Colorado River, west of Granby, Colo) is an example in the third category – human use, human and sacred events.[82]

Victorian place names usually were commemorative, possessive and commendatory than descriptive.[83] These European naming practices were imported into areas that they colonized thus resulting in what has been described as toponymic colonialism as they sought to erase indigenous claims to territory.[84] The practices include adding the prefix "new" to names from Europe into the colonies (New Zealand, New England etc. are examples), naming places after European seafarers (Cook Island or Mount Cook, Tasmania and the Tasman Sea), and an entire continents such as *America*, after the Florentine explorer Amerigo Vespucci![85] These have deep communication significance as

> this practice of naming is linked both to a nostalgia for the native land and to colonial projection. It has a function of a symmetrical axis that favours this doubling, the reflection of the Old World upon the New World. It represents a symbolic taking possession of a territory before the actual event.... The role of colonial placenames has been to serve as a sort of linguistic stamp and symbol, something with which Europeans could mark places and regions and demonstrate ownership of the colonial regions. When, however, Indigenous peoples' placenames were silenced as a result of toponymic colonialism, it reinforced the perception of a terra nullius – as if the regions were not inhabited before the arrival of the Europeans.[86]

This name and claim posture plays out forcefully in Sápmi land that straddles the Scandinavian region. The Sámi name *Leavdnja* referenced the whole region but *Porsángu* a loan word from the Norwegian Porsanger was also in use but now the loan word has become the accepted reference for the area while *Leavdnja* now refers to a town and is no longer the exclusive name for the whole region. The silencing and subjugation of Sámi placenames in Norway has now come to stay since "in maps, a two-way division appeared, with the subjugated use of Sámi names in uninhabited areas and the exclusive use of Norwegian names in settled areas."[87]

Apache place names and their English alternative is also a slight of hand by the settlers similar to Norway and the Sápmi. It attempts to delete the "lived reality of minority populations" and replaces it with the "imagined free-floating ahistorical linguistic example" thus "*Tónoogah* comes to mean the same thing as 'Dripping Springs'.[88] In Canada, scant regard was paid to indigenous people with place names transplanted from Europe such as Thames River and Ontario, while others places were named after Christian saints, Whites, their children, employees and pets.[89] Where there was a passing nod to First people their names were corrupted like *Westaskiwin* derived from the Cree word *Witaskiwinihk* (the hills were peace were made).[90] In other instances there was transliteration of indigenous names into French or English such as Nose Hill or Medicine Hat in Alberta.[91] Jelocan Caves in Australia were originally referred to with the non-Aboriginal names of Binda or Fish River to reflect these landmarks on the way to the caves.[92] Three names of Gundungurra place names for the caves – Binomil, Binoomea, Benomera – have come to light since 1900 but the present name has stuck thus erasing the indigenous one.

The meaning and significance of Indian place names is shrouded in confusion. This is because the names are from several languages and the mixture makes interpretations very problematic.[93] For instance, "there were as many as nine versions of the meaning of Jammu and Kashmir, seven for the name Karnataka, five in the case of Tripur."[94] The names of the country itself is three in number: India, Bharat (named after king Bharata) and Hindustan (the land of Hindus).[95] Place names serve to boost or defame in this environment. Arunachal Pradesh is called the "land of the rising sun", while another name for Jharkhand is "Vananchal" or the "land of trees" but there is also BIMARU or sick states (Bihar, Madhya Pradesh, Rajasthan and Uttar Pradesh) that references their explosive population growth and high rate of poverty.[96]

In the Italian Peninsula, place names had Celtic and divine origins. The former has been described as "comprising antonomastic divine names and nature-deities."[97] There is also a blowback from First Peoples and indigenous people about names imposed by colonialists. American Indian and Native American labels are being discarded in place of names that recognize the nation status of indigenous people, their rights to sovereignty, self-determination, and self-sufficiency.[98]

Conclusion

Even as we see the richness in the discussion of place and personal names, there are still countries that have a prescribed list of personal names that children can be given. Examples are Argentina, Sweden and China with the United States and Germany having prescriptions about names given at birth.[99] To make sure that your child has an indigenous name involves a convoluted process in Argentina before officialdom agrees.[100] Even as we have seen, the damage and marginalization that naming practices have done to indigenous communities, yet "true" names with official sanctions are the "technology of belonging."[101] This raises the question: why can't everyone and every people have a place under the Sun without being erased in favour of others? Just like other kinds of violence visited by settlers on indigenous people toponymic and personal names have not escaped their attention. The light at the end of the tunnel is that indigenous groups are reasserting their identity through personal naming and in some instances drawing attention to the injustices in placenames practices. There is still a long way to go to obtain redress, if ever.

Notes

1. Akinnaso, F. N. (1980). The sociolinguistic basis of Yoruba personal names. *Anthropological Linguistics, 22*(7), 275–304, p. 277.
2. Finch, J. (2008). Naming names: Kinship, individuality and personal names. *Sociology, 42*(4), 709–725.
3. Moore, P. (2007). Negotiated identities: The evolution of Dene Tha and Kaska personal naming systems. *Anthropological Linguistics, 49*(3/4), 283–307.
4. Cahir, F. (David). (2014). Why did squatters in colonial Victoria use Indigenous placenames for their sheep stations? In I. D. Clark, L. Hercus, & L. Kostanski (Eds.), *Indigenous and Minority Placenames: Australian and International Perspectives* (pp. 225–238). ANU Press.
5. Udo, E.A. (1983). *Who are the Ibibio?* African-Fep Publishers.
6. Györffy, G. (1994). Dual kingship and the seven chieftains of the Hungarians in the era of the conquest and the raids. *Acta Orientalia Academiae Scientiarum Hungaricae, 47*(1/2), 87–104, p. 102.
7. Cahir, F. (David). (2014).
8. Kapur, A. (2010). The value of place names in India. *Economic and Political Weekly, 45*(26/27), 410–418.
9. See Chaplin, J.H. (1959). A note on some Central African forenames. *Africa: Journal of International African Institute, 29*(4), 384–390.; Doob, L. (1966). *Communication in Africa: A search for boundaries.* New Haven, Connecticut, CT: Yale University Press.; Leyew, Z. (2003). Amharic personal nomenclature: A grammar and sociolinguistic insight. *Journal of African Cultural Studies, 16*(2), 181–211.
10. Akinnaso, F. N. (1980).
11. Clark, C. (1987). English personal names CA. 650–1300: Some prosopographical bearings. *Medieval Prosopography, 8*(1), 31–60.
12. Akinnaso, F. N. (1980).
13. M'Clure, E. (1879). On Irish personal names. *Proceedings of the Royal Irish Academy. Polite Literature and Antiquities, 1*, 307–314.

14. Hough, C. (2000). Towards an explanation of phonetic differentiation in masculine and feminine personal names. *Journal of Linguistics, 36*(1), 1–11.
15. Finch, J. (2008).
16. Finch, J. (2008).
17. Finch, J. (2008), p. 711.
18. Golub, M. (2014). The distribution of personal names in the land of Israel and Transjordan during the Iron II Period. *Journal of the American Oriental Society, 134*(4), 621–642. https://doi.org/10.7817/jameroriesoci.134.4.621
19. Golub, M. (2014).
20. Golub, M. (2014), p. 624.
21. Chirikba, V. A. (2013). Abaza Personal Names. *Iran & the Caucasus,* 17(4), 391–400, p. 392.
22. Chirikba, V. A. (2013).
23. Chirikba, V. A. (2013).
24. Chirikba, V. A. (2013), p. 392.
25. Moore, P. (2007).
26. Moore, P. (2007).
27. Moore, P. (2007), p. 287.
28. Moore, P. (2007).
29. Goldin, P. R. (2000). Personal names in early China: A research note. *Journal of the American Oriental Society, 120*(1), 77–81. https://doi.org/10.2307/604887, p. 77.
30. Akinnaso, F. N. (1980), p. 277.
31. Akinnaso, F. N. (1980), p. 277.
32. Brewer, J. D. (1981). Bimanese personal names: Meaning and use. *Ethnology, 20*(3), 203–215. https://doi.org/10.2307/3773227
33. Brewer, J. D. (1981).
34. Brewer, J. D. (1981).
35. Clark, C. (1987).
36. Clark, C. (1987).
37. Onukawa, M. C. (2000). The Chi concept in Igbo gender naming. *Africa: Journal of the International African Institute, 70*(1), 107–117. https://doi.org/10.2307/1161403
38. Suzman, S.M. (1994). Names as pointers: Zulu personal naming practices. *Language in Society, 23*(2), 253–272.
39. Finch, J. (2008), p. 712.
40. Finch, J. (2008).
41. Lestremau, A., & Epstein, A. (2017). Gender and naming in the medieval West (sixth-eleventh centuries). *Clio. Women, Gender, History, 45,* 193–215.

42. Lestremau, A., & Epstein, A. (2017).
43. Palsson, G. (2014). Personal names: Embodiment, differentiation, exclusion, and belonging. *Science, Technology, & Human Values, 39*(4), 618–630.
44. Palsson, G. (2014), p. 622.
45. Palsson, G. (2014).
46. Aghbari, K. A. (2010).
47. Aghbari, K. A. (2010), p. 345.
48. Aghbari, K. A. (2010). Derogatory forms of personal names in Omani Arabic. *Anthropological Linguistics, 52*(3/4), 344–357.
49. Finch, J. (2008), p. 713.
50. Palsson, G. (2014).
51. Palsson, G. (2014).
52. Palsson, G. (2014).
53. Lindstrom, L. (1985). Personal names and social reproduction on Tanna, Vanuatu. The Journal of the Polynesian Society, 94(1), 27–45.
54. Aghbari, K. A. (2010).
55. Aghbari, K. A. (2010).
56. Aghbari, K. A. (2010), p. 346.
57. Aghbari, K. A. (2010).
58. Aghbari, K. A. (2010).
59. Palsson, G. (2014).
60. Palsson, G. (2014).
61. Palsson, G. (2014), p. 624.
62. Cooke, C. A. (1952). Iroquois personal names: Their classification. *Proceedings of the American Philosophical Society, 96*(4), 427–438.
63. Cooke, C. A. (1952).
64. Cooke, C. A. (1952).
65. Reinecke, J. E. (1940). Personal names in Hawaii. *American Speech, 15*(4), 345–352. https://doi.org/10.2307/487063
66. Yassin, M. A. F. (1978). Personal names of address in Kuwaiti Arabic. *Anthropological Linguistics, 20*(2), 53–63.
67. Yassin, M. A. F. (1978), p. 53.
68. Yassin, M. A. F. (1978), p. 54.
69. Yassin, M. A. F. (1978).
70. Yassin, M. A. F. (1978).
71. Britto, F. (1986). Personal names in Tamil Society. *Anthropological Linguistics, 28*(3), 349–365, p. 349.
72. Györffy, G. (1994), p. 102.
73. Györffy, G. (1994).
74. Amery, R. (2009). Weeding out spurious etymologies: Toponyms on the Adelaide Plains. In L. Hercus, F. Hodges, & J. Simpson (Eds.), *The land*

is a map: Placenames of Indigenous origin in Australia (pp. 165–180). ANU Press.
75. Amery, R. (2009).
76. Amery, R. (2009), p. 167.
77. Cahir, F. (David). (2014).
78. Dorji, T. C. (2010). Preserving our folktales, myths and legends in the digital era. *Storytelling, Self, Society,* 6(1), 19–38, p. 24.
79. Cowell, A., & Moss, A. (2003). Arapaho place names in Colorado: Form and function, language and culture. *Anthropological Linguistics,* 45(4), 349–389.
80. Cowell, A., & Moss, A. (2003), p. 350.
81. Cowell, A., & Moss, A. (2003).
82. Cowell, A., & Moss, A. (2003).
83. Cahir, F. (David). (2014).
84. Helander, R.K. (n.d.). Sámi placenames, power relations and representation. In I. D. Clark, L. Hercus & L. Kostanski (Eds.). *Indigenous and minority placenames: Australian and international perspectives.* Anu Press.
85. Helander, R.K. (n.d.).
86. Helander, R.K. (n.d.), p. 330.
87. Helander, R.K. (n.d.), p. 339.
88. Webster, A. K. (2017). Why Tséhootsooí Does not equal "Kit Carson Drive": Reflections on Navajo place names and the inequalities of language. Anthropological Linguistics, 59(3), 239–262.
89. Gray, C., & Rück, D. (2019). *Reclaiming indigenous place names.* Yellowhead Institute.
90. Gray, C., & Rück, D. (2019).
91. Gray, C., & Rück, D. (2019).
92. Smith, J. (2014). Illuminating the cave names of Gundungurra country. In I. D. Clark, L. Hercus, & L. Kostanski (Eds.), *Indigenous and Minority Placenames: Australian and International* Perspectives (pp. 83–96). ANU Press.
93. Kapur, A. (2010).
94. Kapur, A. (2010), p. 411.
95. Kapur, A. (2010).
96. Kapur, A. (2010), p. 412.
97. de Bernardo Stempel, P., Hainzmann, M., & Mathieu, N. (2013). Celtic and other indigenous divine names found in the Italian Peninsula. In P. de Bernardo Stempel & A. Hofeneder (Eds.), *Théonymie celtique, cultes, interpretatio – Keltische Theonymie, Kulte, Interpretatio* (1st ed., pp. 73–96). Austrian Academy of Sciences Press.

98. Bird, M. Y. (1999). What we want to be called: Indigenous peoples' perspectives on racial and ethnic identity labels. *American Indian Quarterly, 23*(2), 1–21. https://doi.org/10.2307/1185964
99. Warren, S. D. (2015). Naming regulations and indigenous rights in Argentina. Sociological Forum, 30(3), 764–786.
100. Warren, S. D. (2015).
101. Palsson, G. (2014), p. 622.

CHAPTER 11

Axiomatic Communication

INTRODUCTION

Myths and legends are significant windows into people's worldview. They are an integral part of different cultures around the world as this chapter will clearly point out.[1] Myths and legends remain relevant in spite of whatever our stage of development.[2] Chinese leaders for instance have appealed to them to sanction their policies and programmes.[3] The idea is not to see some as superior to others but to note that myths and legends are a universal attempt to explain natural phenomenon.[4] Myths and legend are said to have the following in common:

> Either or both may be fictitious, the chief distinction being that a legend is popularly regarded as based in fact. Both are closely associated with the supernatural, a possible difference being that myths are concerned with a higher realm of religious philosophizing (that of the gods) while legends are more closely associated with a lower realm of religious philosophizing (that of saints – mere men.) Important here is the fact that myths and legends represent man's desire to explain his fundamental ideas about natural phenomena, supernatural occurrences, the goodness and order of the universe. Myths and legends are basic to man's religious beliefs.[5]

But myths that are widely dispersed are regarded by the tribespeople as clearly factual thus calling into question allegations of fiction levelled against them.[6] But these tribes also make a distinction between some stories which they regard as fairytales and those that "really happened."

Be that as it may, myths supply historical and other information.[7] Myths may have gone through some social filters as they are handed down across generations but this does not detract from their authenticity.[8] This is more so that many early writers used them as illustrations in their expositions and with the passage of time they have sometimes come to be mixed up with histories and facts.[9] They are a sacred history lesson that explains the very beginning of time.[10] They are a repository of indigenous wisdom and values.[11] The central tenets of myths is pluralism and diversity.[12] Myths have to do with the gods and their action with creation, and with the general nature of the universe and of the earth; plus much more.[13]

Legends supply an explanation of the human condition and how people have come to adapt to challenges in their peculiar environments.[14] They have been described as an "artifact of culture."[15] Legends, according to Uzoigwe,[16] though incorporating supernatural elements are historical events that recount general, clan and family histories. As a consequence, they contain crucial data for migration and settlement of groups, evolution of leadership and governance.[17] Their broad appeal makes them useful in effective communication and persuasion.[18] Legends have been described as cultural information that serve to supply explanation during periods of anxiety and ambivalence.[19]

Myths

The Nasa of Colombia have myths related to stones and water which are at the centre of their history given their environment's proximity to a waterfall with lots of stone carvings.[20] Their progenitor, St. Thomas, is the stone incarnation of a powerful force related to earthquakes and the origin of the earth; He turned *pijaos* (enemies) into stone and lent his name to a stone that marks the boundary between two *resguardos* [reservation].[21] For instance, myths were used to pinpoint key landmarks that confirmed their new location which was actually their ancestral land after an earthquake destroyed their dwelling.[22]

The Wawa of Cameroon also have an account of how the masquerade used to mourn the dead came about. According to Gausset,[23] humans and the bush spirit use to live together in harmony so much so that bush spirits were invited to mourn the dead. At such funerals the bush spirits usually ate large quantities of food. At one such funeral, since there was no food, the bush spirit ate a child. To get back at the bush spirit, instead of throwing food at it, they threw a hot stone which he swallowed and then died. The people then made the wooden masks in his image. But the bush spirit is much more than the mask, masquerade and mourning of the dead

> They are also symbolically and cosmologically equivalent. On one hand, the bush spirits are called *ginaji*, a Fulfulde term with the same etymological root as our "genie." They are also called *cicangai*, a Wawa term often translated by informants as "the winds" (these spirits are supposed to travel in the wind and streams), although the term "génies" or "bush spirits" seems more accurate. On the other hand, the spirit of a human being (living or dead) is called either *hakilo* (Fulfulde term) or *foo* (Wawa term meaning "wind"). Both bush spirits and those of the dead are supposed to travel in the wind. When there is a strong wind in the village, pregnant women stay indoors to protect their babies from the bad influence of the bush spirits.[24]

But myths can also contain disinformation meant to gain undue advantage. An example is this Irish myth to the effect that "long before Columbus crossed the Atlantic, the land between Virginia and Florida was 'peopled by the Irish' and formed a 'Great Ireland' beyond the western sea."[25] Thus the Irish can eat their cake and have in that

> bringing up this tradition has three effects. First, it separates Irish people from the "white population" that oppresses these tribes. Second, it reinforces the idea of an Irish cultural past, suggesting that the Irish can claim "the honor of this discovery prior to Columbus." And finally, it imposes an origin story onto Indigenous peoples. This legend of Irish origins produces the ultimate figurative flexibility: Irish people can claim to be Indigenous, while also claiming "the honor of this discovery prior to Columbus."[26]

The myth of the two suns of the Adi people of Arunachal Pradesh in India[27] indicates that there were once two Suns that did not allow human beings to rest hence, they killed off one of them. In protest the second Sun refused to rise causing more misery for people but based on offering of lives and promises to atone for their cruelty, the living Sun, and the injured Sun rose at alternative times of the day – hence the present arrangement involving the Sun and the Moon.

Caddo Indians of the Hasinai confederacy in present day Texas have a creation myth that references a female goddess who taught them survival skills and once they could fish, hunt, build and clothe themselves she disappeared as her work was done.[28] The Khasi which is an indigenous community in Northeast India also have their own myth of origin. Nongbri tells of the tradition that indicates that the Khasi came from heaven as stated in *Ki Khanatang U Hynniewtrep* (Tales of the Seven huts).[29] They originally would climb down a tree from heaven to cultivate their fields until an evil person cut down the tree hence the seven families were stranded here on earth while the remaining nine remained in heaven.

Indra myth embodied in the *Rgveda* martial ideology from India and has three components:

> As a demiurge, Indra is the creator and sustainer of the universe. He pulls apart the world halves, Father Sky and Mother Earth, and, along with the gods *Mitra* and *Varuṇa*, he keeps the primordial parents apart with stabilizing mountains and other cosmic supports. Second, the god battles the cosmic serpent *Vrtra* (literally "Obstacle, Ensnarer") to release primordial waters, especially in the form of spring rains and snowmelt floods. Third, he smashes open a mountain cave (*vaia*) to free the sun and stolen cattle. *Vrtra* is the personification of resistance, and both the serpent and the vala cave are primordial manifestations of an enervating cosmic force that imprisons sunlight, water, life, and prosperity, especially in the form of livestock. In this vein, poets connect Indra with violent storm imagery such as thunder and lightning since such natural phenomena signify heavenly battles.[30]

Initiation ceremony among Manchinery in Western Amazonia feature "the spirits of anaconda (*jibóia*) and jaguar (*onça*), which have traditionally a central role in the Manchinery mythology."[31] As a consequence, participants who take ayahuasca are able to take these animals' perspective and learn from this mutation hence they gain special knowledge and protection.[32] The Amerindian myth of Amazon women who lived by themselves away from men claim that they have objects that allowed for societal maintenance and continuity: *ciba* stones and *guanin* ornaments among the Taino; greenstones in the lower Amazon; the *Yurupari* flutes among Tukanoan and Arawak groups; *Karokó* trumpets among the Mundurucu; ceremonial axes among the Gé-speaking Apinayé and; and bullroarers and ritual masks among the Yamana and Selk'man of Tierra del Fuego.[33]

The exchange of these objects are said to be "a necessary condition for social life."[34]

In the Indo-Iranian myth the sweet nectar of the gods (*haoma* or *soma*) was brought from heaven down to earth by a divine bird.[35] The source of the nectar in the Zoroastrian tradition of old Persia was *Gaokarena*, the tree of life which is also referred to as the White *Haoma*.[36] The sun bird facing off against a snake, reptile or fish is quite common and ubiquitous as the following examples illustrate:

> A very ancient literary source for it can be found in the Old Babylonian myth of *Etana*, in which a huge eagle which sat at the top of a great tree fought with a serpent at its base; and an evil lizard strove to eat the roots of the Old Persian *Gaokerena* Tree on which perched the *Saena*. Even in old Germanic mythology, *Odin* as an eagle, or another divine bird, nests atop the World Tree, *Ygdrasil*, while under its roots lurks the malignant dragon-serpent.[37]

The Haida and Tinglit found in the Pacific Coast (US and Canada) have a variety of myths

> such are the story of the man who was carried off by the salmon people, the story of the woman who was turned into an owl, the story of the man who obtained strength to kill sea-lions, the story of the man who made killer-whales out of wood, and the story of the hunters who changed into supernatural beings by putting themselves into the fire.[38]

The *Ningi* descent myth gives the Japanese royal family a spiritual and heavenly approval.[39] Ningi descended from heaven on Mt. Takachiho haven gotten the seal of the major deities in heaven to be the legitimate ruler of the earth and was accompanied by ancestors of warrior families and deities to serve as priests.[40] He carried the imperial regalia of a mirror, sword, and jewel.[41] Versions of this myth are also found in Korea, Mongolia, Thai of southeast China and Thailand and other parts of east and southeast Asia all attesting to the heavenly origins of their various monarchical institutions.

The Bribri earth myth of Costa Rica tells of the origin of the earth as well as of human beings.[42] At the very beginning there were just spiritual beings and Sibū (God) decides to make other people like Indians that are not spirits. So, he decides to plant corn seeds from another planet called *suLákaska* but how to make them grow became a challenge. In the planet where the corn seed is from is the Tapir who have a little fat little girl Iriria that is bedridden. God instructs his bat to go suck her blood to water the corn seeds which then germinate. Eventually the little girl's grandmother is persuaded to bring her over and during a dance she is trampled to death hence she covers the rocky surface and creates the earth. So, God planted different shades of corn that produced a diversity of Indians. It is also from this process that other races come from.

The Khasi of India's myth tells of a ladder connecting heaven and earth so that traffic was going in both directions unhindered and humans had direct interaction with God until "man's disobedience" cut off the ladder.[43] The ladder was located at "*u Lumsohpetbneng Lum- hill, sohpetbneng* (navel of heaven), a hillock adjacent to the Shillong Gauhati trunk road in Ri Bhoi district."[44] The Maui myths indicates that the *tapua* landed on the east coast of Nieu at Motu from a pool on the reef where Fao climbed up and stood with one foot. He was soon joined by his brother Huanaki and together they worked to make the island habitable.[45]

Legends

In ancient Greece and Rome we have

> UFOs in ancient Rome, prototypical vampire tales, voodoo dolls, "Poison Dresses" in ancient Greek myths, a "Choking Doberman" urban legend in the late Roman empire, the earliest recorded ghost stories Swam Maidens as "runaway brides" Greek epics in modern comics and science fiction, ancient "Ouija boards" and rumors of flexible glass as an "Improved Product" legend in ancient Rome.[46]

The legend of Llynsavathan from Wales[47] tells the story of a poor young man desirous of wining the affections of the great and beautiful heiress who was "covered" by this pool – Llynsavathan. To win her over with gold that he did not have, he killed and buried a "carrier" who had the money that he desired. With the loot in tow, he went on his way to woo the beautiful heiress. The woman of his dreams wanted to know how he came about such wealth insisting that she would not marry him until he reveals his secret. He tells her the unhappy story having sworn her to secrecy. The wedding would have gone on but for reports of a spirit troubling the area where the murdered man was buried upon which she insists that he must go back and appease the spirit as well as hear what it had to say before the wedding could go on. The young man who could kill for love was also ready to face any spirit that would stand in his way, proceeded to the burial site where he heard this sad cry: "Is there no revenge for innocent blood ?"-and another voice answer-"Not until the ninth generation." He goes back to relay the news to his lover, and they proceeded to enjoy marital bliss in the belief that they would have long died and gone to the great beyond by the time this judgement is executed. But they forgot all about this judgment and having lived to a great age called all their children and the entire lineage together for a farewell feast upon which an earthquake struck and swallowed them all alive.

Mexico has two versions of the sun and moon legend. In one a "young, strong but cowardly god" becomes the Moon while a "humble elderly god" becomes the Sun.[48] In the other version a young male god becomes the Moon while a young female goddess who is also a leper becomes the Sun.[49] The marks on the Sun is also explained by a legend. According to Ballesteros,[50] there lived an old man who had no food. He decided to plant vegetables but there was Sun in his part of town. So, he told his magical rabbit to turn into a wheelbarrow that he took to the affluent part of town, threw stones at the Sun and took the pieces that fell off in his wheelbarrow back home. He then threw the pieces as high as he could to create the sun and his fields brought forth in abundance. This explains the big black spots on the Sun. The moon, on the other hand is actually a black cat.[51] The black cat to the townspeople was a bad omen and since people bumped into each other at night as visibility was poor, they threw the poor black cat up using a rubber band and it became fixed in the sky as the Moon.[52]

Thunderbird motif is common among Amerindians from the United States to Canada.[53] It is a sky spirit that protects Indians against the great horned serpent that inhabits the underworld.[54] It is a giant eagle-bird that "causes lightning by flashing its eyes, thunder by beating its wings, and wind through the sky. It lives in the sky and devours serpents."[55] The hornbill, according to the Bambara and Malinke legend, is the king of the birds because none of them had names until they came to pay condolences to the hornbill when his father died. They came away with different names afterwards.[56] According to one version of an Hungarian legend, Almos originating from the *turul* bird-ancestor was the first prince![57]

The raven according to Inuit legend used to be white in colour.[58] Here goes how it got its black colour. The raven and the loon in their prior human form decided to tattoo each other.[59]

> The raven began tattooing the loon first, creating the checkered patterns now characteristic of its plumage. For unknown reasons the raven quickly became impatient and threw ashes all over the loon – forever colouring its back grey. Angrily, the loon scraped soot from the bottom of a cooking pot,

which was often used as pigment for tattoos, and covered the raven with it – turning it completely black.[60]

In Cambodia, there is a legend of a duel between two *Neak Ta*. The father of a beautiful girl decides that his daughter will marry *Neak Ta Phnom* (mountain) but *Neak Ta Dtuek* (water) causes flooding to carry away his rival but *Neak Ta Phnom* creates a mountain that holds the lake at the top thus claiming victory.[61]

Semiramis is celebrated for feats of civil engineering so much so "that towns were called after her name far beyond the limits of the Semitic land."[62] Earthworks, walls, strongholds, aqueducts and stair-like roads over mountains, canals, roads and bridges throughout Euphrates and Iran as well as Behistun inscription of Darius are credited to her. Semiramis was of course "a goddess and a form of Astarte."[63] All her lovers were said to be buried alive but "being gods, they lived and received homage in their graves."[64]

A feared demoness used to live in Dudphung, Bhutan and when a *Masang* playing a *Degor* flew over her abode she issued this threat: "You, come here. I will swallow you at once."[65] The *Masang* threw his *Degor* and *Pungdos* at the clearly irritated demoness. Upon realizing that this was a manifestation of the Buddha she tried to escape by digging a hole, but she was captured upon which she pledged never to attack any human being ever.[66] Then the Masang blessed the environment hence its peace and prosperity till date.[67]

The Bantu legend of how a crocodile became a sacred creature goes to the issue of rivalry between the eldest son of the chief and the son from his youngest wife who is heir to the throne.[68] The former because of his position holding fort for the heir begins to scheme to take over goaded on by the first wife who is now neglected. Eventually his younger brother takes the throne and sends him into exile. While in exile, a crocodile comes along and they had this conversation:

"Hail, chief!"
He replied, "I am no chief, I am an empty-handed wanderer. I came here to die with my friends."
"Hoe a garden and put pumpkin seed in it," said the- crocodile, and departed.[69]

The new chief instead of being content with his position sends soldiers to steal the pumpkin which his older brother planted as advised by the crocodile from which emerged a leopard that killed everyone in the chief's hut and the older brother comes back to the village as the new chief.

Sekatoa of Tonga is the stuff of which legends are indeed made. In one account, imps from Samoa stole Tafahi leaving a crater in its place and Sekatoa saved the day by sending a devil to crow like a cock after them.[70] The second and third crow be sent served to increase the speed of the fleeing thieves hence he arranged for an impromptu sunrise which made the imps drop off their ill-gotten goods in the sea which accounts for the present location of the island.[71] But if the thieves had paid attention to the sunrise they would have realized that it was the head of Sekatoa rising from the sea and not from the horizon as the Sun was wont to![72]

The Irish popular legend seems to involve extending generosity to those not in need with drinking at the heart of it all. Take this typically interesting account from the home of Guinness:

> the kamikaze Irish drinker who will continue to coma or until all available liquor is consumed. The object is not to forget but to make something happen. Imminence of revelation – the most exciting (no, second most exciting) sensation known to man. If you are making an *eejit* of yourself or look like doing so soon there will be plenty to buy you as much as you can hold (or more). This is money invested, not given. Kavanagh has pointed out that when he was penniless and starving there was always somebody buying drink but no one to give him a shilling for a chop. Similarly, to refuse a drink is to reject not just a glass of liquid **but an entire culture** (emphasis added).[73]

The nature of popular legends like in this instance is that they are sometimes associated with a particular geographic location.[74]

The Bigfoot phenomena seems to bridge cultural boundaries as it is not just a Western concept more so as there have been increased Bigfoot sightings from the 1940s.[75] In fact, the medieval wild man is impacted by the prevailing social, political, and economic conditions that in turn affects people's cosmology and their relationship with nature.[76] Parallels to the bigfoot phenomena include *sasquatch* and *yeti*. Other manifestations of wild humanoids have been reported "throughout Asia from the steppes to the forests; Southeast Asia, Indonesia and Australia; and throughout the Americas."[77] Changes in people's perception of such phenomenon indicates a longing for the pristine in nature and are also fairly consistent across the ages from medieval times to the present: "from fear, to sympathy, to neutrality and finally to admiration."[78]

New legends which are a rehash of the past is also making inroads. The baby parts and satanic legends are quite common in western Europe and the United States.[79] For the latter the rationale is that the blood of preadolescent children is efficacious, but the grand plan is to subvert the entire social system.[80] But this killing and dismembering of children as well as other satanic practices also go way back and is quite widespread. It was

> attributed to Jews before the Christian era by Greeks; by Romans to first century Christians; even by Christians to other sects of Christians ... Its attachment by Christians to Jews in the 14th to 17th centuries became very elaborate .... It is not uniquely Western; it has been recorded in Islamized areas, and in all regions of the world by tribal peoples against each other, against colonial government and even against anthropologists.[81]

Still on the baby parts and satanism, anti-Jewish demonology legend involves the "Black Mass" whose Eucharist is the blood and flesh of a virgin girl or infant as well as the inverted cross.[82] Clearly, Africa and Asia are not alone when occultic and satanic practices come up for mention.

Conclusion

Making sense of the world we live in was the raison détre for myths and legends among societies and peoples from the very beginning. But their continued relevance is also shown in appeals to stories of origin, accomplishments of ancestors, superiority of the tribe and other sentiments to achieve contemporary goals. Myths and legends are available everywhere in the world in spite of our level of development and civilization sometimes taking the form of popular culture that assists in passing them along to the next generation. The communication properties inherent therein are numerous including cementing tribal and national identity as well as sense of pride, conveying s sense of our common humanity given the similarities in the myths and legends and conveying valuable lessons, morals and values as well as their entertainment value amongst others.

Notes

1. Canizo, T.L. (1994). Legends and myths of the sky. *Science Scope*, 17(6), Special issue: Science for All, 31–33.
2. Nongbri, T. (2006). Culture and biodiversity: Myths, legends and the conservation of nature in the hills of North-East India. *Indian Anthropologist*, (36) 1/2, Special issue on Folk narratives 1–21.
3. Price, M.T. (1946). Differentiating Myth, legend, and history in Ancient Chinese Culture. *American Anthropologist*, 48(1), 31–42.
4. Canizo, T.L. (1994).
5. Peyton, H.H. (1969). Myths and legends. *Interpretations*, 2(1), 31–36, pp. 31–32.
6. Swanton, J.R. (1910). Some practical aspects of the study of myths. *The Journal of American Folklore*, 23 (87), 1–7.
7. Carloye, J.C. (1980). Myths as religious explanations. *Journal of the American Academy of Religion*, 48(2), 175–189.
8. Nongbri, T. (2006).
9. Price, M.T. (1946).
10. Carloye, J.C. (1980).
11. Nongbri, T. (2006).
12. Sandor. A. (1991). Myths and the fantastic. *New Literary History*, 22(2), Probings: Art, Criticism, Genre (Spring), 339–358.
13. Sandor. A. (1991), p. 484.
14. Stevens, Jr., P. (1990). "New" legends: Some perspectives from Anthropology. Western Folklore, (49)1, Contemporary Legends in Emergence, 121–133.
15. Stevens, Jr., P. (1990), p. 122.
16. Uzoigwe, G.N. (1980). Oral literature and African history. *Transafrican Journal of History*, 9(1–2), 18–41.
17. Uzoigwe, G.N. (1980).
18. Uzoigwe, G.N. (1980).
19. Stevens, P. (1990). "New" Legends: Some perspectives from anthropology. *Western Folklore*, 49(1), Contemporary Legends in Emergence, 121–133.
20. Gnecco, C., & Hernández, C. (2008). History and Its discontents: Stone Statues, native histories, and archaeologists. Current Anthropology, 49(3), 439–466. https://doi.org/10.1086/588497
21. Gnecco, C., & Hernández, C. (2008), pp. 442–443.
22. Gnecco, C., & Hernández, C. (2008).
23. Gausset, Q. (2001). Masks and identity. The significance of masquerades in the symbolic cycle linking the living, the dead, and the bush spirits among the Wawa (Cameroon). Anthropos, 96(1), 193–200.

24. Gausset, Q. (2001), p. 196.
25. Mullen, M. L. (2016). How the Irish Became Settlers: Metaphors of Indigeneity and the Erasure of Indigenous Peoples. *New Hibernia Review/Iris Éireannach Nua*, 20(3), 81–96, p. 88.
26. Mullen, M. L. (2016), p. 88.
27. Chaudhuri, S. K. (2013). The *Institutionalization of Tribal Religion*: Recasting the Donyi-Polo movement in Arunachal Pradesh. *Asian Ethnology*, 72(2), 259–277.
28. Barr, J. (2004). A diplomacy of gender: Rituals of first contact in the "Land of the Tejas." *The William and Mary Quarterly*, 61(3), 393–434. https://doi.org/10.2307/3491803
29. Nongbri, T. (2006).
30. Whitaker, J. (2016). I Boldly Took the Mace (Vájra) for Might: Ritually Weaponizing a Warrior's Body in Ancient India. *International Journal of Hindu Studies*, 20(1), 51–94.
31. Virtanen, P. K. (2006). The urban Manchinery youth and social capital in Western Amazonian contemporary rituals. *Anthropos*, 101(1), 159–167.
32. Virtanen, P. K. (2006), p. 163.
33. Steverlynck, A. (2008). Amerindian Amazons: Women, exchange, and the origins of society. *The Journal of the Royal Anthropological Institute*, 14(3), 572–589.
34. Steverlynck, A. (2008), p. 573.
35. Cammann, S. (1957). Ancient symbols in modern Afghanistan. *Ars Orientalis*, 2, 5–34.
36. Cammann, S. (1957).
37. Cammann, S. (1957), p. 9.
38. Swanton, J.R. (1905). Types of Haida and Tlingit myths. *American Anthropologist*, New Series, 7(1), 94–103M, p. 94.
39. Taryō, Ō. (1984). Japanese myths of descent from Heaven and their Korean parallels. *Asian Folklore Studies*, 43(2), 171–184. https://doi.org/10.2307/1178007
40. Taryō, Ō. (1984).
41. Taryō, Ō. (1984).
42. Nygren, A. (1998). Struggle over meanings: Reconstruction of *Indigenous Mythology, Cultural Identity, and Social Representation*. *Ethnohistory*, 45(1), 31–63.
43. Nongbri, T. (2006), p. 3.
44. Nongbri, T. (2006), pp. 3–4.
45. Nunn, P. D. (2004). Myths and the formation of Niue Island, Central South Pacific. *The Journal of Pacific History*, 39(1), 99–108.

46. Mayor, A. (2000). Bibliography of classical folklore scholarship: Myths, legends, and popular beliefs of Ancient Greece and Rome. *Folklore*, (111)1, 123–138, p. 124.
47. The Cambro-Briton (1821). *The Legend of Llynsavathan*, 2(21), 399–402.
48. Canizo, T.L. (1994), pp. 31–32.
49. Canizo, T.L. (1994).
50. Ballesteros, M. (1994). Marks on the Sun. *Science Scope*, 17(6), Special issue: Science for All, 32.
51. Verdugo, R. (1994). How the black cat is the Moon. Marks on the Sun. *Science Scope*, 17(6), Special issue: Science for All, 32.
52. Verdugo, R. (1994).
53. Lenik, E.J. (2012). The thunderbird motif in Northeastern Indian art. *Archaeology of Eastern North America*, 40, 163–185.
54. Lenik, E.J. (2012).
55. Lenik, E.J. (2012), p. 163.
56. Imperato, P. J. (1980). Bambara and Malinke Ton masquerades. *African Arts*, 13(4), 47–87. https://doi.org/10.2307/3335784
57. Györffy, G. (1994). Dual kingship and the seven chieftains of the Hungarians in the era of the conquest and the raids. *Acta Orientalia Academiae Scientiarum Hungaricae*, 47(1/2), 87–104.
58. Jelinski, J. (2018). "If only it makes them pretty". *Collections arctiques/Arctic Collections*, 42 (1), 211–242.
59. Jelinski, J. (2018).
60. Jelinski, J. (2018), p. 212.
61. O'Lemmon, M. (2014). Spirit cults and Buddhist practice in Kep Province, Cambodia. *Journal of Southeast Asian Studies*, 45(1), 25–49.
    Smith, W. R. (1887). Ctesias and the Semiramis Legend. *The English Historical Review*, 2(6), 303–317.
62. Smith, W. R. (1887). Ctesias and the Semiramis legend. The English Historical Review, 2(6), 303–317, p. 304.
63. Smith, W. R. (1887), p. 305.
64. Smith, W. R. (1887), p. 307.
65. Dorji, T. C. (2010). Preserving our folktales, myths and legends in the digital era. *Storytelling, Self, Society*, 6(1), 19–38, p. 25.
66. Dorji, T. C. (2010).
67. Dorji, T. C. (2010).
68. Macdonald, J. (1892). Bantu customs and legends. *Folklore*, 3(3), 337–359.
69. Macdonald, J. (1892), pp. 340–341.
70. Taylor, P. W. (1995). Myths, legends and volcanic activity: An example from northern Tonga. *The Journal of the Polynesian Society*, 104(3), 323–346.
71. Taylor, P. W. (1995).

72. Taylor, P. W. (1995).
73. Foley, M. (1987). Irish myths and legends. *Fortnight, 248*, 25.
74. Sandor. A. (1991).
75. Stevens, P. (1990).
76. Stevens, P. (1990).
77. Stevens, P. (1990), p. 123.
78. Stevens, P. (1990), p. 123.
79. Stevens, P. (1990).
80. Stevens, P. (1990).
81. Stevens, P. (1990), p. 129.
82. Stevens, P. (1990).

CHAPTER 12

Conclusion – Indigenous Communication Around the World

Documentation of indigenous communication across the globe involving instrumental communication, demonstrative communication, iconographic communication, extra-mundane communication, visual communication, institutional communication, venue-oriented communication, taxonomic communication and axiomatic communication has been the focus of this excursion. It also covered some philosophical and epistemological issues that served to compare and contrast indigenous scholarship with Western paradigms. All in all, this has served to underline the global nature of indigenous communication and hopefully make it take its pride of place in the pantheon of media and communication studies. More so as there are increasing calls to have indigenous intellectual and cultural heritage recognized as legitimate knowledge systems just like their Western counterparts.[1] This excursion attempts to bring indigenous communication into the fold. But in doing this, to be avoided in seeking validation based on Western knowledge as this results in "appropriating, tokenizing, and exploiting these knowledges."[2] So we approach this on an equal footing, as it should be.

In Chap. 1 we see the ubiquity of colonized and oppressed peoples with some estimate of 350 million indigenous people in 70 countries worldwide.[3] The oppression they were subjected to was not only intended to break their spirit but to ensure that they discard their tried and tested ways of life for those of the oppressors and colonizers. While colonialists have done the most damage and this continues in some instances till today, other settler groups are equally complicit. In many instances, the new way of life has damaged the environment and decimated indigenous peoples and impaired their way of life irretrievably. The ray of hope is that indigenous studies and research are reviving these cultural practices and showing to Western scholars and others that their existence is no threat as the sky is big enough to accommodate all viewpoints. Indigenous communication is located within Indigenous Knowledge Systems (IKS) and as the acknowledgement and revival of IKS takes hold scholars from every hue and cry must make their voices heard. This is one such attempt from a communication perspective. Just as the revival of IKS has clearly indicated that such knowledge and resources are tailored to and effective in meeting local needs so also this treatise that is intended to make indigenous communication takes its pride of place in the IKS pantheon. The various elements we have looked at can be deployed for effective communication that is targeting indigenous people because of the emotional connections and cues that they elicit.

In Chap. 2 we review literature that point to the fact that indigenous scholarship is at par with that of their western counterparts given the effort put in by indigenous scholars to make it come into its own. These efforts revolve around surfacing indigenous philosophical worldview, research methodologies and designs. We endorse the constructivist and transformative worldviews which rightly offers redress in scholarship on indigenous studies. This chapter also locates and properly situates indigenous paradigms, methodologies and designs in any investigation into indigenous communities. This would assist scholars interested in doing research in indigenous communities. But we cannot but also mention that the inequities and injustices that have pervaded relationships between settlers/colonialists and indigenous groups have also reared it ugly head here with scholarship privileging Western perspectives over and above those of others. The bad blood may throw spanners in the works as regards collaborative research given the abuses and denial of research benefits to indigenous peoples whose gems have been stolen, whose resources have been appropriated and whose lives have been negatively impacted. That this discussion even taking place shows some progress towards the table of brotherhood and mutual understanding.

In Chap. 3 we discuss instrumental communication that say a lot about society in which they found in that they have symbolic roles and meanings

12 CONCLUSION – INDIGENOUS COMMUNICATION AROUND THE WORLD

as well as play significant roles in ritual, music and dance.[4] Musical instruments – drums, chordophones, aerophones, bells, gongs and cymbals; trumpets, clarinet and animal horns and; clappers and rattles have a critical role to play in cultural research in addition to communicating about the mental and spiritual life of a people through their secular and ritual deployments.[5] They speak to the musical achievement of a people as well as the cultural importance of their music.[6] They are made from locally available material and their effective deployment in personal and community affairs is worth noting. Whether it is a love interest recognizing your peculiar tune and responding to the overtures or for occupational uses of for the enactment of a unified community response these speak to the effectiveness of these instruments and it is best to continue to deploy them given the resonance they have in these communities and people living therein.

Chapter 4 excursion into music shows it connection to every aspect of life such as entertainment, religious and sacred occasions, funerals, education, travel, comforting and soothing children to sleep, love and the entirety of life. Indigenous communities have their own peculiar songs and themes, but music also serve communication functions reflecting longings of the heart, philosophies of life, hope for the future etc. They take on local colorations not just in terms of categorizations but also in deployment and use. The chapter surfaces various types of music and performances from around the world thus pointing to our common humanity. But very unique ways in which music comes into play in the affairs of various groups makes this chapter a gem with lots of takeaways from a communication perspective. As it is music is deployed in movies and other forms of popular culture quite effectively. This offers more variety that can be tapped into for social marketing, products, survive advertising and content production. Let every music from every part of the globe play on.

Chapter 5 explores signs and symbols that through heavy use have acquired rich connotations and consequently convey powerful meanings that are clearly understood and are recognizable by members of a community. They include feathered ornaments, canoes, nudity, penis sheath, lip plugs, body paint, shell middens, eucalyptus smoke, rock engravings headdress, ear plugs, beads, headdress, feathers, Pollera, whips, rock paintings, Indian heads, tomahawk, and teepees, hei tiki, tā moko, stone carvings, water, black pottery of San Bartolo, the weavings of Teotitlán, the ceramic skeletons of Capula, the lacquered boxes of Olinalá, marks on the barks of trees, floral patterns, message sticks, shells, *Ulu* or crescent-shaped knives, Twill-plaited baskets, rice, water buffaloes, bison horns and peacock feathers Indigenous signs and symbols have evolved from being derided and looked down upon to been accepted and even misappropriated and misused. The interests in the forms of iconographic communication makes them a work in progress as there is a lot to learn from these indigenous forms particularly the forms of writing to which a lot of scholarly attention has been devoted. But more work is still required to fully understand the length and breadth of these indigenous forms of communication so that these communities take their pride of place in the narrative about human progress and civilization.

Chapter 6 discuses extra-mundane communication that goes beyond the realm of intra-personal, interpersonal and mass communication to embrace supernatural beings – ancestors, spirits, gods, the supreme God – or when they involve processes, elements or abilities that are superhuman as in witchcraft, reincarnation etc. More so as the supernatural is a natural part of the indigenous experience and worldview with the earth, the seen and unseen world perceived as intimately linked and connected. The global outlook of this chapter takes a sweep at indigenous religious practices across the globe. The syncretism that is apparent in this excursion is unmissable. Indigenous religious practices have not remained untouched by the goings-on around them. The numerous examples from every part of the world adds to the richness of this chapter and clearly indicates that spiritually is part and parcel of the human experience in spite of all attempts to scientifically explain everything which is akin to fetching water in a basket – a clearly impossible undertaking.

Chapter 7 details the cues supplied by one's physical appearance, clothing, hairdo, tribal marks, tattoos, incisions and other marks on the body. It showed that the skin can be encoded to convey messages. While indigenous clothing, accessories, body art in general have experienced a revival, they have also been impacted by colonialists and encounters with other cultures as this excursion has demonstrated. We have equally come a long way from the dark age of equating body modification with self-harm that requires psychiatric intervention.[7] The modern iteration manifested in plastic surgery has taken on a life of its own but, sadly, the art form is dying off apart from tattoos that have become quite popular. Clearly, indigenous forms of body art have rich communication properties from clan identification to aesthetics and spiritual purposes.

Chapter 8 discussed indigenous institutions such as the traditional ruler, secret societies, age grades, kinship and family, masquerade and marriage. The institutions are revered for reasons which include powers – spiritual and temporal – which they possess. They make for good order in society and they played their role before the colonialists came along to displace, replace and change them. Indigenous forms of leadership have seen more interventions that the other institutions. Interestingly, the institutions seem to have a global spread particularly secret societies and masquerades and have the same roles and function across the board which speaks to commonalities among human beings despite all the othering taking place in our world today. The communication component of the masquerades clearly points to democratization across classes and gender. Even though the repertoire of communication media we have today was not present, the kinship and family descent groups still could tell their roles and enacted same given the socialization process they had undergone. This speaks to effective communication with the little that was available.

Chapter 9 focus was the sites in which indigenous communication take place. Of course, communication is a continuing activity that is not limited to any site. It involved a sweep of habitation patterns, markets, whose primary purpose is buying and selling of goods but that also exhibit communication function is within the ambit of this chapter. The communication function in settlements is clear from the ties between indigenous people and the lands they occupy as these have deep spiritual and sentimental values. Markets also exhibit communication functions in a variety of ways including differentiating between various classes.

Chapter 10's focus was on names and the fact they communicate lots of information about their owners, his or her family and communal values. In addition to being markers of family connections, names have been deployed to effect social and political changes are reflective of various circumstances surrounding the coming into being of a people, their location, special or unique features, identification with animals (totems), their particular behaviour, strengths or skills amongst others. This of study of naming does reveal a lot about the cultural attitudes.[8]

Chapter 11's covered myths and legends which are significant windows into people's worldview. They are an integral part of different cultures around the world. Be that as it may, myths supply historical and other information while legends supply an explanation of the human condition and how people have come to adapt to challenges in their peculiar environments. The ubiquity of myths and legends point to our common humanity as there are no societies in which they are not present. They have made their presence felt in popular culture as well as village folktales.

Conclusions and Way Forward

A takeaway from this excursion is that cultures are clearly porous and embrace other cultures and their practices.[9] This is a recurring theme that indicates that we do not live in an insular world. We hope that this discussion shows that decimating whole cultures and people does not add any value as everyone can make a worthwhile contribution to human progress. But this sadly was the case as colonialists and settler groups made superiority and ethnocentrism central to their need to dominate and decimate indigenous groups and their sentient landscape. However, the fact remains that progress of any kind and in any field whether acknowledged or not involved stolen indigenous knowledges based on early and continuing human contact. This is apparent from our discussion of colonial architecture in West Africa but even science is not immune as "many elements of *modern* science (modern medicine, agriculture, mathematics, etc.) are partly rooted in indigenous knowledge principles, a historical truism which is often neglected."[10]

The movement of people back and forth is an ongoing and continuing phenomenon that clearly has no end in sight. Whether it is colonialists seeking new territories to "discover", people fleeing wars and natural disaster, seeking for a better income and way of life etc., migration has come to stay, and we need to have a way of making the most of it for everyone. The UK is a good example because in 2021

> a third of pupils in the UK come from an ethnic minority background (33.9% of primary school pupils and 32.1% of secondary school pupils). While 80.3% of pupils were recorded as having a first language known or believed to be English, some 1.6 million (19.2%) were recorded as having a first language other than English.[11]

Even Japan which appears homogenous to outsiders is clearly not. In fact, this viewpoint has been characterized as an "invented tradition".[12] This is because there are indigenous groups such as the "Ainu people of the northern island of Hokkaidō; the Burakumin, who are commonly described as descendants of outcast groups in feudal Japan; the Ryūkyū Islanders from the prefecture of Okinawa; and Korean long-term residents known as *zainichi Kankokujin*".

While we do not seek a united front informed by conceit and arrogance of the Babel that wanted a tower that would make a name for themselves, there is clearly room under the sky for human diversity to thrive and flourish. It is known fact that in the field of science, technology, engineering, and mathematics (STEM), for instance, diverse groups outperform homogenous groups in the indices of innovation, creativity, problem solving and innovation.[13] Even though there exists evidence of geothermal exploitation in Peru during the Inca and Pre-Inca times, yet these resources have remained unexploited and it is only in recent times that the regions sitting on this gold mine are awakening to its use and making efforts in this direction.[14] This failure speaks to the marginalization of indigenous knowledge in favour of received wisdom which has damaged the planet when there is clean energy for the taking. An approach that is diverse and accommodating has implication for communication effectiveness. For instance, a diverse team is more likely to come up with messaging that is least likely to cause offence and be rejected outright as such an issue can be flagged and addressed before flighting the message thus ensuring acceptance and effectiveness.

The rich communication properties of this discussion should not escape our attention. The emotional connection that these elements and cues have, given their intimate connections with these communities offer a window of opportunity for their effective deployment in any communication endeavour from getting attention, generating interest as well as behaviour change. In climate change literacy such an approach is already in play by ensuring that "climate information is available through trusted information and service providers and in languages that minorities and migrant and displaced populations understand, and is shared through communication channels that are accessible, including through local, traditional, and indigenous knowledge systems."[15] Communities in Nepal are being engaged with to reduce biological hazards, risks, and disasters as we speak.[16] More so as a marginalized communities such as the Chepang Indigenous group reported that they did not have the information required to assist them navigate health and financial issues. In the United States "Black, Indigenous, people of color (BIPOC), low income, and rural communities have borne the disproportionate effects of air pollution, hazardous chemicals, contaminated drinking water, and other environmental hazards."[17]

This is the bane of outreach efforts to many rural and indigenous communities globally and deploying the systems we have identified will make for effective communication, behavior change as well as the achievement of whatever other objectives such initiatives and programmes were set up to achieve in the first place. But to be acknowledged is the ambivalent relationship between the past in which many of these indigenous knowledges occupy or come from and the present. This recourse to the past "highlight injustices that require redress ... [and} ancient glories that should be restored" but it also "contains politically potent symbols of old loyalties that new ruling groups would prefer to expunge from the collective consciousness."[18] Yet, there is room for this discussion and engagement as the advantages to be gained far outweigh the ethnocentricity and arrogance that are evil winds that add no value to humanity. A better ending to this book cannot be better that the example of Young Timorese who travel to Australia for seasonal work because for these workers "leaving their homeland to work was not so much an opportunity to escape social and ritual duties to which their families hold them accountable **as to acquire the wealth to service them better** (emphasis added)."[19] In other words, no sunset in the horizon for IKS.

NOTES

1. Knopf, K. (2015). The turn toward the indigenous: knowledge systems and practices in the academy. *Amerikastudien/American Studies, 60*(2/3), 179–200.
2. Knopf, K. (2015), p. 183.
3. Alfred, T., & Corntassel, J. (2005). Politics of identity – IX: Being indigenous: Resurgences against contemporary colonialism. *Government and Opposition, 40*(4), 597–614.
4. Oliver, P. (1988). Musico-ethnological approaches to musical instruments. *Popular Music, 7*(2), 216–218.
5. Boulton, L. (1974). The Laura Boulton Collection of world music and musical instruments. *College Music Symposium, 14*, 127–130.
6. Boulton, L. (1974).
7. Pitts, V. (2004). Debating body projects: Reading "Tattooed" [Review of Tattooed: The sociogenesis of a body art, by M. Atkinson]. Health, 8(3), 380–386.
8. Clark, C. (1987). English personal names CA. 650–1300: Some prosopographical bearings. *Medieval Prosopography, 8*(1), 31–60.
9. Moore, P. (2007). Negotiated Identities: The evolution of Dene Tha and Kaska personal naming systems. *Anthropological Linguistics, 49*(3/4), 283–307.
10. Fre, Z. (2018). The case for indigenous knowledge systems and knowledge sovereignty. In Knowledge Sovereignty Among African Cattle

Herders (pp. 12–32). UCL Press. https://doi.org/10.2307/j.ctv3hvc5n.7, p. 12.
11. Williams, C. H. (2023). Creating synergies in comparative multilingualism: An epilogue. In S. Björklund & M. Björklund (Eds.), Policy and practice for multilingual educational settings: Comparisons across Contexts (Vol. 138, pp. 198–212). Multilingual Matters / Channel View Publications. https://doi.org/10.2307/jj.1231861.12
12. Malitz, D. (2023). Shinkoku: Reconsidering the concept of sentient landscapes from Japan. In A. Coțofană & H. Kuran (Eds.), Sentient ecologies: Xenophobic imaginaries of landscape (Vol. 31, pp. 160–185). Berghahn Books. https://doi.org/10.2307/j.ctv36cj81n.11
13. Meyer-Gutbrod, E. L., Pierson, J. J., & Behl, M. (2023). Community perspectives on justice, equity, diversity, and inclusion in ocean sciences: A town hall discussion. *Oceanography, 36*(1), 67–73.
14. Berg, R. C., Cohen, K., Rubio, J., & Guzman, A. (2023). Turning up the heat on geothermal energy development in Latin America: Varying scenarios for Costa Rica, El Salvador, and Peru. Center for Strategic and International Studies (CSIS).
15. Simpson, N., & Rosengaertner, S. (2023). Boosting Adaptation Through Climate Change Literacy in Africa. South African Institute of International Affairs, p. 1.
16. Tran, M., Niraula, D., Pottinger-Glass, C., Khoza, S., Dhungana, G., & Nitsch, C. (2023). *Inclusive urban development to reduce biological hazards and disaster risks: A case study of Bharatpur, Nepal.* Stockholm Environment Institute.
17. Union of Concerned Scientists. (2023). Getting science back on track: Voices of scientists across six federal agencies. Union of Concerned Scientists, p. 1.
18. Ginsberg, B., & Bachner, J. (2023). Reshaping the past to change the present. In Warping time: How contending political forces manipulate the past, present, and future (pp. 18–52). University of Michigan Press, p. 18.
19. Rose, M. (2023). The frente ekonomika (economic front): Timorese perspectives on seasonal work in Australia. In K. Silva, L. Palmer, & T. Cunha (Eds.), *Economic diversity in contemporary Timor-Leste* (pp. 295–312). Leiden University Press, p. 298.

Index

A
Aerophones, 38–42, 48
  pipes and flutes, 38, 39, 41
  whistles, 38
Africa, 10, 96
African Americans, 142
African indigenous knowledge, 10
Age grades, 138–140
Ancestors, 97
Ancestral homes, 5
Ancestral land, 151
Ancient Egypt, 58
Anglo-indigenous historical identification, 173
Animal horns, 43–47
Arizona, 3
  Mount Graham, 3
Atoin Meto-culture, 118
Australia, 2, 70
  Australian Aborigines, 3
  Indigenous Australians, 3
Australian, 2
Axiomatic communication, 181–190
  legends, 181, 182
  myths, 181, 182

B
Bagpipe, 41
Bangladesh, 8
Bantu legend, 188
Belgian, 18
"The bell of kings," 43
Bells, 42–43
  big bell (*see* Gōzen Glocken)
  Church bells, 42
  small metal bells, 42
  war bells (*see* Campanas)
Boasting songs, 69
Botswana, 57, 79
British colonialists, 125, 140
Bronze gong, 43

C
Cameroon marriage, 134
Cameroon's masquerades, 137
Campanas, 42
Canada, 3
  First Nation Peoples (*see* Poachers)
Candles and scented perfume, 103
Catholic missionaries, 39

Chieftaincy, 140–142
Chile, 48, 58
Chinese, 5
Chordophones, 35–38
Clappers, 47–48
Clarinet, 43–47
Classical dance ritual, 99
Colonial settlers, 153
Columbia, 2
  Wounaan people, 2
  Wounaan's cultural survival, 3
Community-Based Participatory Research (CBPR), 20
Congo, 35
Critical Indigenous Research Methodologies (CIRM), 21
Cylindrical drums, 34
Cymbals, 42–43

D
Dances, 61
  gender dimension, 61
Dar es Salaam, 98
Decolonizing Methodologies, 8
Dehumanize, 18
Demonstrative communication, 57–72
Denmark, 41
Dirge, 64–65
Double bell, *see* The bell of kings

E
Egypt, 58
Elgeeii centralized farm system, 4
Emancipatory methodologies, 19
Entertainment, 60–62
Epistemology of indigenous knowledge, 19
Estonians, 41
Ethiopia, 154
Ethnomusicologist, 57
European colonialism, 4
European colonialists, 5
European settlers, 5
Experiential knowledge, 11
Extra-mundane communication, 26, 95–109, 198
  bottom-up communication, 102
  global outlook, 96
  top-down communication, 104

F
Finnish, 18
Folk music, 66
French colonialists, 18

G
Ga community, 34
Game songs, 61
Ghana, 34
Ginguru, 38
Goat horn, 44
Gongs, 42–43
Gōzen Glocken, 42
Graphical scripts, 88
Group mimetic dance, 60

H
Hainan Island, 39
Hoklo
  native Taiwanese, 5
Holism, 11

I
Iconic, 83–84
Iconographic communication, 77–89
  types and uses, 77
Indexical, 84
Indigeneity, 78
  See also Indigenous
Indigenist Research Methodology, 21

Indigenous Australians, 21
Indigenous clothing, 126, 198
Indigenous communication, 11–12, 17–26, 149, 195–202
　classification, 17, 22–26
　gesture, 25
　models, 17, 22–26
Indigenous communities, 7, 24, 72, 151, 196
Indigenous culture, 11, 70
Indigenous dispossession, 78
Indigenous epistemologies, 21
Indigenous ethnic group, 170
Indigenous forms, 82
Indigenous group, 4, 5, 8
　Ecuadorian Amazon, 5
Indigenous icons and symbols, 80
Indigenous inhabitants, 159
Indigenous knowledge, 4, 8–11, 200
　philosophical worldview, 17–19
Indigenous Koori, 78
Indigenous language, 24
Indigenous methodologies, 20
Indigenous names, 173
Indigenous people, 4, 5, 9, 11, 18, 59, 62, 81, 107, 115, 196
　dehumanization (*see* Dehumanize)
　marginalized indigenous peoples, 5
Indigenous religious, 9, 97
Indigenous research methodologies, 19–22
Indigenous rights, 5
Indigenous settlements, 153
Indigenous signs and symbols, 89, 198
Indigenous societies, 6
Indigenous values, 19
Institutional communication, 133–144
　marriage, 133
Instrumental communication, 31–48, 196
　Ancient Chinese drums, 32
　Bombitos or little drums, 33
　drums, 32
　Marquesan drum, 33
　Pohnpei of Micronesia's drum, 33
　Stone drum or Keho, 33
Instruments
　goat horn, 44
Intra-village communication, 24
Irish people, 5
Irish popular legend, 189
Italian, 18
Ivory horn, 45

J
Juggling game song, 61
Jump rope song, 62

K
Kalirangwe, 37
Kanaka Maoli, 8
Kenya, 37
Kettle drums, 34
Khweru, 41
Kinship, 138–140
Korea, 8
KwaZulu-Natal, 141

L
Latvia, 37
Latvian folk, 59
Latvians, 41
Leadership, 140–142
Legends, 186–190
Lilieh, 40
Lithuania, 37
Lithuanian music, 44
Lithuanian musical instrument, 60
Local Chinese markets, 156
Long drum, 35
Love songs, 69
Lullaby, 67–68
Lyrics, 68

M
Malay music, 35
Malaysia, 34
Malay traditional musical performances, 43
Mantra culture, 63
Markets, 155–159
Masquerade, 135–138
Maya scripts, 86
Message sticks, 82
Metal horns, 45
Methodology, 20
Mixtec tradition, 107
Mochica, 45
Modelling, 23
Mondo, Mbudikidi, 35
Mourning ritual, 65
  acoustics, 65
  ancestor worship, 65
  musicality, 65
  stylized, 65
Murali, 40
Musical instruments, 45, 48, 58, 197
Myths, 183

N
Namibia, 2, 117
  Himbas, 117
  Katutura, 2
  Kavango, 64
  Namibian, 2
Native American, 7
Native inhabitants, 78
Nature of popular legends, 189
New legends, 190
Nghana
  Akan, 34
Nigeria, 34
Nigerian markets, 157

O
Occupation of ancestral lands, 7
One indigenous group, 6

P
Periodic markets, 155
Personal knowledge, 11
Philippines, 5
Philosophical worldview of Indigenous knowledge, 17–19
Pictographic decorations, 97
Pipes
  bagpipe, 41
  and flutes, 38
  Panpipe, 41
Poachers, 18
Poncho market, 158
Portuguese, 2
Postpositivist approach, 9
Pragmatic, 10
Praise songs, 70–71
Private communication, 37

R
Rattles, 47–48
Religious, 62–64
Religious music, 63
Ritual dance, 107
Rituals, 107

S
Same-sex marriage, 9
Sámi people, 2, 4, 18
Secret rites, 143
Secret societies, 142–143
Segaba, 35–36
Settlement patterns, 150–155

Settler groups, 5
Seventeenth century Swedish masquerades, 136
Signs and symbols, 197
Slit drum, *see* Mondo, Mbudikidi
Source, Message Channel, Receiver (SMCR), 24
South Africa, 2, 141
  South Africans, 2
Soviet Union, 4
Spiritual communication, 43
Statues of gods, 99
String instruments, 36
Sub-Saharan Africa, 9, 153
Syllabic writing, 88

T
Taiwan, 8
Tanzania, 9
  culture, 9
Tattoos and scars, 121–123, 125
Taxonomic communication, 165–176
  personal names, 166
  tribal and ethnic names, 172
Teasing songs, 69
Top-down communication, 95
TPR, *see* Tribal participatory research
Traditional Cultural Expressions (TCE), 80
Traditional music, 35, 57
Transactional model, 24
Transformative worldviews, 19
Travelling songs, 71
Treaty of Waitangi, 5
Triad Society, 142
Tribal identity, 173
Tribal participatory research, 21
Trumpets, 43–47
  military trumpet, 44
  shell trumpet, 46
  wooden trumpet, 46
Turner and West's holistic model, 24

U
Ugboajah's traditional-urban model, 24
United Nations Declaration on the Rights of Indigenous Peoples, 9
United States (US), 2, 80

V
Venue-oriented communication, 149–159
Visual communication, 115–126
  accessories, 118
  body art, 120
  clothes, 115
  colours, 119

W
Wars and conflict, 69–70
West Africa, 34
West African, 154
Western Apache, 3
Western Caroline Island, 40
Western model, 10
Western paradigms, 195
Whistles
  Single-pitched whistles, 39
Work songs, 65–67
Worldviews, 17
  epistemologies, 17
  ontologies, 17
  paradigms, 17
  research methodologies, 17

Y
Yupic Eskimos, 67
Yupik dance song, 61

Z
Zither, *see* Segaba

Printed in the United States
by Baker & Taylor Publisher Services